Resources for Teaching

THE STORY AND ITS WRITER

An Introduction to Short Fiction

Compact Seventh Edition

PREPARED BY

Ann Charters
University of Connecticut

Samuel Charters

William E. Sheidley
University of Southern Colorado

BEDFORD/ST. MARTIN'S   Boston ◆ New York

For information, write: Bedford/St. Martin's, 75 Arlington Street, Boston, MA
02116 (617-399-4000)

ISBN-10: 0–312–45237–3
ISBN-13: 978–0–312–45237–7

PREFACE

The entries in this manual include commentaries on each story in the anthology, along with questions for discussion, writing assignments, and suggested readings. The commentaries offer brief critical analyses of the stories and suggest ways to approach them in class. Like the questions that follow, the commentaries aim to promote a lively exchange of responses and perceptions without insisting on any particular interpretation or critical methodology.

Within many of the Topics for Writing are Connections questions, which ask students to link selections in the book. These questions promote critical thinking and are designed to provide both stimulating topics for writing assignments and material for fruitful class discussions. We have also added Responding Creatively questions, which enable you to incorporate creative writing assignments into your course. Instructors using these resources will readily see ways to rephrase, restructure, and reapply these assignments to suit their own purposes and the needs of their students. Some writing topics may serve equally well as discussion questions, and vice versa.

The suggested reading lists that conclude most entries are neither exhaustive nor highly selective; they simply cite interesting and, when possible, readily available criticism that proved useful in preparing the manual or that contains information and approaches to the stories that could not be incorporated in the commentaries. Thanks are due to the authors mentioned, to whose insights and scholarship these resources are generally indebted.

At the end of these resources are a thematic index of stories, a guide to commentaries, and a directory of short stories on film and video.

CONTENTS

STORIES

Chinua Achebe

Civil Peace (p. 10)

Achebe narrates this story about the "civil peace" prevailing in war-torn Nigeria after the Biafran war with an ironic control that provides a strong contrast to the human suffering portrayed in the story. When the story opens, we learn that the protagonist, Jonathan Iwegbu, considers himself lucky to have survived the war with his wife and three of their four children. The terms of his survival, and the price he continues to pay for his own and his family's safekeeping despite the official end to the civil war, are dramatized in the events of the story.

Jonathan Iwegbu is an excellent example of what the critic Frank O'Connor called "the little Man" in short story literature, a figure projecting a distinctive aura of human dignity despite his all-too-apparent vulnerability and isolation. Jonathan Iwegbu is tormented by the people around him (the soldiers who threaten to shoot up his house and force him to give up his money), yet his fundamental decency speaks so directly to us that we seem to hear him say, "Why do you [bother] me? . . . I am your brother."

Questions for Discussion

1. Is "Civil Peace" a fully developed short story or an anecdote? What qualities in the narrative — characterization, setting, plot — lead you to your answer?
2. Explain the irony in the title of the story.
3. Jonathan Iwegbu acts as a self-reliant head of his family throughout the narrative. Why then does Achebe emphasize the "miracle" of his family's survival and the "monumental blessing" of his house's survival, and why does he repeat the phrase "nothing puzzles God" at the end of the story?

Topic for Writing

1. **RESPONDING CREATIVELY** Translate into conventional English the words of the leader of the group who knocks on the door of Jonathan's house and demands money from him in the middle of the night. Analyze the dramatic effect of this dialogue as the climax of the story.

Related Commentary

Chinua Achebe, An Image of Africa: Conrad's "Heart of Darkness," p. 827.

Suggested Readings

Achebe, Chinua. *Girls at War and Other Stories.* New York: Ballantine, 1973.
Chargois, J. A. *Two Views of Black Alienation: A Comparative Study of Chinua Achebe and Ralph Ellison.* Bloomington: Indiana UP, 1973.
Wren, R. W. *Achebe's World.* Washington, DC: Three Continents, 1980.

SHERMAN ALEXIE

The Lone Ranger and Tonto Fistfight in Heaven (p. 15)

Although students will have little difficulty understanding the content of Alexie's story, they may be unfamiliar with the reference of the story's title, which seems to have no immediate connection to the story itself. In the story there is no specific mention of the Lone Ranger or Tonto, and nothing about a fistfight, in heaven or on earth. Some students will be familiar with the fictional characters in the title, but there may be students who are not, since it has been many years since they were a ubiquitous presence in American popular culture.

The Lone Ranger was a member of the Texas Rangers, a law enforcement group that was instituted in the nineteenth century to bring justice to the wild Texas frontier. In the fictional story, a group of rangers riding in a deserted area were ambushed by bandits, and all but one of them was killed. The survivor, severely wounded, was found by an "Indian," Tonto, who nursed him back to health. Together they set out to find the killers, and then rode on together through a long career, bringing justice to the West in Saturday matinee film serials, books, comic books, radio programs, and television. The Lone Ranger wore a mask to protect his identity and fought his enemies with silver bullets. When they had accomplished their mission, he and Tonto would move on, always leaving behind one of the silver bullets as a sign to the people he had helped.

The characters have obvious connections to other figures of myth and legend, such as Robin Hood, who also reinforced the belief in the power of the lone individual to effect change in society. The role of the "Indian," who was usually played by a white actor in dark make-up, was secondary, even though Tonto saved the Lone Ranger's life again in several episodes. There was also a suggestion of the fictional characters Don Quixote and Sancho Panza in the Lone Ranger's idealism and in Tonto's dependent role. Despite their years together, Tonto never learned English, expressing himself in a kind of pidgin English dialect. With the title of the story Alexie seems to be telling the reader that the myth is dead, and with the death of the myth the natural antagonism between the white man and the Indian can now be openly expressed. Native Americans had long complained about Tonto's role as a virtual servant to the white ranger, and in the years when the figures became fixtures of popular culture there were already cynical jokes questioning the relationship.

As students read the story more closely, they will realize that on another level Alexie is suggesting that the fistfight between the Lone Ranger, who represents white society, and Tonto, who represents Indian society, reflects a deep conflict within himself. There is almost no plot to the story. The only thing that happens — and we don't learn about it until close to the end — is that the narrator receives a phone call from the white woman whom he once lived with, abused emotionally, and finally left in the middle of the night. The story is a series of remembered incidents through which he is made conscious of the conflict he feels between his Indian background and the white culture he has chosen to enter. By presenting the story as memory, he is able to introduce other elements that his memory dredges up — from failed treaties between the Indians and the whites, to memories of old basketball games, to his self-conscious description of his attempt to frighten the clerk of an all-night store. The reader is aware that Alexie himself was a good basketball player, and that he consciously participated in white culture on many levels, so the story has a strong element of autobiography.

Questions for Discussion

1. Is the title of the story meant seriously or ironically?
2. Why does the protagonist purposefully frighten the clerk of the 7-Eleven?
3. When he describes the clerk swallowing hard "like a white man does," is he suggesting that someone else — an African American or an Asian American — would not be frightened in the same situation?
4. In the italicized sentence beginning "We'll take Washington and Oregon," to what is the author referring? Is it a specific or a general reference?
5. When he describes three white soldiers playing polo with a dead Indian woman's head and compares this to the U.S. policy in Central America, what is he saying about America's treatment of other races and peoples?
6. When he says that his failure to do anything with his life is normal "for almost any other Indian in the country," is he speaking cynically or out of genuine despair?

Topics for Writing

1. Some critics have suggested that Alexie is making a career by manipulating white Americans' guilt over the destruction of the Native American peoples. Discuss this idea in terms of the actions of the protagonist in the story.
2. In the story, there are two examples of police mistrust of minority peoples. Have students discuss whether these are, or are not, valid descriptions of police attitudes.

Related Commentary

Sherman Alexie, Superman and Me, p. 832.

Suggested Reading

Alexie, Sherman. *The Lone Ranger and Tonto Fistfight in Heaven.* New York: HarperCollins, 1994.

ISABEL ALLENDE

An Act of Vengeance (p. 21)

Allende has said that "a good short story begins with the overpowering need to communicate a single idea or feeling. . . . It's like shooting an arrow. There is no second chance, it's a make-or-break proposition." She also believes that writing clearly is the first duty of the storyteller: "Not simply — that only works with soap advertising; we don't have to sacrifice aesthetics for the sake of ethics. On the contrary, only if we are able to say it beautifully can we be convincing."

"An Act of Vengeance" begins clearly and powerfully with an opening paragraph foreshadowing the plot of the story while suggesting the individuality of the protagonist Dulce Rosa Orellano, the Senator's daughter. Her father's high position may have gotten her elected Carnival Queen, but she is no stereotype. She is an independent young woman who will be forced to confront her terrible destiny — committing an act of vengeance that will avenge her father's death by the man with whom she allows herself to fall in love thirty years later.

The setting of Allende's magical realist story could occur in any fantasy land of the author's imagination, but its details reinforce the stereotypes about the conventional separation of women's and men's lives in her fictional country south of the border — the women in the local Ladies' Club are peaceful and plant trees in the town square; the men are violent and shoot out the windows in the public buildings, bullheadedly determined "to teach everyone a lesson." Dulce Rosa, the untypical heroine, thinks for herself even if she follows her culture's code of honor. To avenge her family's good name, she must kill the lover who was the young man who raped her after murdering and dishonoring her father. Forced to choose between the Senator's ghost and the man she loves, she stabs herself in her wedding dress before the ceremony.

Questions for Discussion

1. Discuss the style of the opening paragraph. How does it foreshadow the conclusion of the story?
2. Discuss the irony of the title. Is Rosa avenging her father's death, or her own independent "melancholy" character because she found herself unable to carry out her "perfect plan of vengeance"?
3. Is Rosa's change of heart toward her father's killer realistic? Did Allende mean it to be realistic, or does it suit the magical realist circumstances of the story?

Topics for Writing

1. **RESPONDING CREATIVELY** Write a book review of Allende's novel *Eva Luna.*

2. Allende has said that "it's hard for a book to stand against the message of the mass media; it's an unfair battle. Writers should therefore look for other forms of expressing their thoughts, avoiding the prejudice that only in books can they make literature. All means are legitimate, not only the cultivated language of academia but also the direct language of journalism, the mass language of radio, television and the movies, the poetic language of popular songs and the passionate language of talking face to face with an audience. These are all forms of literature." Agree or disagree with her statement.

Suggested Readings

Allende, Isabel. *The Stories of Eva Luna.* Trans. Margaret Sayers Peden. New York Atheneum, 1991.

De Zapata, Celia Correas, ed. *Short Stories by Latin American Women: The Magic and the Real.* Houston: Arte Público, 1990.

Zinsser, William, ed. *Paths of Resistance: The Art and Craft of the Political Novel.* Boston: Houghton, 1989. Contains Isabel Allende's "Writing as an Act of Hope."

SHERWOOD ANDERSON

Hands (p. 28)

Anderson's story "Hands" might be called a portrait. Like a formal painted portrait, it depicts Wing Biddlebaum not only as he exists at a given moment but also in conjunction with certain props in the background that reveal who he is by recalling his past and defining his circumstances. The focal image of the portrait is Wing's hands, around which the other elements of the picture are organized and to which they lend meaning. Further, the story depends for a portion of its effect upon a series of painterly tableaux, from the sunset landscape with berry pickers with which it begins to the silhouette of Wing as a holy hermit, saying over and over the rosary of his lonely years of penance for a sin he did not commit.

In keeping with this achronological narration (which William L. Phillips has shown may in part result from Anderson's thinking his way through the story as he wrote it), neither Wing nor George Willard experiences any clear revelation or makes any climactic decision. Wing never understands why he was driven out of Pennsylvania, and George is afraid to ask the questions that might lead them both to a liberating understanding of Wing's experience.

The reader, however, is not permitted to remain in the dark. With the clear understanding of how the crudity and narrow-minded suspicion of his neighbors have perverted Wing's selfless, "diffused" love for his students into a source of fear and shame comes a poignant sorrow for what is being wasted. Wing's hands may be the pride of Winesburg for their agility at picking strawberries, but the nurturing love that they betoken is feared by everyone, including George, including even Wing himself, whose loneliness is as great as his capacity to love — from which, by a cruel irony, it arises.

WILLIAM E. SHEIDLEY

Questions for Discussion

1. Define Wing Biddlebaum's relationship to his community as it is implied in the first paragraph. To what extent is the impression created here borne out?

2. Why does Wing hope George Willard will come to visit? Does George ever arrive?

3. Wing's name, which refers to his hands, was given to him by "some obscure poet of the town," and telling the full story of those hands "is a job for a poet." What connotations of "wings" are appropriate? Why is "Wing" a better name for Biddlebaum than, say, "Claw," or "Hook," or "Picker"?

4. Could Wing himself have been a poet? Why does he tell his dreams only to George?

5. Why did the people of the town in Pennsylvania nearly lynch Adolph Myers? Why was he unable to defend himself?

6. Are the people in Ohio any different from those in Pennsylvania? Explain. What about George Willard? Evaluate his decision not to ask Wing about his hands.

7. What other hands do we see in the story? Compare them with Wing's.

8. Explain the implications of our last view of Wing. What is the pun in the last line?

Topics for Writing

1. Write an essay analyzing the crucifixion of Wing Biddlebaum.

2. Consider Anderson's comments in "Form, Not Plot, in the Short Story" (included in Part Two, p. 835) as a key to his art in "Hands."

3. After reading the story once, jot down your response, including your feelings about Wing, George, the townspeople, and the narrator. Also write, in one or two sentences, a summation of the story's theme as you understand it. Then reread the paragraphs in the order they would have followed had Anderson told the story in chronological order. Would your responses differ? Would the story have an identical theme? Explain.

4. **RESPONDING CREATIVELY**   Anderson claimed to have written this story at a sitting and to have published it without rearrangements or major additions or deletions of material. Imitating his process, write a vignette about a person unknown to you whom you see in a photograph. Start with the scene in the photo and end with the same, interpolating previous incidents and background information as they occur to you.

Related Commentary

Sherwood Anderson, Form, Not Plot, in the Short Story, p. 835.

Suggested Readings

Anderson, David, ed. *Critical Essays on Sherwood Anderson.* Boston: G. K. Hall, 1981.
Anderson, Sherwood. *The Portable Sherwood Anderson.* New York: Viking, 1972.
———. *A Story Teller's Story.* Cleveland: The UP of Case Western Reserve, 1968.
———. *The Teller's Tales.* Introduction by Frank Gado. Schenectady, NY: Union College P, 1983.
Burbank, Rex. *Sherwood Anderson.* Twayne's United States Authors Series 65. New York: Twayne, 1964. 64–66.
Crowley, John W., ed. *New Essays on Winesburg, Ohio.* New York: Cambridge UP, 1990.
Joselyn, Sister Mary. "Some Artistic Dimensions of Sherwood Anderson's 'Death in the Woods.'" *Studies in Short Fiction* 4 (1967): 252–59.
Phillips, William L. "How Sherwood Anderson Wrote *Winesburg, Ohio.*" *The Achievement of Sherwood Anderson.* Ed. Ray Lewis White. Chapel Hill: U of North Carolina P, 1966. 62–84, esp. 74–78. Originally published in American Literature 23 (1951): 7–30.
Rideout, Walter B., ed. *Sherwood Anderson.* Englewood Cliffs, NJ: Prentice, 1974.
Scheick, William J. "Compulsion toward Repetition: Sherwood Anderson's 'Death in the Woods.'" *Studies in Short Fiction* 11 (1974): 141–46.
Townsend, Kim. *Sherwood Anderson.* Boston: Houghton, 1987.
White, Ray Lewis. Winesburg, Ohio: *An Explanation.* Boston: Twayne, 1990.

MARGARET ATWOOD

Happy Endings (p. 33)

Atwood's story can be read profitably in conjunction with Grace Paley's "A Conversation with My Father." In both, the authors use humor to suggest a certain impatience with the traditional short story form. Both stories can be read as "metafictions," fictions that comment on the art of telling stories. Atwood's piece is harsher than Paley's in its insistence that happy endings are impossible in stories; Atwood tells us clearly that death is "the only authentic ending" to everyone's story. Paley, in contrast, clearly values both her relationship with her dying father and her own imagination, allowing (even half-jokingly) her fictional heroine the possibility of rehabilitation after her drug addiction and a valued place in society as a counselor in a center for young addicts.

The first time students read "Happy Endings," they may miss the way Atwood connects the stories from "A" to "F." "B" is the first unhappy ending (as Atwood warns us in the third sentence), with the "worst possible scenario" worked out in John and Mary's love affair. Atwood's vocabulary here is deliberately harsh and unromantic, unlike the sentimental clichés of the "A" scenario.

As Atwood continues her permutations of the couples' possible relation-ships, her stories get shorter and more perfunctory. Her language becomes more elemental, preparing the reader for her summary dismissal of all plots, since they all end in death. In the final three paragraphs, Atwood drops all pretense that she is telling stories and directly addresses her readers, revealing that her true subject is not the emotional life she is creating for her characters but her awareness of the elements of fiction. She defines plot as "what" or "just one thing after another." Then, like the instructor's manual of a short story anthology, she leaves the rest up to her reader: "Now try How [character] and Why [theme]."

Questions for Discussion

1. Atwood's authorial presence is the strongest element in "Happy Endings" — does this make the text closer to an essay than a short story? Explain.
2. How does Atwood elicit your curiosity, so that you continue to read this short story? Would you say that she has proven that plot is the most essen-tial element in a story? Is there also an underlying, coherent theme to "Happy Endings"?
3. Would the story still be effective if Atwood omitted her direct address to the reader ("If you want a happy ending, try A.")? Explain.

Topics for Writing

1. **RESPONDING CREATIVELY** Rewrite the story, inventing additional out-comes for John and Mary's relationship.
2. In "Reading Blind" (p. 837), Atwood gives her criteria for judging whether a story is "good." Using these criteria, how would you rate "Happy Endings"?
3. Ray Bradbury, in his book *Zen in the Art of Writing: Essays on Creativity* (Capra, 1990), writes, "The writer must let his fingers run out the story of his characters, who, being only human and full of strange dreams and obsessions, are only too glad to run. . . . Remember: *Plot* is no more than footprints left in the snow after your characters have run by on their way to incredible destinations. *Plot* is observed after the fact rather than before. It cannot precede action. It is the chart that remains when an action is through." Apply Bradbury's analysis to "Happy Endings."

Related Commentary

Margaret Atwood, Reading Blind, p. 837.

Suggested Readings

Atwood, Margaret. *Murder in the Dark.* Toronto: Coach House, 1983.
———. *Second Words.* Toronto: Anansi, 1982.
Grace, Sherrill E., and Lorraine Weir. *Margaret Atwood: Language, Text and System.* Vancouver: U of British Columbia P, 1983.

Rigney, Barbara Hill. *Margaret Atwood*. Totowa, NJ: Barnes & Noble, 1987.
Stouck, David. *Major Canadian Authors*. Lincoln: U of Nebraska P, 1988.

JAMES BALDWIN

Sonny's Blues (p. 37)

The marvel of this story is the way the narrator — Sonny's older brother — narrows the physical and emotional distance between himself and Sonny until Sonny's plight is revealed and illuminated in a remarkable moment of empathy and insight. This story of drug addiction in the inner city's black ghetto is as valid today as it was when it was written. By juxtaposing the two brothers — a straight high school math teacher and a heroin addict blues pianist — Baldwin makes it possible for readers to enter the world of the story regardless of their racial background or their opinions about drugs. The author doesn't judge Sonny's plight. Instead, through the brother, he helps us understand it, sympathize with it, and transcend it in a brief shared experience of Sonny's inspired musical improvisation.

This is a long story, and its plot consists mostly of flashbacks, more "told" than "shown" in the reminiscences of Sonny's older brother. Yet the power of Baldwin's sympathy for his characters and his eloquent style move the reader along. Baldwin captures the African American culture of strong family allegiances in the face of American racism. Both Sonny and his brother are trying to survive, and we respect them for their courage.

One of the ways to discuss the story is through an analysis of the narrator's growing sympathy for Sonny. Baldwin tells us that the narrator thinks, after the death of his little daughter Grace from polio, "My trouble made his real." This realization motivates the first scene with the two brothers in which Baldwin begins to build the bridge between them. Separately they watch three sisters and a brother hold a revival meeting on the sidewalk opposite the narrator's apartment, and after they hear the gospel music, the silence between Sonny and his brother begins to give way to shared sound. The scene leads directly to the two brothers going to the bar where Sonny plays and creates an opportunity for the narrator (and the reader) to enter Sonny's world and satisfy his anguished need to share his music with someone who will listen to it and understand.

Questions for Discussion

1. Analyze the following speech, in which Sonny explains to his brother how he has survived (however tenuously) the experience of racism in America:

   "It's terrible sometimes, inside," he said, "that's what's the trouble. You walk these streets, black and funky and cold, and there's not really a living ass to talk to, and there's nothing shaking, and there's no way of getting it out — that storm inside. You can't talk it and you can't make love with it, and when you finally try to get with it and play it, you realize nobody's listening. So you've got to listen. You got to find a way to listen."

   How does this explanation make Sonny a sympathetic character?

2. Discuss Baldwin's comment on the blues Sonny plays with Creole and the two other musicians at the end of the story:

    > Creole began to tell us what the blues were all about. They were not about anything very new. He and his boys up there were keeping it new, at the risk of ruin, destruction, madness, and death, in order to find new ways to make us listen. For, while the tale of how we suffer, and how we are delighted, and how we may triumph is never new, it always must be heard. There isn't any other tale to tell, it's the only light we've got in all this darkness.

    Baldwin's subject is the music, of course, but he is also talking about other forms of creation. What might they be?

Topics for Writing

1. Chinua Achebe describes Baldwin as having brought "a new sharpness of vision, a new energy of passion, a new perfection of language to battle the incubus of race" in a eulogy titled "Postscript: James Baldwin (1924–1987)" (*Hopes and Impediments,* 1990). How does "Sonny's Blues" embody these qualities?
2. **CONNECTIONS** Baldwin's commentary "Autobiographical Notes" (p. 841) states that he found it difficult to be a writer because he was forced to become a spokesman for his race: "I have not written about being a Negro at such length because I expect that to be my only subject, but only because it was the gate I had to unlock before I could hope to write about anything else." Yet Baldwin's depiction of the life lived by African Americans is unique and very different from Richard Wright's or Ralph Ellison's, Toni Cade Bambara's or Alice Walker's accounts. Compare and contrast "Sonny's Blues" with a story by one or more of these writers to describe how each finds his or her own way to dramatize what Baldwin calls "the ambiguity and irony of Negro life." Could "Sonny's Blues" be set in an Italian American or Jewish American family?
3. **CONNECTIONS** Compare and contrast "Sonny's Blues" with Willa Cather's "Paul's Case."

Related Commentary

James Baldwin, Autobiographical Notes, p. 841.

Suggested Readings

Bloom, Harold. *James Baldwin.* New York: Chelsea House, 1986.
Burt, Nancy. *Critical Essays on James Baldwin.* Boston: G. K. Hall, 1986.
Campbell, James. *Talking at the Gates: A Life of James Baldwin.* New York: Viking, 1991.
Chametzky, Jules, ed. *A Tribute to James Baldwin: Black Writers Redefine the Struggle.* Amherst: U of Massachusetts P, 1989.
Kinnamon, Kenneth, ed. *James Baldwin.* Englewood Cliffs, NJ: Prentice, 1974.
Macebuh, Stanley. *James Baldwin: A Critical Study.* New York: Third, 1973.

Pratt, Louis H. *James Baldwin*. Twayne's United States Authors Series 290. Boston: G. K. Hall, 1978.

Standley, F. L., ed. *Conversations with James Baldwin*. Jackson: U of Mississippi P, 1989.

Toni Cade Bambara

The Lesson (p. 61)

Relationships are an organizational key to this story. "The Lesson" is narrated by Sylvia, one of a group of eight African American children living in an uptown slum in New York City who are "treated" by their neighborhood guide Miss Moore to an educational visit to the F.A.O. Schwarz toy store at Fifth Avenue and Fifty-seventh Street. The group consists of four girls (Sylvia and her best friend Sugar, the relatively affluent Mercedes and her friend Rosie Giraffe) and four boys (Big Butt [Ronald] and Junebug, and Little Q.T. and Flyboy).

The "lesson" of the story is learned first by Sugar and then by Sylvia. All along Sylvia has assumed Sugar to be her ally, sharing her hostility to all adults as authority figures and to the idea of education. There's a suggestion of foreshadowing when the girls pay the taxicab driver outside F.A.O. Schwarz and Sugar steps in when Sylvia can't figure out the 10 percent tip on the 85-cent fare — "Give him a dime." (This is a taxi fare from twenty-five years ago, when the story was written.) But Sugar plays dumb as usual in her next appearance in the story, when she asks Miss Moore outside the toy store, "Can we steal?"

After the children learn about the high prices of the luxury toys at F.A.O. Schwarz, they return to their homes uptown. Sugar's remark to Miss Moore before they disperse reveals that the afternoon's lesson in economics hasn't been wasted: "This is not much of a democracy if you ask me. Equal chance to pursue happiness means an equal crack at the dough, don't it?" Bambara doesn't tell us whether Sugar intends to begin studying hard in school or to begin dealing drugs (this is the early 1970s), but the blinders formed by her life in the inner-city ghetto have fallen away, and she's clearly dissatisfied with her customary smart-aleck role. In her first response Sylvia is dumbfounded by her friend's betrayal, but within a few minutes she awakens to a sense of rivalry: "But ain't nobody gonna beat me at nuthin." Again Bambara leaves the lesson unspecified, and the reader must imagine how Sylvia intends to win the new game she's playing.

Questions for Discussion

1. What is the effect of the inner-city ghetto language in the story?
2. Is Sylvia a reliable or an unreliable narrator?
3. How does Bambara evoke a sense of sympathy for the people enduring the poverty and filth in Sylvia's neighborhood through her descriptions of the relationship of the winos and the newly arrived families from the South?
4. Describe the eight children and their relationships within the neighborhood group. How dependent is Sylvia on her friend Sugar?

5. Who is Miss Moore? Why does she personify the hostile force of "education" to the ghetto children?
6. Why does Sylvia keep the four dollars' change from the taxi fare? What does she do with the money? Is this a convincing ending to the story?

Topics for Writing

1. **RESPONDING CREATIVELY**   Write a story using a special dialect that you have learned from your family or friends.
2. **CONNECTIONS**   Compare and contrast the authors' uses of African American speech in this story and in Richard Wright's "The Man Who Was Almost a Man." Analyze the different ways the two writers keep the dialect from distracting readers and causing them to lose interest in the stories.

Suggested Readings

Bambara, Toni Cade. *The Sea Birds Are Still Alive: Stories.* New York: Vintage, 1982.
Bell, Roseann P., Bettye J. Parker, and Beverly Guy-Sheftall, eds. *Sturdy Black Bridges: Visions of Black Women in Literature.* New York: Anchor, 1979.
Butler-Evans, Elliot. *Race, Gender, and Desire: Narrative Strategies in the Fiction of Toni Cade Bambara, Toni Morrison, and Alice Walker.* Philadelphia: Temple UP, 1989.
Cartwright, Jerome. "Bambara's 'The Lesson.'" *Explicator* 47.3 (Spring 1989): 61–63.
Evans, Mari, ed. *Black Women Writers (1950–1980): A Critical Evaluation.* New York: Anchor, 1984. 41–71.
Giddings, P. "Call to Wholeness from a Gifted Storyteller." *Encore* 9 (1980): 48–49.
Lyles, Lois F. "Time, Motion, Sound and Fury in *The Sea Birds Are Still Alive.*" *College Language Association Journal* 36.2 (December 1992): 134–44.
Morrison, Toni. "City Limits, Village Values: Concepts of the Neighborhood in Black Fiction." *Literature and the Urban Experience: Essays on the City and Literature.* Ed. Ann Chalmers Watts and Michael C. Jaye. New Brunswick: Rutgers UP, 1981.
Tate, Claudia, ed. *Black Women Writers at Work.* New York: Continuum, 1983. 12–38.
Vertreace, Martha M. "A Bibliography of Writings about Toni Cade Bambara." *American Women Writing Fiction: Memory, Identity, Family, and Space.* Ed. Mickey Pearlman. Lexington: U of Kentucky P, 1989.
———. "Toni Cade Bambara: The Dance of Character and Community." *American Women Writing Fiction: Memory, Identity, Family, and Space.* Ed. Mickey Pearlman. Lexington: U of Kentucky P, 1989.

RUSSELL BANKS

Black Man and White Woman in Dark Green Rowboat (p. 68)

In an afterword to a collection of his short stories (*The Angel on the Roof,* 2000), Russell Banks justified his interest in the short story by explaining, "I've written a dozen or so novels, but the story form thrills me still. It invites me today, as it did back then, to behave on the page in a way that is more reckless, more steadily painful."

"Black Man and White Woman in Dark Green Rowboat" is a painful story, although on its quiet surface it could be said that the prevailing mood is a calm that matches the day Banks describes. He has left it to the reader to intuit the pain of each of the protagonists. We know the boundaries and the dimensions of the pain because the story at its deepest level is about something we live with daily; it is a story about race. The event that the author narrates, the young woman's decision to have an abortion, is just one incident in lives that have known many similar. To allow us to judge the effect of the woman's decision on the life of the man she is with in the green rowboat, as well as on her own life, the author has stripped the story of any secondary action. We see everything with the bright clarity of the sunlight on the hot summer day. A man swims, people leave for work, a woman sits and reads a book, a second woman walks to get her mail, a teenager sits on his trailer steps and smokes a joint, an old man scrapes paint from the bottom of a boat. The scene is set for the couple and their afternoon of fishing in the dark green rowboat.

Everything about the scene is completely ordinary, except that the man is black. His blackness, because of the reader's consciousness of the implications of this blackness, places him just outside the scene. As both the man and woman are aware, the decision she has made, despite her denials, will shut him outside of the scene forever. If the author had chosen to allow her any other explanation for her decision — she is young, they aren't married, she has recently been ill — we might have been presented with a plausible justification for her decision. She says that her mother is concerned because of her problems with depression, but she never offers a reason of her own, and so we are left with an awareness that to her race is in itself sufficient reason for what she is going to do.

One of the brilliant technical aspects of the story is its use of color as a series of symbols for the events of the afternoon. At no point in the story is the phrase African American or the word Negro used to describe the man. We are told only the color of his skin. The word *nigger* appears once, but it is used by the man himself in angry derision. Instead, the ordinary scene of the lake and the trailers is given a spare, stripped dimension that is clarified with moments of color. The title itself gives us colors — black, white, and dark green — and the other tonalities in the story are set against them. The morning haze is blue-gray, the swimmer is wearing a white bathing cap, the water is a dark green plain. The woman who comes out to read is wearing white shorts and halter, the skin of the swimmer is a chestnut color, the woman going for her mail is wearing a T-shirt that had turned pink in the wash. The boy smoking the joint is blond, the blonde girl who walks toward the rowboat is wearing a lime-green bikini, and her skin is tanned a light brown. The trailers, from the lake, are like "pastel-colored shoe boxes." The reader is given continual, almost subliminal hints throughout the story to be conscious of color.

Although students probably have no familiarity with other stories by Russell Banks, they would be interested to learn that he has written about this group of people many times. The trailer park is outside a small, imaginary New Hampshire mill town named Catamount, and the people who have jobs work in the town. The man taking the early swim is a retired captain in the American army, Dewey Knox; the woman reading the book, the girl's mother, is named Nancy Hubner; and the girl herself is Noni Hubner. She is home from college and recuperating from a nervous breakdown. Her father died two years earlier, and she and her mother are still struggling to go on with their lives. The boy smoking the joint is named Bruce Severance, and he will be shot to death in a few months as the result of a bad drug deal. The manager's name is Marcelle Chagnon, and the man scraping down the boat is named Merle Ring. He brought considerable confusion to the trailer park the winter before by winning $50,000 in the state lottery and showing a complete lack of interest in what might become of the money. This is the world of the little trailer park backed up against the boundary of the state forest at the edge of the lake. Did the author mean to emphasize the black man's inability to enter the white world at even this level by having his rejection come from someone who would be described as "trailer trash"?

Students will find it interesting to contrast this story with Ernest Hemingway's "Hills Like White Elephants (p. 540). This is also a story about a young woman who is about to have an abortion, but the circumstances and emotions of the two stories reflect entirely different social and personal conditions.

Questions for Discussion

1. The author has been careful to describe the setting of his story in considerable detail, but could the same story have been set in another part of the United States with the same effect?
2. How much of the emotional effect of the story depends on the events that are described, and how much depends on the reader's understanding of the implication of the woman's decision?
3. Does the young woman's lack of interest in fishing and the contents of the magazine she is reading suggest some of the emotional uncertainties that have gone into her decision?
4. Although no direct reference is made to the man's race, there is emphasis on the historical implications of his color, first when he ties his shirt over his head so that he looks, in her words, like an Arab sheik and, in his words, like a galley-slave, then when his face is described as "somber and ancient." What is the author suggesting with these allusions?
5. Is there any moment in the story when the man is given an opportunity to express his wishes regarding the situation? What is the implication of her statement, "Well. We've been through all this before. A hundred times"?

Topics for Writing

1. Discuss the way in which colors are used in the story.

2. **CONNECTIONS** Contrast this story with Hemingway's "Hills Like White Elephants" and discuss the similarities and the differences in the woman's role in the decision she has made.
3. Discuss how the reader's consciousness of race is crucial to his or her understanding of the story.

Related Story

Ernest Hemingway, Hills Like White Elephants, p. 350.

Related Commentary

Russell Banks, Author's Note, p. 845.

Suggested Reading

Niemi, Robert. *Russell Banks.* New York: Twayne; London: Prentice-Hall International, 1997.

AMBROSE BIERCE

An Occurrence at Owl Creek Bridge (p. 75)

What is the reason for the enduring interest of this contrived and improbable tale? Surprise endings frequently draw groans similar to those that greet bad puns, but Bierce's final twist is more likely to elicit shock and recoil. Perhaps the story's success results more from its realization of an intimate and familiar fear than from its sharp, vivid style or its tense pacing. The idea of continued life is all that the human mind, unable to imagine mere "darkness and silence," can propose in view of impending death. By narrating a fantasy of escape so persuasively that we succumb to it, and then by revealing it with the snap of a neck to have been only a fantasy, Bierce forces us to recognize once again the reality of our mortal situation.

If, out of the desire to evade that recognition, the reader seeks to repudiate the story as a piece of literary chicanery, he or she will not succeed. A clearheaded review of section III reveals that the exciting tale of escape could not have been real. Even before Farquhar enters the nightmare forest with its strange constellations and peculiar, untraveled roadway, he has experienced a preternatural heightening of sensory awareness that happens only when one sees with the eyes of the mind, and he has undergone sensations better explained by reference to a slow-motion expansion of a hanging than to his imagined plunge into Owl Creek. The images of his dream emerge from Farquhar's instinctual desire to live, and Bierce renders them with such clarity that the reader can cherish them as well. The same intensity of sensory awareness marks Bierce's conjecture about what it must be like when the noose jerks tight. We feel the constriction, see the flash of nervous discharge, and hear the cracking vertebrae.

Our close participation in the imaginary and real sensations of dying countervails the doomed man's symbolic isolation, which is the burden of section I. While the executioners enact the formal rituals that establish distance from the victim, who is being expelled from the human community (even the sentinels are turning their backs on him), Bierce leads the reader into an empathic communion with him. The agency of this imaginative projection is the coolly exact observational style, which carries us across the plank — Farquhar's first thought to which we are privy is his approval of this device — and into the psyche of the condemned.

Before launching into Farquhar's dying fantasy, however, Bierce goes back, in section II, to narrate the events leading up to the execution. Besides establishing for Farquhar an identity with which we can sympathize, this passage presents him as active rather than acted upon, and so generates a momentum that continues into the story of his escape. The section ends with one of several stark, one-line revelations that conclude passages of uncertainty, illusion, or false conjecture in the story: "He was a Federal scout"; "What he heard was the ticking of his watch"; "Peyton Farquhar was dead." This device of style expresses Bierce's major theme: Whatever we dream of, life is entrapment by death, and time is running out.

WILLIAM E. SHEIDLEY

Questions for Discussion

1. In what ways does section I suggest a psychological time much slower than actual time?
2. Why is it appropriate that the execution take place on a bridge over a river?
3. What is the function of Farquhar's conjectures about escape at the end of section I?
4. In what ways does Bierce try to gain the reader's sympathy for Farquhar? Why does he need to do this?
5. Which events in section III might be read as dislocations of sensations experienced by a man in the process of being hanged?
6. Contrast the descriptive style of a passage from section III with that of a passage from section I.
7. What would be the result if Farquhar's imagined reunion with his wife took place *after* the snapping of his neck?

Topics for Writing

1. Analyze Bierce's handling of time and chronology in "An Occurrence at Owl Creek Bridge."
2. **CONNECTIONS**   Discuss the fiction of effect as a fiction of despair in the works of Bierce and Poe.

Suggested Readings

Bierce, Ambrose. *The Complete Short Stories of Ambrose Bierce.* Lincoln: U of Nebraska P, 1984.

Davidson, Cathy N. *The Experimental Fictions of Ambrose Bierce.* Lincoln: U of Nebraska P, 1984.

Grenander, Mary E. *Ambrose Bierce.* New York: Twayne, 1971.

Stoicheff, Peter. "'Something Uncanny': The Dream Structure in Ambrose Bierce's 'An Occurrence at Owl Creek Bridge.'" *Studies in Short Fiction* 30.3 (Summer 1993): 349–58.

Wolotkiewicz, Diana. "Ambrose Bierce's Use of the Grotesque Mode: The Pathology of Society." *Journal of the Short Story in English* 16 (Spring 1991): 81–92.

JORGE LUIS BORGES

The Circular Ruins (p. 83)

In Julio Cortázar's commentary, he maintains that "The Circular Ruins" is a perfect story in its "insistent race against the clock." Borges has relentlessly eliminated "all the elements proper to the novella and the novel." While relying only on the employment of "a minimum of elements," he has transformed "certain situations or narrative territories into a story with ramifications as extensive as those of the most developed novella."

Fascinated with philosophical puzzles since childhood, Borges created a story-within-a-story-within-a-story in "The Circular Ruins" that has no beginning and no ending. In this fantasy, the unnamed gray man who is the protagonist from the South arrives at the circular enclosure during the night, and we are told that "his immediate obligation was to dream." We are in a land of dream, myth, and fable — one in a series of similar locations described as circular ruins which we learn at the conclusion of the story is part of a series without beginning or end. We have no flesh-and-blood characters, no realistic setting, no conflict. Borges has eliminated the three most tangible elements of short fiction in "The Circular Ruins," and yet he has created one of the most memorable races against the clock in modern storytelling.

Questions for Discussion

1. What details in the opening paragraph of "The Circular Ruins" make Borges's story appear to be a conventional tale?
2. Why do the "men of the region" supply the protagonist with figs, rice, and a jug of water while he is sleeping?
3. Describe the process by which the dreamer sets about his "magic project" of dreaming the man who becomes his son.
4. How different — and how similar — is this fictional dream process from Borges's own creative process when he wrote "The Circular Ruins"?
5. How serious was Borges when he wrote that "it would have been better had he destroyed it" when the wizard almost destroyed his entire work?
6. What surprise awaited the wizard at the end of the story? How does this conclusion relate to the title Borges has chosen for his tale?

Topics for Writing

1.   Compare and contrast the different ways that the authors create their "story's insistent race against the clock" in Borges's "The Circular Ruins" and Poe's "The Cask of Amontillado."
2.   Revise Borges's story so that it becomes comic. Change it only as much as is necessary to achieve the desired effect. What changes do you find essential?

Related Commentary

Julio Cortázar, On the Short Story and Its Environs, p. 859.

Suggested Readings

Agheana, Ion Tudro. *The Meaning of Experience in the Prose of Jorge Luis Borges.* New York: P. Lang, 1988.
Alazraki, Jaime. *Critical Essays on Jorge Luis Borges.* Boston: Twayne, 1987.
Borges, Jorge Luis. *The Book of Fantasy.* New York: Carroll and Graf, 1990.
———. *The Book of Sand.* New York: NAL-Dutton, 1979.
———. *Dream Tigers.* Austin: U of Texas P, 1984.
———. *A Personal Anthology.* New York: Grove Weidenfeld, 1961.
Christ, Ronald J. *The Narrow Act: Borges's Art of Allusion.* New York: New York UP, 1969.
Lindstrom, Naomi. *Jorge Luis Borges: A Study of Short Fiction.* Boston: Twayne, 1990.
McMurray, George R. *Jorge Luis Borges.* Modern Literature Monographs. New York: Ungar, 1980.
Stabb, Martin S. *Borges Revisited.* Boston: Twayne, 1991.

RAYMOND CARVER

Cathedral (p. 88)

"Cathedral" is a story about alienation, isolation, and the cure for both. The narrator is an insecure, jealous man, more dead than alive — a man who has constructed a virtual prison in which he exists emotionally detached from his wife and cut off from any active participation in what makes life worth living. He anesthetizes his pain with drink and marijuana while making comments that reveal his feelings of inferiority, confusion, and resentment.

When the story opens, the narrator's tone is anecdotal and familiar ("this blind man, an old friend of my wife's, he was on his way to spend the night . . . I wasn't enthusiastic about his visit"); at the conclusion, however, his tone has become one of awe ("'it's really something,' I said"). We are aware that he has undergone an important transformation, an almost mystical experience that comes to him at an unexpected moment from an unexpected source and literally frees him from the prison his life had become. Despite his jealousy of blind

Robert, and his professed resistance to the other's intrusion, the narrator unwittingly makes a friend of the blind man and in the process comes to understand something about himself. As he begins, ironically, to see through Robert's eyes, to experience the world through Robert's perceptions, his own horizons are expanded ("my eyes were still closed. I was in my house. I knew that. But I didn't feel like I was inside anything"). Robert contradicts every stereotypical idea the narrator holds about the blind, and with his commanding presence, his vitality, his sensitivity, and his engagement with life, he forces the narrator to see.

Contrasts abound between Robert and the narrator and between their respective relationships with the narrator's wife. The blind man is infinitely more alive than the narrator ("I don't have any blind friends," the narrator tells his wife; "you don't have *any* friends," she replies. "The blind man was also a ham radio operator. He talked in his loud voice about conversations he'd had with fellow operators in Guam, in the Philippines, in Alaska, and even in Tahiti. He said he'd have a lot of friends there if he ever wanted to go visit those places"). Robert and the narrator's wife (whom the narrator never calls by name but refers to, significantly, as "my wife") have a special and long-lasting friendship that involves a level of intimacy conspicuously absent from the narrator's marital relationship, the cause of much jealousy and resentment. An underlying tension is constantly present in the conversations between the couple, but with Robert the woman is a different person: "I saw my wife laughing as she parked the car. I saw her get out of the car and shut the door. She was still wearing a smile. Just amazing." We infer from this observation that she does not laugh much with her husband. His wife and Robert approach the house, "talking all the way." Earlier the narrator had commented, "right then my wife filled me in with more detail than I cared to know." Talking and the emotional sharing that results have played a vital role in the enduring relationship between the woman and the blind man; they are obviously not an integral part of the marital relationship.

"I want you to feel comfortable in this house," the wife says to her friend. "I am comfortable," Robert replies. Oddly, it is the narrator who is uncomfortable, and this discomfort prompts his pathetic attempts to feel superior to the blind man. Offering him marijuana, the narrator observes: "I could tell he didn't know the first thing." But soon he grudgingly acknowledges, "it was like he'd been doing it since he was nine years old," and the dynamics of the relationship slowly begin to change. After his wife falls asleep, the narrator offers to take Robert up to bed, but Robert declines and the narrator comments, "I'm glad for the company" and adds, "and I guess I was." They watch television together, Robert telling his host, "Whatever you want to watch is okay. I'm always learning something. Learning never ends. It won't hurt me to learn something tonight," but it is the narrator, not the blind man, who will learn something important tonight. The image of the two men's hands tracing the cathedral together is dramatic, striking, and poignant. Robert asks him if he is religious, and the narrator realizes that he truly does not know how to talk to Robert, but the difference now is that he begins to care that he doesn't ("I guess I don't believe in it. In anything. Sometimes it's hard. You know what I'm saying?" "Sure, I do," Robert answers. "Right," the narrator replies).

As the two men's hands trace the cathedral, we are reminded of the time when Robert touched the woman's face. Perhaps the connection that has been forged between the men will influence the marriage as well. The narrator's awkward and inadequate attempts at conversation with Robert are a form of engagement, and his hand speeding across the page drawing windows and arches and buttresses is truly a liberating experience. Inspired by the man who cannot see, he has literally drawn himself out of the prison to which his own limited perceptions had restricted him.

Questions for Discussion

1. Is the narrator a sympathetic protagonist? Does our opinion of him change as the story progresses?
2. What does the narrator learn from his encounter with Robert? Do you believe that there will be a significant change in his outlook from this point on?
3. What is the significance of Carver's choice of a cathedral as catalyst for the narrator's learning experience? What added dimension does this symbol bring to our understanding of the story? Can you tie it to any previous detail?
4. Contrast the author's tone and the narrator's mood at the opening of the story with the tone and mood at the end. How does the change in style reflect the change that has occurred in the narrator?
5. What is the narrator's attitude toward his wife? What kind of marriage do they have, and what evidence do you find to support your conclusion? Is the narrator's jealousy of Robert irrational?
6. What are the primary emotions displayed by the narrator throughout, and how can we understand them in terms of the life he leads? What are some adjectives you would use to characterize him? What role does alcohol play in his life?
7. What is it about Robert that unsettles the narrator? How do his appearance and bearing resist every stereotypical image the narrator has about blind people, and why is this so upsetting?

Topics for Writing

1. For Carver, salvation lies in human contact and connection. Comment critically.
2. Create a conversation between the narrator and his wife after Robert's departure.
3. Discuss "Cathedral" as a story about "the blind leading the blind."

Related Casebook

Raymond Carver, On Writing, p. 941.
Raymond Carver, Creative Writing 101, p. 946.
Raymond Carver, The Ashtray, p. 949.
Raymond Carver, On "Errand," p. 950.
Olga Knipper, Remembering Chekhov, p. 952.
Henri Troyat, Chekhov's Last Days, p. 953.
Tom Jenks, The Origin of "Cathedral," p. 956.
Arthur M. Saltzman, A Reading of "What We Talk About When We Talk About Love," p. 957.
A. O. Scott, Looking for Raymond Carver, p. 959.

Suggested Readings

See page 25.

RAYMOND CARVER

Errand (p. 98)

Carver's story may be instructively compared with the excerpt from Henri Troyat's biography of Anton Chekhov describing Chekhov's death (included with other commentary in the Carver Casebook in this anthology). In addition to providing a considerable amount of factual background about Chekhov and the last years of his century, this comparison may shed light on a question that could conceivably be asked by students in the course: What is the difference between a short story and an essay?

In comparing the fiction and nonfiction descriptions of Chekhov's last days, students will notice that Carver has based a good deal of his story on Troyat's biography of Chekhov, which Carver read and enjoyed. A knowledgeable and highly skilled literary biographer, Troyat wrote prose that (even in translation) moves briskly along almost like a short story, since Troyat eliminates editorial digressions and commentary in his desire to dramatize his account of Chekhov's last illness.

Carver has absorbed Troyat's style in addition to information about the people and places involved in Chekhov's death. The pace of the narrative is calm and unhurried, the tone unassuming and authoritative. To make "Errand" complete unto itself as a short narrative, Carver includes information about Chekhov's life — the hemorrhage he suffered while dining with Suvorin, his marriage to the actress Olga Knipper — found in earlier pages in Troyat's biography. These details provide the reader with the information necessary to appreciate the background of the story.

Perhaps most significant, Carver, unlike Troyat, invents details in telling the story of Chekhov's death. "Errand" contains the fictional character of the blond young man who works at the hotel. He brings up the bottle of champagne that Doctor Schwöhrer has ordered for Chekhov in the middle of the night. Later in the morning, the young man reappears at the door of the suite with a vase containing three yellow roses to announce to Olga Knipper that breakfast will be served that day in the garden of the hotel because of the heat wave.

Carver ingeniously introduces this fictional character by having Doctor Schwöhrer summon him from the hotel kitchen by using the telephone in Chekhov's room. This would have been a newfangled gadget in 1904, and the doctor's meticulous way of following the "instructions for using the device" makes his action believable to the reader, thus preparing the way for a fictional rather than a historical character to enter the story. Carver then tells us everything we need to know to accept the "lie": First we visualize the appearance of the young man, who was awakened from sleep and who dressed so hastily that his jacket is carelessly buttoned. Then we see what he sees when he brings his tray into Chekhov's hotel suite, and hear what he hears — the "dreadful, harrowing sound" of the dying writer's "ratchety breathing."

With the young man's reappearance in the concluding paragraphs of the story, Carver's imagination sets to work dramatizing the way that Chekhov's widow entrusts the waiter with the precious errand of notifying the mortician of Chekhov's death. Olga Knipper was an actress, and her way of explaining the errand is an actress's visualization technique. "If it would help keep his movements purposeful he should imagine himself as someone moving down the busy sidewalk carrying in his arms a porcelain vase of roses that he had to deliver to an important man." Chekhov, of course, is the precious "porcelain vase of roses," but to keep the story from veering off into sentimentality, Carver must keep imagining. He succeeds by balancing the widow's beautiful image of the precious vase with the prosaic fact of the champagne cork in the last paragraph of the narrative. The young servant, totally alive and believable as he functions in the story, has been superbly trained in this elegant Swiss hotel to do his duty. "He leaned over. Without looking down, he reached out and closed it into his hand."

Questions for Discussion

1. Why does Carver begin "Errand" with an account of Chekhov's meeting with Alexei Suvorin in 1897, four years before the writer's death?
2. Why does Carver allow Leo Tolstoy to appear in this story?
3. What have you learned about the difference between Tolstoy and Chekhov from this fictionalized encounter? (Refer to Tolstoy's commentary on Chekhov's "The Darling" in this anthology; see p. 919.)
4. What do Chekhov's efforts to minimize the seriousness of his tuberculosis tell you about him?
5. How effective was the medical treatment of tuberculosis at the turn of the century, judging from Doctor Schwöhrer's prescription for Chekhov's diet?
6. Why does Doctor Schwöhrer try to muffle "the festive explosion" when he uncorks the champagne? Why does he push the cork back into the bottle after he pours three glasses of the wine? Why does the champagne cork reappear in the story?

Topics for Writing

1. Write a short story based on an incident you have read in a biography of a famous person.
2. **CONNECTIONS**   Write an essay comparing and contrasting Carver's treatment of death and dying with Tolstoy's in "The Death of Ivan Ilych."

Related Casebook

See page 20.

Suggested Readings

See page 25.

RAYMOND CARVER

What We Talk About When We Talk About Love (p. 107)

The scarcely veiled animosity between Dr. Mel McGinnis and his wife, Terri, gives tension to this story of three married couples. Through Mel's thoughts and experiences, Carver is investigating the nature of married love. Like the naive boy in Sherwood Anderson's classic short story "I Want to Know Why," Mel insists on asking an impossible question: What is the nature of love? What is the meaning of sharing?

The three pairs of lovers represent different stages of marriage. At one end of a spectrum are Laura and Nick (the narrator), married only a year and a half, still infatuated, glowing with the power of their attraction for each other.

At the other end of the spectrum are the old married pair in the hospital whom Mel and the other doctors have patched up after a catastrophic highway accident. Glad to learn his wife has survived, the old man — as Mel tells the story — is depressed, not because of their physical suffering but because he can't see his wife through the eye holes in his bandages. As Mel says, "Can you imagine? I'm telling you, the man's heart was breaking because he couldn't turn his goddamn head and see his goddamn wife."

Between the two extremes of perfect love, Mel and Terri are veterans (four years married to each other), who are past the bliss of their first attraction and not yet two halves of a whole because they've survived the long haul together. Each has been married before, and each is obsessed with the earlier partner. First Terri talks too much about her sadistic ex-husband Ed; then Mel reveals that he hates his first wife because she kept their kids. Terri says, "she's bankrupting us." The talk appears to ramble, but Carver keeps it under control by sticking to his subject — specific examples of the different varieties of love — and organizing the four friends' conversation by chronicling the stages of their drunkenness as they go through two bottles of gin in the afternoon.

The passing of time is brilliantly described, paralleling the waxing and waning of the stages of love. When the story opens, sunlight fills the New Mexico kitchen where the four friends with their gin and tonics are talking around the table. Midway, when the narrator is beginning to feel the drinks, he describes the sun like the warmth and lift of the gin in his body. "The afternoon sun was like a presence in this room, the spacious light of ease and generosity." As the conversation wears on and Mel tells Terri to shut up after she's interrupted one too many times, the light shifts again, the sunshine getting thinner. The narrator is a shade drunker, and his gaze fixes on the pattern of leaves on the windowpanes and on the Formica kitchen counter, as if he's staying alert by focusing deliberately on the edges of the objects around him. "They weren't the same patterns, of course." Finally, mysteriously, the light drains out of the room, "going back through the window where it had come from." The alcoholic elation has evaporated. At the end of the story, the couples sit in darkness on their kitchen chairs, not moving. The only sound the narrator hears is everyone's hearts beating, separately.

The person we know least about is the narrator, Nick. Perhaps Carver deliberately echoes the name of Nick Adams, Hemingway's autobiographical narrator in his stories of initiation; or Nick Carraway, the narrator of Fitzgerald's *The Great*

Gatsby. The role of Carver's Nick in the story is also like that of Marlow in Conrad's "Heart of Darkness," as Nick voyages through the conversation of Mel and Terri into uncharted, deep waters of the heart. But this Nick is also a participant, through the gin and the sunlight, in the feelings of his troubled, overworked doctor friend.

Questions for Discussion

1. As the story opens, what is the setting in time, place, and situation?
2. How would you describe Terri? What type of person is Mel?
3. What was Terri's experience with her first husband, Ed? In what way was Mel involved in this experience? How does Terri's view of Ed contrast with Mel's view of him? What does this contrast reveal about the character of Mel and Terri's relationship?
4. In the discussion about Ed, what do we discover about the couple with whom Mel and Terri are socializing? What is their relationship both to each other and to Mel and Terri? Compare and contrast their marriage with Terri and Mel's.
5. What is the point of view in this story? Who is the narrator? How reliable is he?
6. Does Mel view his first wife in the same way he does Terri? What are we told about his first wife?
7. What are some of the questions about love that Carver raises through his characters? Does he offer any answers to these questions?
8. A third couple is introduced in the story. What astonishes Mel about their relationship?
9. What changes in the setting, if any, can you identify over the course of the story? In what way does the setting mirror Carver's message about the stages of love?
10. What does each of the couples represent? What is the significance of the last paragraph?

Topics for Writing

1. Write an essay discussing theme and characterization in "What We Talk About When We Talk About Love."
2. Explore the question posed by the title of this story: What does Carver (and the reader) talk about when he (and we) talks about love?
3. Think about married couples you know and discuss what their views on love might be as well as the quality of their relationships.
4. **CONNECTIONS**   Compare and contrast the types of love in Carver's story and Joyce's "The Dead."

Related Casebook

See page 20.

Suggested Readings

Adelman, Bob. *Carver Country — The World of Raymond Carver.* New York: Scribner's, 1991. A photographic essay with quotations from Carver's writing.

Carver, Raymond. "The Art of Fiction LXXVI." Interview in the *Paris Review,* No. 88 (Summer, 1983).

———. *Fires: Essays, Poems, Stories.* Santa Barbara, CA: Capra, 1983.

———. *Where I'm Calling From: New and Selected Stories.* New York: Atlantic Monthly, 1988.

Gentry, Marshall B., and William A. Stuff, eds. *Conversations with Raymond Carver.* Jackson, UP of Mississippi, 1990.

Halpert, Sam, ed. *When We Talk About Raymond Carver.* Layton, UT: Gibbs Smith, 1991.

Stull, W. L. "Beyond Hopelessville: Another Side of Raymond Carver." *Philological Quarterly* 64 (1985): 1–15.

WILLA CATHER

Paul's Case (p. 117)

Students may feel repelled by this story and reject its ending as heavy-handed. The structure of the plot, which pits a sensitive adolescent against an ugly and confining bourgeois society, invites us to admire Paul's rebellion and to glamorize his suicide, but Cather takes great pains to make Paul as unattractive in his way as the family, school, and neighborhood he hates. Quite apart from his supercilious mannerisms, which his teachers feel some inclination to forgive, Paul's quest for brightness and beauty in the world of art and imagination is subjected to Cather's devastating criticism, so readers who were ready to make a stock tragic response to his demise may find it difficult to care.

Try meeting this objection directly by examining the implications of the story's concluding passage. The vision presented here comes close to formulaic naturalism. Paul is not only caught in a universal machine, he is himself a machine. The imagination that has sustained him against the ugliness of his surroundings is dismissed as a "picture making mechanism," now crushed. The world against which Paul rebels is plain, gray, narrow, and monotonous. Its combination of saints (Calvin, Washington) and customary homilies precludes all that is in itself beautiful, pleasant, and fulfilling in the present moment. Paul's reaction, however, is merely the obverse. His habitual lies reflect his general resort to the artificial. He may be "artistic," but not in the sense of being creative, and his romantic fantasies involve no more satisfactory relations with others than does his ordinary life. Paul's world is so intolerable to his sensitivity that he is driven to escape from it, even at the cost of sitting in the cellar with the rats watching him from the corners. His escape inevitably becomes a form of self-destruction, as manifested in his criminal act — which to him feels like confronting "the thing in the corner" — and finally in his suicide. Paul passes through the "portal of Romance" for good, into a dream from which "there would be no awakening."

If it could be termed a choice, it would clearly be a bad choice, but Cather presents it rather as a symptom of Paul's "case," a disease of life from which he suffers, has suffered perhaps since his mother died when he was an infant, and for which, at first glance, there seems to be no cure. No wonder readers may be inclined to dismiss the story as unduly negative because unduly narrow. But Cather, at the same time that she meticulously documents the inexorable progress of Paul's illness, defines by implication a condition of health whose possible existence gives meaning to Paul's demise. As Philip L. Gerber explains: "Although [Cather] extolled the imaginative, her definition of imagination is all-important; for rather than meaning an ability 'to weave pretty stories out of nothing,' imagination conveyed to her 'a response to what is going on — a sensitiveness to which outside things appeal' and was an amalgam of sympathy and observation."

Paul's refuge is the product of the first, false kind of imagination, but the reality and the power of an imagination of the second sort is evident throughout the story, in the masterful evocations of Cordelia Street, of the school and its all-too-human teachers, and not least of Paul himself. When Paul's case finally becomes extreme enough to break through the insensitivity of bourgeois Pittsburgh, the world of the street that bears the name of King Lear's faithful daughter at last begins to live up to its name, sympathizing with Paul's plight and offering to embrace him with its love. To Paul, however, whose own unregenerate imagination is still confined to making pretty pictures rather than sympathetic observations, the advances of Cordelia Street seem like tepid waters of boredom in which he is called upon to submerge himself. The potential for growth and change that is reflected in his father's abandoning his usual frugality to pay back the money Paul has stolen and in his coming down from the top of the stairs into Paul's world to reach out to him, escape Paul's notice — but not that of the reader.

WILLIAM E. SHEIDLEY

Questions for Discussion

1. Describe Paul's personality as Cather sets it forth in the opening paragraph of the story. Is this someone we like and admire?
2. Why do Paul's teachers have so much difficulty dealing with him? What does the knowledge that Cather was a teacher in Pittsburgh at the time she wrote this story suggest about her perspective on Paul's case?
3. What techniques does Cather use to establish the reader's sympathy for Paul? What limits that sympathy?
4. Contrast the three worlds — school, Carnegie Hall, and Cordelia Street — in which Paul moves. Why does Cather introduce them in that order?
5. What is the effect of Cather's capitalizing the word *Romance*?
6. Discuss the three decorations that hang above Paul's bed. What aspects of American culture do they refer to? What do they leave out?
7. Explore the allusion embodied in the name "Cordelia Street." Why does Paul feel he is drowning there?
8. Discuss Paul's fear of rats. Why does he feel that he has "thrown down the gauntlet to the thing in the corner" when he steals the money and leaves for New York?
9. Explicate the paragraph that begins "Perhaps it was because, in Paul's world, the natural nearly always wore the guise of ugliness." To what extent does this paragraph offer a key to the story's structure and theme?

10. Describe the effect of the leap forward in time that occurs in the white space before we find Paul on the train to New York. Why does Cather withhold for so long her account of what has taken place?
11. What is admirable about Paul's entry into and sojourn in New York? What is missing from his new life?
12. Why does Paul wink at himself in the mirror after reading the newspaper account of his deeds?
13. On the morning of his suicide, Paul recognizes that "money was everything." Why does he think so? Does the story bear him out?
14. What is the effect of Paul's burying his carnation in the snow? of his last thoughts?

Topics for Writing

1. Analyze "Paul's Case" as an attack on American society.
2. In an essay argue that Cather's commentary on Mansfield (printed in Part Two, p. 847) is a basis for criticism of "Paul's Case."
3. Cather's story is punctuated by several recurrent images and turns of phrase. Locate as many as you can and take note of their contexts. What does this network of internal connections reveal?
4. **CONNECTIONS** Compare Cather's account of Paul's death with accounts of dying in other stories, such as Tolstoy's "The Death of Ivan Ilych" and Bierce's "An Occurrence at Owl Creek Bridge."

Related Commentary

Willa Cather, The Stories of Katherine Mansfield, p. 847.

Suggested Readings

Arnold, Marilyn. *Willa Cather: A Reference Guide.* Boston: G. K. Hall, 1986.
———. *Willa Cather's Short Fiction.* Athens: Ohio UP, 1984.
Brown, E. K., and Leon Edel. *Willa Cather: A Critical Biography.* Lincoln: U of Nebraska P, 1987.
Callander, Marilyn B. *Willa Cather and the Fairy Tale.* Ann Arbor: UMI Research P, 1989.
Cather, Willa. *Collected Short Fiction 1892–1912.* Introduction by Mildred R. Bennett. Lincoln: U of Nebraska P, 1965.
———. *Early Novels and Stories.* The Library of America. New York: Viking, 1986.
Daiches, David. *Willa Cather: A Critical Introduction.* Ithaca: Cornell UP, 1951. 144–47.
Gerber, Philip L. *Willa Cather.* Twayne's United States Authors Series 258. Boston: G. K. Hall, 1975. 72–73, 101, 141, 163.
Murphy, John J. *Critical Essays on Willa Cather.* Boston: G. K. Hall, 1984.
Thomas, Susie. *Willa Cather.* Savage, MD: Barnes and Noble, 1990.
Wasserman, Loretta. *Willa Cather: A Study of Short Fiction.* Boston: Twayne, 1991.

JOHN CHEEVER

The Swimmer (p. 133)

One way to reconstruct a naturalistic time scheme for the story, so Neddy's "misfortunes," the awareness of which he seems to have repressed, can be dated with regard to the other events in the narrative, is to imagine a gap in time covered by the line "He stayed in the Levys' gazebo until the storm had passed." The authoritative point of view in the opening paragraphs seems to preclude placing the misfortunes before Neddy begins his swim, while the gathering clouds and circling de Haviland trainer assert the continuity of the first phase of his journey. After the storm, however, signs of change appear, and it is possible to reconcile Neddy's subsequent encounters with the proposition that he is continuing his swim on another day or days under quite different circumstances. Before the storm, he visits the Grahams and the Bunkers, who greet him as the prosperous and popular Neddy Merrill described at the beginning of the story, but after the storm Neddy visits only the empty houses of the Lindleys and the Welchers; the public pool where any derelict may swim; the peculiar Hallorans, who mention his troubles; the Sachses, who have problems of their own and refuse him a drink; the socially inferior Biswangers, who snub him; and his old mistress Shirley, who implies that this call is not the first he has paid in this condition.

But Cheever is not interested in a realistic time scheme. If he were, he would not have burned the 250-page novelistic version of the story (mentioned in the headnote) that presumably filled in the blanks. Instead, he has constructed the story so Neddy's recognition of his loss strikes the reader with the same impact it has on Neddy. By telescoping time, Cheever thrusts us forward into a state of affairs that exists only as a dim cloud on the horizon on the day the story begins and at first seems to be entirely taking place.

What accounts for the reversal in Neddy's life? Surely it is possible to tax Neddy for irresponsibility and childishness in turning his back on his friends and family and so casually setting off on an odyssey from which he returns far too late. Neddy's own view of his adventure is considerably more attractive. The only member of his society who seems free from a hangover on this midsummer Sunday, Neddy simply wishes to savor the pleasures of his fortunate life: "The day was beautiful and it seemed to him that a long swim might enlarge and celebrate its beauty." Although he has been (or will be) unfaithful to his wife with Shirley Adams, and although he kisses close to a dozen other women on his journey, Neddy does not construe his departure as infidelity to Lucinda. Rather, to swim the string of pools across the suburban county is to travel along "the Lucinda River." As "a pilgrim, an explorer, a man with a destiny," Neddy plunges into this river of life aware of the gathering storm on the horizon but regarding it with pleasurable anticipation. When it finally breaks over the Levys' gazebo, he savors the exciting release of tension that accompanies the arrival of a thunder shower, but with the explosion of thunder and the smell of gunpowder that ensues, Neddy finds his happy illusions, his world of "youth, sport, and clement weather," lashed by a more unpleasant reality, just as the "rain lashed the Japanese lanterns that Mrs. Levy had bought in Kyoto the year before last, or was it the year before that?"

What Neddy now confronts, though he tries gamely to ignore it, are the twin recognitions that his youth is not eternal and that the pleasant society of the "bonny and lush . . . banks of the Lucinda River" is unstable, exclusive, and cruel. Grass grows in the Lindleys' riding ring, the Welchers have moved away, and the sky is now overcast. Crossing Route 424 in his swimming suit, Neddy is subjected to the ridicule of the public, and at the Recreation Center he finds that swimming does not convey the same sense of elegance, pleasure, and freedom that it does in the pools of his affluent friends. The validity of the society Neddy has previously enjoyed is called further into question by the very existence of the self-contradictory Hallorans, whose personal eccentricity is matched by their political hypocrisy. Neddy's visits to the Biswangers and to Shirley Adams complete the destruction of his illusions, but it is Eric Sachs, disfigured by surgery and (with the loss of his navel) symbolically cut off from the human community, who embodies the most troubling reflection of Neddy's condition. "I'm not alone," Shirley proclaims, but Neddy is, and as this man who "might have been compared to a summer's day" recognizes that his summer is over, it is not surprising that for "the first time in his adult life" he begins to cry. While the reader may relish Cheever's indictment of a society whose values have so betrayed Neddy, it is hard not to feel some admiration for a man who, by executing his plan to swim the county through the now icy autumn waters, has indeed become a legendary figure, an epic hero of a sort.

WILLIAM E. SHEIDLEY

Questions for Discussion

1. Who is referred to by the word "everyone" in the opening sentence? Who is not?
2. How does Neddy Merrill relate to the world in which he moves? Why does he decide to swim home?
3. Why does Neddy name his route "the Lucinda River"? The Levys live on "Alewives Lane." Alewives are a kind of fish that swim upriver to spawn. Is there a sexual component to Neddy's journey?
4. Is the storm that breaks a surprise? How does Neddy feel about the beginning of the rain?
5. What differences can be noticed between what Neddy experiences before and after the storm? How might they be explained?
6. What new elements enter the story when Neddy crosses Route 424? Why do the drivers jeer at him?
7. Before he dives into the unappealing public swimming pool, Neddy tells himself "that this was merely a stagnant bend in the Lucinda River." How characteristic is this effort to assuage his own doubts and discontents?
8. Based on what the Hallorans, the Sachses, the Biswangers, and Shirley Adams say to Neddy, what is the truth about himself and his life of which he is unaware?
9. Cheever has his hero discover the season by observing the stars. What effect does that choice among various possibilities have on our attitude toward Neddy?
10. It is not difficult to say what Neddy has lost. What has he gained?

Topics for Writing

1. Explain why Neddy Merrill talks only with women.
2. Analyze the characters Rusty Towers, Eric Sachs, and Neddy Merrill.
3. Write an essay discussing Neddy Merrill's voyage of exploration and discovery.
4. Evaluate Cheever's attitude toward the swimmer.

Related Commentary

John Cheever, Why I Write Short Stories, p. 855.

Suggested Readings

Cheever, John. *The Journals of John Cheever.* New York: Knopf, 1991.
Cheever, Susan. *Home before Dark.* Boston: Houghton, 1984.
Coale, Samuel. *John Cheever.* New York: Ungar, 1977. 43–47.
Collins, R. G., ed. *Critical Essays on John Cheever.* Boston: G. K. Hall, 1982.
O'Hara, James E. *John Cheever: A Study of the Short Fiction.* Boston: Twayne, 1989.
Waldeland, Lynne. *John Cheever.* Boston: Twayne, 1979.
Writers at Work, Fifth Series. New York: Penguin, 1981. Interview with John Cheever by Annette Grant, Fall 1976.

ANTON CHEKHOV

The Darling (p. 143)

One of the liveliest discussions about a short story in this anthology could be started by a class debate based on contradictory interpretations of "The Darling." Was Chekhov misguided in satirizing women's tendency to depend on men for meaning and direction in their lives? In Tolstoy's view (see "Chekhov's Intent in 'The Darling,'" page 919), Chekhov had allowed himself to become a women's rights advocate under the pernicious influence of his "liberated" wife, the actress Olga Knipper. Other interpretations, in contrast, reveal the subtle emotional tyranny of the protagonist, Olga. Students could be assigned an interpretation and asked to either support or refute it.

Other critical perspectives can also be applied to this provocative story. A feminist reader could argue that Olga has been handicapped by the environment around her: Uneducated for a profession, she can have no ideas or life of her own. A psychological interpretation could concentrate on the darling's early, possibly traumatic fixation on her father and his long mortal illness just as she reaches manageable age. A formalist approach might look closely at the words the schoolboy uses as he cries out in his sleep: "You watch out! You go away! Don't you pick quarrels with me!," or in another translation, "I'll give it you! Get away! Shut up!" Basing her analysis on the latter translation, Welty assumes that the boy is dreaming of Olga. He could just as well be dreaming of his teacher at school, other students fighting with him in the schoolyard, or his own mother, who appears to have abandoned him. He could even be repeating the cruel words his mother might have said to drive him away from her before she left him with Olga.

The English short story writer H. E. Bates interpreted the story yet another way. Comparing Chekhov's technique with Maupassant's, Bates writes, "Both like to portray a certain type of weak, stupid, thoughtless woman, a sort of yes-woman who can unwittingly impose tragedy or happiness on others. Maupassant had no patience with the type; but in Olenka [Olga], in the 'The Darling,' it is precisely a quality of tender patience, the judgment of the heart and not the head, that gives Chekhov's story its effect of uncommon understanding and radiance."

Bates saw Chekhov as subtle: His

> receptivity, his capacity for compassion, are both enormous. Of his characters he seems to say, "I know what they are doing is their own responsibility. But how did they come to this, how did it happen? There may be some trivial thing that will explain." That triviality, discovered, held for a moment in the light, is the key to Chekhov's emotional solution. In Maupassant's case the importance of that key would have been inexorably driven home; but as we turn to ask of Chekhov if we have caught his meaning aright, it is to discover that we must answer that question for ourselves — for Chekhov has gone. . . . Both [Maupassant and Chekhov] knew to perfection when they had said enough; an acute instinct continually reminded them of the fatal tedium of explanation, of going on a second too long. In Chekhov this sense of impatience, almost a fear, caused him frequently to stop speaking, as it were, in mid-air. It was this which gave his stories an air of remaining unfinished, of leaving the reader to his own explanations, of imposing on each story's end a note of suspense so abrupt and yet refined that it produced on the reader an effect of delayed shock.

Questions for Discussion

1. How does Chekhov characterize Olga at the beginning of the story?
2. Why are the "lady visitors" the first ones to call her a "darling"?
3. Olga "mothers" each of her husbands. Could she have been both a good wife and a good mother if she had had children of her own?

Topics for Writing

1. Interpret Sasha's words at the end of "The Darling." Identify the person he is talking to, and find details in the story that justify your interpretation.
2. **RESPONDING CREATIVELY** Continue "The Darling," supposing that the "loud knock at the gate" is a message from Sasha's mother, who wants him to join her in Harkov.

Related Commentaries

Anton Chekhov, Technique in Writing the Short Story, p. 857.
Leo Tolstoy, Chekhov's Intent in "The Darling," p. 919.

Suggested Readings

Bates, H. E. *The Modern Short Story.* Boston: The Writer, 1972.

Eekman, Thomas. *Critical Essays on Anton Chekhov.* Boston: G. K. Hall, 1989.

Friedland, Louis S., ed. *Anton Chekhov's Letters on the Short Story, the Drama, and Other Topics.* Salem, NH: Ayer, 1965.

Kramer, Karl D. *The Chameleon and the Dream: The Image of Reality in Chekhov's Stories.* The Hague: Mouton, 1970. 171.

Matlaw, Ralph E., ed. *Anton Chekhov's Short Stories.* New York: Norton, 1979.

Meister, Charles W. *Chekhov Criticism, 1880 through 1986.* New York: St. Martin's, 1990.

Pritchett, V. S. *Chekhov: A Spirit Set Free.* New York: Random, 1988.

Rayfield, Donald. *Chekhov: The Evolution of His Art.* New York: Barnes, 1975. 197–200.

Smith, Virginia Llewellyn. "The Lady with the Dog." Anton Chekhov's Short Stories: Texts of the Stories, Backgrounds, Criticism. Ed. Ralph E. Matlaw. New York: Norton, 1979. Excerpted from Smith, *Anton Chekhov and the Lady with the Dog* (New York: Oxford UP, 1973). 96–97, 212–18.

Troyat, Henri. *Chekhov.* Trans. Michael Henry Heim. New York: Dutton, 1986.

KATE CHOPIN

Désirée's Baby (p. 154)

It is difficult to imagine a reader who would not be horrified and disgusted by the tragic results of the racism and sexism that permeate this story. No one could believe that Armand Aubigny's inhuman cruelty to his wife Désirée and his child is warranted. The only real uncertainty the reader confronts regards Armand's foreknowledge of his own parentage: Did he know that his mother had "negro blood" before he married Désirée, or did he discover her revealing letter later on? If he *did* know beforehand (and it is difficult to believe that he did not), his courtship of and marriage to Désirée were highly calculated actions, with Désirée chosen because she was the perfect woman to be used in an "experimental" reproduction. If their child(ren) "passed" as white, everything would be fine. If not, Désirée, the foundling, would be the perfect victim to take the blame.

This may seem to be judging Armand too harshly, because the narrator does describe his great passion for Désirée, so suddenly and furiously ignited. Certainly Armand behaves like a man in love. But Chopin inserts a few subtle remarks that allow us to question this, at least in hindsight: "The wonder was that he had not loved her before; for he had known her since his father brought him home from Paris, a boy of eight, after his mother died there." It does seem unlikely that a man of Armand's temperament would conceive this sudden intense desire for "the girl next door," a sweet, naive young woman whom he has known for most of his life. Right from the beginning, Chopin also reveals details about his character that are unsettling, even to the innocent and loving Désirée. The basic cruelty of Armand's nature is hinted at throughout the story, particularly regarding his severe treatment of "his negroes," which is notably in sharp contrast to his father's example.

Armand's reputation as a harsh slavemaster supports the presumption that he has known about his own part-negro ancestry all along. He did not learn this behavior from his father, who was "easy-going and indulgent" in his dealings with the slaves. The knowledge that some of his own ancestors spring from the same "race of slavery" would surely be unbearable to the proud, "imperious" Armand, and the rage and shame that his knowledge brings would easily be turned against the blacks around him. In much the same way, when Armand realizes that his baby is visibly racially mixed, he vents his fury viciously on his slaves, the "very spirit of Satan [taking] hold of him."

Modern readers will find many disturbing aspects to this story. The seemingly casual racism is horrifying. And feminists will be likely to take exception (as they sometimes do to Chopin's *The Awakening*) to Désirée's passive acceptance of Armand's rejection of her and his child, and her apparently deliberate walk into the bayou. Suicide is not the strong woman's answer to the situation, but Désirée is definitely not a strong woman. What she does have is wealthy parents who love her and are willing to take care of her and the baby. So why would she feel that she has to end her life? Discussion of this issue will have to focus on the historical period and social setting of the story. Gender and class roles and structures were so rigid that it was impossible for a woman to cross those lines very far. If she tried, what would the cost be to her children? And of course, the most rigid barrier of all was racial. No mixing of black and white blood would ever be condoned in that society (thus, Armand's mother remained in France, keeping her family secrets), so Désirée's baby would never have acceptance anywhere. Désirée isn't able to see any viable way out of her terrifying situation, and her view is not entirely unrealistic, considering her time and place. Once again, Chopin realistically depicts the cruelty and horror of a social structure that totally denies power to women, children, the poor, and most of all, to blacks.

Questions for Discussion

1. Describe your feelings toward Armand at the end of the story. What aspect of this last scene do you find the most shocking? Are you completely surprised by his behavior here? See if you can trace Chopin's gradual building of Armand's character, noting the things she chooses to reveal to us throughout the story.

2. What kind of person is Désirée? Does she seem to be a good match for Armand? Does your opinion of her change as the story progresses? How consistent is she as a character?

3. How do you feel about Désirée's final choice? Is suicide an understandable choice, or is she simply a weak character? What other options do you think she may have?

4. Should Madame Valmondé have told Désirée of her realization about the baby? When she sees the baby at four weeks of age, she obviously is startled by something in its appearance, but doesn't mention it. Then, she returns home and seems to wait for disaster to strike, never returning to visit Désirée. How do you explain this behavior, coming from an obviously protective, loving mother?

5. Armand is shown to be a very cruel master to his slaves, a direct contrast to the way in which his father ran the plantation. Does learning his family secret in the last scene suggest any explanation for this?

6. Do you think Armand knew about his own mother's negro ancestry before he courted and married Désirée? Look for evidence from the story to support your opinion.

Topics for Writing

1. Discuss the way the setting affects the action in this story.
2. Should Désirée have returned to her family home with her baby? Consider the pros and cons of her future there.
3. According to the critic Wai-chee Dimock, the racial injustice in "Désirée's Baby" is "only a necessary background against which Chopin stages her deadly dramatic irony. . . . The injustice here is not the injustice of racial oppression but the injustice of a wrongly attributed racial identity." Agree or disagree with this interpretation of the story.

Related Commentary

Kate Chopin, How I Stumbled upon Maupassant, p. 858.

Suggested Readings

See page 35.

Kate Chopin

The Story of an Hour (p. 158)

Does the O. Henryesque trick ending of this story merely surprise us, or does Chopin arrange to have Louise Mallard expire at the sight of her unexpectedly still living husband in order to make a thematic point? Students inclined to groan when Brently Mallard returns "composedly carrying his gripsack and umbrella" may come to think better of the ending if you ask them to evaluate the doctors' conclusions about the cause of Mrs. Mallard's death. Although Richards and Josephine take "great care . . . to break to her as gently as possible the news of her husband's death," what actually kills Mrs. Mallard is the news that he is still alive. The experience of regeneration and freedom that she undergoes in the armchair looking out upon a springtime vista involves an almost sexual surrender of conventional repressions and restraints. As she abandons herself to the realization of her freedom that approaches to possess her, Mrs. Mallard enjoys a hitherto forbidden physical and spiritual excitement. The presumption that she would be devastated by the death of her husband, like the presumption that she needs to be protected by watchful, "tender" friends, reduces Mrs. Mallard to a dependency from which she is joyful at last to escape. Chopin best images this oppressive, debilitating concern in what Mrs. Mallard thinks she will weep again to see: "the kind, tender hands folded in death; the face that had never looked save with love upon her, fixed and gray and dead." Although had she lived Mrs. Mallard might have felt guilty for, as it were, taking her selfhood like a lover and pridefully stepping forth "like a goddess of Victory," Chopin effectively suggests that the guilt belongs instead to the caretakers, the "travel-stained" Brently, the discomfited Josephine, and Richards, whose "quick motion" to conceal his error comes "too late."

WILLIAM E. SHEIDLEY

Questions for Discussion

1. In view of Mrs. Mallard's eventual reactions, evaluate the efforts of Josephine and Richards to break the news of her husband's death gently.
2. What purpose might Chopin have in stressing that Mrs. Mallard does not block out the realization that her husband has died?
3. What might be the cause or causes of the "physical exhaustion that haunted her body and seemed to reach into her soul" that Mrs. Mallard feels as she sinks into the armchair?
4. Describe your reaction to the view out the window the first time you read the story. Did it change on a second reading?
5. Mrs. Mallard's face bespeaks repression. What has she been repressing?
6. Discuss the imagery Chopin uses to describe Mrs. Mallard's recognition of her new freedom.
7. What kind of man is Brently Mallard, as Mrs. Mallard remembers him? In what ways does he resemble Josephine and Richards?
8. Describe your feelings about Mrs. Mallard as she emerges from her room. Is the saying "Pride goeth before a fall" relevant here?
9. In what way is the doctors' pronouncement on the cause of Mrs. Mallard's death ironic? In what sense is it nonetheless correct?

Topics for Writing

1. Discuss the imagery of life and the imagery of death in "The Story of an Hour."
2. Write a paper analyzing "The Story of an Hour" as a thwarted awakening.
3. Describe the tragic irony in "The Story of an Hour."
4. On a second reading of "The Story of an Hour," try to recall how you responded to each paragraph or significant passage when you read it the first time. Write short explanations of any significant changes in your reactions. To what extent are those changes the result of knowing the story's ending? What other factors are at work?
5. **RESPONDING CREATIVELY** Can falsehood be the key to truth? Narrate a personal experience in which your own or someone else's reaction to misinformation revealed something meaningful and true.
6. **RESPONDING CREATIVELY** How long is a turning point? Tell a story covering a brief span of time — a few minutes or an hour — in which the central character's life is permanently changed. Study Chopin's techniques for summarizing and condensing information.

Related Commentary

See page 34.

Suggested Readings

Bender, B. "Kate Chopin's Lyrical Short Stories." *Studies in Short Fiction* 11 (1974): 257–66.

Chopin, Kate. *The Complete Works of Kate Chopin.* Baton Rouge: Louisiana State UP, 1970.

Dimock, Wai-chee. "Kate Chopin." *Modern American Women Writers.* Ed. Elaine Showalter et al. New York: Collier, 1993.

Fluck, Winifred. "Tentative Transgressions: Kate Chopin's Fiction as a Mode of Symbolic Action." *Studies in American Fiction* 10 (1982): 151–71.

Miner, Madonne M. "Veiled Hints: An Affected Stylist's Reading of Kate Chopin's 'Story of an Hour.'" *Markham Review* 11 (1982): 29–32.

Seyersted, Per. *Kate Chopin: A Critical Biography.* Baton Rouge: Louisiana State UP, 1969. 57–59.

Skaggs, Peggy. *Kate Chopin.* Boston: Twayne, 1985.

Toth, Emily. *Kate Chopin.* New York: Morrow, 1990.

SANDRA CISNEROS

The House on Mango Street (p. 162)

Cisneros credits Jorge Luis Borges's *Dreamtigers* as an important influence on her choice of form in *The House on Mango Street*. Like Borges in "Everything and Nothing," a short piece from *Dreamtigers,* Cisneros works within short narrative forms, writing sketches rather than stories. Where Borges develops an idea about Shakespeare as his theme, Cisneros dramatizes emotions in her sketches. These emotions belong to the young narrator as she tells about her experiences of economic hardship and social marginalization within a Mexican American family. The economic and social realities of her life are difficult, but the emotional security she finds within her tightly knit family appears to have given her the strength to survive the difficulties she faces and enables her to speak in the positive tone of her stories.

"The House on Mango Street" starts in a voice that suggests muted protest, foreshadowing our awareness of the narrator's developing strength of character. In the opening paragraph, the narrator names the various streets her family has lived on as they moved from apartment to apartment during her early childhood. Her memories center on the difficult living conditions in the different rental apartments — for example, broken water pipes and a hostile landlord "banging on the ceiling with a broom" if the six members of her family made too much noise. Her parents have told their four children that they would eventually own their own home, and this promise gives them hope. Cisneros's book begins when the family has achieved its dream of home ownership. Then the author takes the difference between the American dream and its economic and social reality as the subject of her book.

Students should be aware that Cisneros and her young narrator are not identical. Cisneros has chosen the persona of a young girl to tell her stories, and this choice of first-person point of view adds considerable poignancy to her narratives. Reading "The House on Mango Street," we are aware that the (imaginary) narrator's naiveté is part of the emotional effect of what she tells us. We become emotionally involved in the story through her shy pride at moving into her "own" house on Mango Street, and through her confusion after she realizes that the dream house her parents have promised her isn't at all what she dreamed it would be.

We understand how important the house is to the narrator when she tells us about the apartment on Loomis where the family lived before moving to Mango Street. There a nun from her school made her "feel like nothing" by tactlessly wondering how her young pupil could live in a building that had been so brazenly burglarized. Yet among the descriptive details of the way the Loomis building looked, the narrator discloses that her father had nailed wooden bars on the windows of the family's third-floor apartment so that she and her brother Carlos and sister Nenny and the baby Kiki wouldn't fall out. The significance of this detail doesn't weigh as heavily on the narrator as her memory of her shame before the nun, but we register the father's concern for his young children's safety. There is little character description in Cisneros's stories, but the essential details giving coherence to the narrative are there.

Questions for Discussion

1. How does your awareness of the author's background help you to understand "The House on Mango Street"?
2. What clues does Cisneros give you to help you understand that she has created a fictional narrator in this story?
3. How does Cisneros's choice of a first-person narrator shape the way she tells her story?

Topic for Writing

1. **RESPONDING CREATIVELY**   Write a sketch of your earliest memories of the home(s) you lived in as a young child.

Suggested Reading

Cisneros, Sandra. *Woman Hollering Creek.* New York: Random, 1991.

JOSEPH CONRAD

Heart of Darkness (p. 165)

At the center of the concentric layers out of which Conrad constructs this story lies a case of atavism and the collapse of civilized morality. Kurtz casts aside all restraint and becomes as wild as his surroundings; or rather, the darkness around him calls out the darkness within his innermost being. Kurtz is a man of heroic abilities and exemplary ideals, yet at the end of the story, he explodes, unable to control his own strength.

Conrad does not provide an intimate inside view of Kurtz. To do so would destroy the aura of mystery and special significance that marks the story's theme as a profound revelation, the "culminating point of [Marlow's] experience," gained at "the farthest point of navigation." Instead, Conrad positions Kurtz in the midst of an impenetrable jungle, at "the very heart of darkness," as far from home and as remote from familiar frames of reference as possible. Then he causes the reader to approach Kurtz through a series of identifications that make the revelation of his debasement a statement not just about Kurtz, but about us all.

Conrad creates this effect mainly through his use of Marlow as narrator, and no discussion of the story can avoid exploring his function. He is on one hand a kind of prophet — his pose resembles that of an idol or Buddha — whose wisdom arises from his having looked beyond the veil that screens the truth from common view ("the inner truth is hidden — luckily, luckily"), and on the other hand an adventurer like the heroes of epic poems, descending into Hades and emerging shaken with his dark illumination. But Marlow's vision is neither of heaven nor of hell. His journey up the Congo River is in fact a descent into the inner reaches of the human soul. Forced by a combination of circumstances and preconceptions into a special association with Kurtz, Marlow recognizes in that "shadow" the intrinsic darkness of human nature, in which he shares. When he plunges into the jungle to redeem Kurtz, who has crawled away on all fours to rejoin the "unspeakable rites" of his worshipers, Marlow embraces what Kurtz has become no less than what he once was or might have been, acknowledging his own kinship with the deepest depravity. Kurtz dies crying, "The horror! The horror!" — apparently having regained from his rescuer enough of his moral bearings to recoil from his own behavior. Marlow, who judges the truth "too dark —too dark altogether," preserves the innocence of Kurtz's "Intended," leaving her "great and saving illusion" intact.

Conrad may be suggesting that only by a conscious lie or by willful blindness can we avoid sinking into the savagery that surrounds us, that dwells under externally maintained restraint within us, and that animates our civilization in various guises, such as the "flabby, pretending, weak-eyed devil of a rapacious and pitiless folly." The conquest of the earth, which is what the civilized society portrayed in the story is engaged in, "is not a pretty thing when you look into it too much," Marlow says. "What redeems it is the idea only . . . an unselfish belief in the idea — something you can set up, and bow down before, and offer sacrifice to." But such idolatry of our own idea is not far from its horrible perversion into the worship of himself that the would-be civilizer Kurtz sets up. It leads to a civilization aptly portrayed in Kurtz's symbolic painting of a blindfolded woman carrying a torch through darkness. If Conrad offers a glimmer of light in the dark world he envisions, it is in the sympathetic understanding that enables Marlow to befriend Kurtz and to lie for Kurtz and his Intended, even at the cost of having to taste the "flavor of mortality" he finds in lies, which he detests like the death it suggests to him.

WILLIAM E. SHEIDLEY

Questions for Discussion

1. What does Conrad gain by having his story told by Marlow to a group of important Londoners on a yacht in the Thames estuary? What is implied by the association of the Thames with the Congo? by Marlow's assertion, "And this also . . . has been one of the dark places on the earth"?

2. Marlow enters on his adventure through a city he associates with "a whited sepulcher"; he passes old women knitting who remind him of the Fates; the Company office is "as still as a house in a city of the dead." Locate other indications that Marlow's journey is like a trip into the underworld. What do they suggest about the story's meaning?

3. In what ways is the French warship "shelling the bush" an apt image of the European conquest of Africa? What does this historical theme contribute to our understanding of Marlow and Kurtz?

4. Discuss the Company's chief accountant. Why is it appropriate that Marlow first hears of Kurtz from him?

5. Marlow calls the men waiting for a post in the interior "pilgrims." Explain the irony in his use of the term.

6. Marlow is associated with Kurtz as a member of "the gang of virtue." Explain the resonance of that phrase.

7. Describe the journey up the Congo as Marlow reports it in the pages that follow his remark, "Going up that river was like traveling back to the earliest beginnings of the world." In what ways does Conrad make it a symbolic journey as well as an actual one?

8. Discuss Marlow's attitudes toward the natives. What do they mean to him?

9. As the boat draws near Kurtz's station, people cry out "with unrestrained grief" from the jungle. Why?

10. After the attack of the natives is repulsed and the narrative seems at the point of reaching the climax toward which so much suspense has been built — the meeting with Kurtz — Conrad throws it away by having Marlow stop to light his pipe and speak offhandedly and abstractly about what he learned. Why? Does this passage actually destroy the suspense? Is the story rendered anticlimactic? Or is the climax changed? What is the true climax of the story?

11. Why do you think the heads on stakes are facing Kurtz's house?

12. Discuss the Russian and his attitude toward Kurtz. Why does Conrad trouble to add this European to Kurtz's train of cultists?

13. Marlow is astonished that the Manager calls Kurtz's methods "unsound." Why? What does this passage reveal about each of them?

14. Explain what happens to Marlow when he goes into the bush after Kurtz. Explain what happens to Kurtz. Why does Marlow call Kurtz "that shadow"?

15. Marlow claims to have "struggled with a soul"; he tells Kurtz that if he does not come back he will be "utterly lost." Is Marlow a savior for Kurtz? Is Kurtz saved?

16. Why does Marlow lie to Kurtz's "Intended"?

17. Contrast the last paragraph of the story with the opening.

18. Comment on the title of Kurtz's pamphlet, about the "Suppression of Savage Customs," and on the significance of its scrawled postscript, "Exterminate all the brutes."

Topics for Writing

1. In an essay, explore Conrad's use of foreshadowing.

2. Discuss traditional symbolism and literary allusion as a way of universalizing the theme of "Heart of Darkness."

3. Analyze the function of the frame in this novella.
4. Marlow frequently concludes a segment of his narrative with a generalization that sums it up and takes on a quality of special significance, such as, "I felt as though, instead of going to the center of a continent, I were about to set off for the center of the earth"; or, "It was like a weary pilgrimage among hints for nightmares." Locate as many such passages as you can. What do they reveal about the mind of the narrator?
5. Conrad frequently uses an impressionist technique that Ian Watt has called "delayed decoding." When the steamboat is attacked, for example, Marlow first sees "little sticks" flying about, and only later recognizes them as arrows. Find other instances of delayed decoding in the story, and then write a narrative of your own using a similar method.
6. **CONNECTIONS**   Analyze the journey into madness in Conrad's "Heart of Darkness" and Gilman's "The Yellow Wallpaper."

Related Commentaries

Chinua Achebe, An Image of Africa: Conrad's "Heart of Darkness," p. 827.

Suggested Readings

Bender, Todd K. *Concordances to Conrad's "The Shadow Line" and "Youth": A Narrative.* New York: Garland, 1980.

Bennett, Carl D. *Joseph Conrad.* New York: Continuum, 1991.

Berthoud, Jacques. *Joseph Conrad: The Major Phase.* New York: Cambridge UP, 1978. 41–63.

Billy, Ted. *Critical Essays on Joseph Conrad.* Boston: G. K. Hall, 1987.

Cohen, Michael. "Sailing through The Secret Sharer: The End of Conrad's Story." *Studies in English* 10.2 (Fall 1988): 102–09.

Conrad, Joseph. *Heart of Darkness: An Authoritative Text, Backgrounds and Sources, Criticism.* Ed. Robert Kimbrough. Rev. ed. New York: Norton, 1971.

———. *Portable Conrad.* New York: Penguin, 1991.

Gekoski, R. A. *Conrad: The Moral World of the Novelist.* New York: Barnes, 1978. 72–90.

Gillon, Adam. *Joseph Conrad.* Boston: Twayne, 1982.

Graver, Lawrence. *Conrad's Short Fiction.* Berkeley: U of California P, 1969.

Hynes, Samuel, ed. *The Complete Short Fiction of Joseph Conrad. The Stories, Volume I.* New York: Ecco, 1991.

Page, Norman. *A Conrad Companion.* New York: St. Martin's, 1986.

STEPHEN CRANE

The Open Boat (p. 228)

Crane's story fictionalizes an actual experience. A correspondent himself, Crane happened to be aboard the *Commodore* when it went down, and he included in his newspaper report of the event this passage (as quoted by E. R. Hagemann):

> The history of life in an open boat for thirty hours would no doubt be instructive for the young, but none is to be told here now. For my part I would prefer to tell the story at once, because from it would shine the splendid manhood of Captain Edward Murphy and of William Higgins, the oiler, but let it suffice at this time to say that when we were swamped in the surf and making the best of our way toward the shore the captain gave orders amid the wildness of the breakers as clearly as if he had been on the quarter deck of a battleship.

It is good that Crane did not write "at once" but let his experience take shape as a work of art which, instead of celebrating the "splendid manhood" of two or four individuals, recognizes a profound truth about human life in general — about the puniness of humankind in the face of an indifferent nature and about the consequent value of the solidarity and compassion that arise from an awareness of our common fate. Crane's meditation on his experience "after the fact" enables him to become not simply a reporter but, as he puts it in the last line of the story, an *interpreter* of the message spoken to us by the world we confront.

Crane portrays the exertions of the four men in the boat without glamorizing them. His extended and intimate account of their hard work and weariness wrings out any false emotion from the reader's view of the situation. By varying the narrative point of view from a coolly detached objective observer to a plural account of all four men's shared feelings and perceptions to the correspondent's rueful, self-mocking cogitations, Crane defeats our impulse to choose a hero for adulation, at the same time driving home the point that the condition of the men in the dinghy — their longing, their fear, and their powerlessness before nature and destiny — reflects our own. By the end, what has been revealed is so horrible that there can be no triumph in survival. The good fortune of a rescue brings only a reprieve, not an escape from what awaits us. Billie the oiler drowns, but there is no reason it should have been he, or only he. His death could be anybody's death.

Crane's narration builds suspense through rhythmic repetition, foreshadowing, and irony. We hear the surf periodically: Our hopes for rescue are repeatedly raised and dashed; night follows day, wave follows wave, and the endless struggle goes on. The correspondent's complaint against the cruelty of fate recurs in diminuendo, with less whimsy and self-consciousness each time.

These recurrences mark the men's changes in attitude — from the egocentric viewpoint they start with, imagining that the whole world is watching them and working for their survival, to the perception of the utter indifference of nature with which the story ends. Some stages in this progression include their false sense of security when they light up the cigars; their isolation from the people on shore, epitomized by their inability to interpret the signal of the man waving his coat (whose apparent advice to try another stretch of beach they nonetheless inadvertently follow); their experience of aloneness at night; their confrontation with the hostility of nature in the shark; and, finally, their recognition that death might be a welcome release from toil and suffering. They respond by drawing together in a communion that sustains them, sharing their labor and their body heat, huddled together in their tiny, helpless dinghy. Even their strong bond of comradeship, however, cannot withstand the onslaught of the waves. When the boat is swamped, it is every man for himself: Each individual must face death alone. Because of the fellowship that has grown up among them, however, when Billie dies, each of the others feels the oiler's death as his own. The reader, whom Crane's narrative has caused to share thirty hours at sea in an open boat, may recognize the implication in what is spoken by "the sound of the great sea's voice to the men on shore."

WILLIAM E. SHEIDLEY

Questions for Discussion

1. Contrast the imagery and the tone of the first paragraph with those of the second. Why does Crane continually seek to magnify nature and to belittle the men who are struggling with it? Find other instances of Crane's reductive irony, and discuss their effects.

2. How does Crane convey the men's concentration on keeping the boat afloat?

3. Explain Crane's use of the word "probably" in the first paragraph of section II.

4. Why does the seagull seem "somehow gruesome and ominous" to the men in the boat? Compare and contrast the seagull with the shark that appears later.

5. Comment on the imagery Crane uses to describe changing seats in the dinghy (stealing eggs, Sèvres).

6. What is it that the correspondent "knew even at the time was the best experience of his life"? Why is it the best?

7. What is the purpose of Crane's understatement in the line "neither the oiler nor the correspondent was fond of rowing at this time"?

8. What is the effect on the reader of the men's lighting up cigars?

9. Discuss the meaning of the correspondent's question "Was I brought here merely to have my nose dragged away as I was about to nibble the sacred cheese of life?"

10. What do you think the man waving a coat means? Why is it impossible for him to communicate with the men in the boat?

11. "A night on the sea in an open boat is a long night," says Crane. How does he make the reader feel the truth of that assertion?

12. At one point the correspondent thinks that he is "the one man afloat on all the oceans." Explain that sensation. Why does the wind he hears sound "sadder than the end"? Why does he later wish he had known the captain was awake when the shark came by?

13. Why does the correspondent have a different attitude toward the poem about the dying soldier in Algiers from the one he had as a boy?

14. Examine the third paragraph of section VII. How important are the thoughts of the correspondent to our understanding of the story? What would the story lose if they were omitted? What would the effect of this passage have been if Crane had narrated the story in the first person? If he had made these comments in the voice of an omniscient third-person narrator?

15. Define the correspondent's physical, mental, and emotional condition during his final moments on the boat and during his swim to the beach.

16. Characterize and explain the tone of Crane's description of the man who pulls the castaways from the sea.

17. Why does Crane make fun of the women who bring coffee to the survivors?

Topics for Writing

1. Consider Crane's handling of point of view in "The Open Boat."
2. Discuss the importance of repetition in Crane's narrative.
3. Analyze imagery as a key to tone in "The Open Boat."
4. After reading the story once rapidly, read it again with a pencil in hand, marking every simile and metaphor. Then sort them into categories. What realms of experience does Crane bring into view through these devices that are not actually part of the simple boat-sea-sky-beach world in which the story is set? Why?
5. **RESPONDING CREATIVELY**   Write an eyewitness account of some experience you have undergone that would be suitable for newspaper publication. Then note the changes you would make to turn it into a fictional narrative with broader or more profound implications — or write that story.

Related Commentary

Stephen Crane, The Sinking of the *Commodore*, p. 861.

Suggested Readings

Adams, Richard P. "Naturalistic Fiction: 'The Open Boat.'" *Stephen Crane's Career: Perspectives and Evaluations.* Ed. Thomas A. Gullason. New York: New York UP, 1972. 421–29. Originally published in *Tulane Studies in English* 4 (1954): 137–46.

Cady, Edwin H. *Stephen Crane.* Twayne's United States Authors Series 23. Rev. ed. Boston: G. K. Hall, 1980. 150–54.

Colvert, James B. *Stephen Crane.* New York: Ungar, 1987.

Follett, Wilson, ed. *The Work of Stephen Crane.* New York: Knopf, 1925.

Fryckstedt, O. W., ed. *Stephen Crane: Uncollected Writings.* Uppsala: Studia Anglistica Upsaliensia, 1963.

Hagemann, E. R. "'Sadder Than the End': Another Look at 'The Open Boat.'" *Stephen Crane in Transition: Centenary Essays.* Ed. Joseph Katz. DeKalb: Northern Illinois UP, 1972. 66–85.

Johnson, Glen M. "Stephen Crane." *American Short-Story Writers, 1880–1910.* Dictionary of Literary Biography, vol. 78. Detroit: Gale, 1989.

Katz, Joseph, ed. *The Portable Stephen Crane.* New York: Viking, 1985.

Kissane, Leedice. "Interpretation through Language: A Study of the Metaphors in Stephen Crane's 'The Open Boat.'" Gullason, cited above. 410–16. Originally published in *Rendezvous* (Idaho State U) 1 (1966): 18–22.

Knapp, Bettina L. *Stephen Crane.* New York: Ungar, 1987.

Stallman, R. W. *Stephen Crane: A Critical Bibliography.* Ames: Iowa State UP, 1972.

———. *Stories and Tales/Stephen Crane.* New York: Vintage, 1955.

Wolford, Chester L. *Stephen Crane: A Study of the Short Fiction.* Boston: Twayne, 1989.

JUNOT DÍAZ

How to Date a Browngirl, Blackgirl, Whitegirl, or Halfie (p. 247)

Díaz has chosen the second-person point of view for his narrative, and he keeps it short and simple, as if expecting his reader to be on the same educational level as his narrator. Yet the language of the story is deceptively simple; Díaz also slips in words such as "nemesis" (instead of "enemy") that give his story the smooth finish of a creative writing class exercise that's been polished in draft after draft. The audacity of Díaz's subject is what grabs the reader's attention: "If she's a whitegirl you know you'll at least get a hand job."

As the speaker continues to outline the action he anticipates happening on the date, he grows progressively less confident, expecting less and less from the girls he is with. The tone of the story darkens as he fails to make any significant human contact with his dates, even the white girl whom he imagines permits sexual intercourse. The clash of the different cultures isn't the only communication barrier; the speaker includes "a local girl" among the hypothetical dates he's describing, so he doesn't need to pretend with her that he's a "Spanish" guy instead of a Dominican.

The mood of disenchantment extends past the narrator's personal encounters into the broader area of politics — there are references to the United States' invasion of the Dominican Republic. While moving to the United States apparently hasn't given the narrator immediate access to the American Dream of economic prosperity — he lives "in the Terrace," a housing project in New Jersey — he still can dream of sexual conquest with the ready supply of "strong-headed" young girls he meets at school.

Questions for Discussion

1. What are the cultural differences in the expectations of a "Browngirl, Blackgirl, Whitegirl, or Halfie"?
2. How do their different expectations cause the narrator to treat them differently on the date?
3. To whom is the narrator talking in the story? Who is his ideal reader?
4. Why is the narrator so conscious of his hairstyle?
5. How does the narrator establish the setting of the story and give a sense of the atmosphere of the housing project where he lives?
6. Why does the narrator include his reference to the tear gas used by the United States when the Dominican Republic was invaded?

Topics for Writing

1. The syntax of the story is weighted with many contemporary colloquialisms. Discuss whether these terms will present difficulties for future readers or whether they help lend the story a stronger sense of verisimilitude.

2. Discuss this story in the context of other immigrant literature and the themes of assimilation and loss of identity.

Suggested Reading

Díaz, Junot. *Drown*. New York: Riverhead, 1996.

CHITRA BANERJEE DIVAKARUNI

Mrs. Dutta Writes a Letter (p. 250)

This long story is told from the third-person point of view of Mrs. Dutta, the sixtyish widow from India who has moved to the United States to live with her son Sagar, her daughter-in-law Shyamoli, and her two grandchildren. Divakaruni understands the cultural shock of such a move for an older woman who has spent her entire life as a traditional wife and mother in her native culture. Mrs. Dutta is a sympathetic character: She loves her son and grandchildren, she means well, and she does her best to adjust to family life in the United States, but she is unable to change her traditional ways of living and thinking.

Nearly a half century ago, as a bride, she lived with a domineering mother-in-law, but times have changed. Her daughter-in-law Shyamoli is a well-paid executive, no longer the shy bride in India whom Mrs. Dutta remembers from a decade before; now Shyamoli is more concerned with fitting into the American way of life than appeasing her mother-in-law. But the experiences in the new country have also opened the way for Mrs. Dutta to change. When she left India after her bout with pneumonia to live with her son's family, she was still acting as an obedient, traditional woman. At the end of the story she looks deeply into her heart and acts for herself. As she writes in her letter to her friend Roma, what she really wants is to return home to India. Allowing herself to do as she pleases for the first time in her life, she is free from conventional restraints. "Now that she no longer cares whether tears blotch her letter, she feels no need to weep."

Questions for Discussion

1. Why does Divakaruni open her story by showing Mrs. Dutta unable to turn off her alarm clock? What other modern appliances does she have trouble with in her son's household?
2. Are Mrs. Dutta's grandchildren sympathetic or unsympathetic characters? In what ways are they typical American children?
3. What is Mrs. Dutta's relationship with her son? Why doesn't he take her side in the family arguments?
4. How does American life in the suburbs appear to Mrs. Dutta? In what ways is she correct in her judgment? In what ways is she incorrect?
5. What kind of life does Mrs. Dutta return to in India? Do you think that she will be happy there?

Topics for Writing

1. The critic Elizabeth Stuckey-French has said that Divakaruni broke a cardinal rule of fiction writing when she started her story by describing Mrs. Dutta's struggle with her alarm clock:

   > In this story, the rattling alarm is not a signal that the writer is merely doing warm-ups before the real story begins — if it ever does. The alarm clock is doing more than that. In fact, it's doing lots of things.

   > First of all, the habit of rising early evokes Mrs. Dutta's past as a young wife in India, when she had to get up early each morning to start the fire before the rest of the household got up. Mrs. Dutta felt useful then, as opposed to now, in California, when nobody cares when she gets up.

   > She sets her alarm clock because rising early is one of a number of old habits she can't break, even though she knows these habits will get her in trouble. Mrs. Dutta has done something wrong by setting her alarm — she's done it even though she knows it will annoy her son and daughter-in-law, even though her son has asked her not to do it. We keep reading, hoping she won't get into trouble. But we know she will. Trouble is what stories are all about.

   Write a short essay in which you discuss Stuckey-French's assertion that "trouble is what stories are all about."

2. Compare and contrast the situation of immigrants from India and Pakistan in "Mrs. Dutta Writes a Letter" and Lahiri's "When Mr. Pirzada Came to Dine."

RALPH ELLISON

Battle Royal (p. 266)

In the headnote to his comments on "Battle Royal" reprinted in Part Two (p. 864), Ellison is quoted expounding on the importance of "converting experience into symbolic action" in fiction. One of the major triumphs of "Battle Royal" (and of Invisible Man as a whole) is Ellison's success in the realistic rendering of experiences that are in themselves so obviously significant of larger social, psychological, and moral truths that explication is unnecessary. From the small American flag tattooed on the nude dancer's belly to the "rope of bloody saliva forming a shape like an undiscovered continent" that the narrator drools on his new briefcase, Ellison's account of the festivities at the men's smoker effectively symbolizes the condition of blacks in America while remaining thoroughly persuasive in its verisimilitude. Both the broader structure of the evening and the finer details of narration and description carry the force of Ellison's theme. The young blacks are tortured first by having the most forbidden of America's riches dangled before them, then by being put through their paces in a melee in which their only victims are their fellows and the whites look on with glee, and finally by being debased into groveling for money (some of it counterfeit) on a rug whose electrification underlines their own powerlessness. In one brief passage, the nightmare of such an existence appears in a strange subaqueous vision of primitive life: "The boys groped about like blind, cautious crabs crouching to protect their mid-sections, their heads pulled in short against their shoulders, their arms stretched nervously before them, with their fists testing the smoke-filled air like the knobbed feelers of hypersensitive snails."

Because his actual experience forms itself into such revealing images, the narrator's dream of his grandfather seems all the more credible as a statement of his position. "Keep This Nigger-Boy Running," he dreams the message of his briefcase says — not far from "You've got to know your place at all times." The narrator's grandfather knew his place and played his role, but he never believed a word of it. It is this assurance of an inner being quite different from the face he turned toward the world that makes him so troubling to his descendants. In his effort to please the white folks and in so doing to get ahead, the narrator seeks alliance rather than secret enmity with his antagonists. As a result he subjects himself to the trickery and delusions the white community chooses to impose on him. Dependent for his sense of himself on his ability to guess what they want him to do, the narrator finds himself groping in a fog deeper than the swirls of cigar smoke that hang over the scene of the battle royal. When the smoke clears and the blindfold comes off, he will recognize, as he puts it at the start, that he is invisible to the whites and may therefore discover his own identity within himself.

The first episode of a long novel does not accomplish the narrator's enlightenment, but it constitutes his initiation into the realities of the world he must eventually come to understand. Ellison says (in the Commentary in Part Two, p. 864) that the battle royal "is a ritual in preservation of caste lines, a keeping of taboo to appease the gods and ward off bad luck," and that "it is also the initiation ritual to which all greenhorns are subjected." This rite of initiation bears a revealing relation to the primitive initiation ceremonies known to anthropologists. The battle royal, for example, separates the boys from their families, challenges them to prove their valor, and subjects them to instruction by the tribal elders in a sort of men's house. The boys are stripped and introduced to sexual mysteries. But the hazing of women that is a frequent feature of such initiations is not carried on here by the boys but by the gross elders, whose savagery is barely under control; the ritual ends not with the entry of the initiates into the larger community but with their pointed exclusion; and the sacred lore embodied in the narrator's recital of his graduation speech makes explicit the contradictions inherent in the society it describes. To cast down his bucket where he is forces him to swallow his own blood. The narrator is delighted with the scholarship to "the state college for Negroes" that he wins by toeing the line and knowing his place, and he does not object that the "gold" coins he groveled for are fraudulent. His education in the meaning of his grandfather's troubling injunctions will continue, but the reader has already seen enough to recognize their validity.

WILLIAM E. SHEIDLEY

Questions for Discussion

1. In the opening paragraph the narrator says, "I was naive." In what ways is his naiveté revealed in the story that follows?
2. Why does the narrator feel guilty when praised?

3. What is the message to the narrator behind the suggestion "that since I was to be there anyway I might as well take part in the battle royal"? Explain his hesitation. What is the most important part of the evening for the whites?
4. Who is present at the smoker? Discuss the role of the school superintendent.
5. What techniques does Ellison use to convey to the reader the impact that seeing the stripper has on the boys?
6. What does the stripper have in common with the boys? Why are both a stripper and a battle royal part of the evening's entertainment?
7. During the chaos of the battle, the narrator worries about how his speech will be received. Is that absurd or understandable?
8. Does the deathbed advice of the narrator's grandfather offer a way to handle the battle royal?
9. Why does Tatlock refuse to take a dive?
10. Explain the narrator's first reaction to seeing the "small square rug." In what sense is his instinct correct?
11. What is the meaning of the electric rug to the whites? What do they wish it to demonstrate to the blacks?
12. Explain Mr. Colcord's reaction when the narrator tries to topple him onto the rug.
13. Analyze the narrator's speech. What is the implication of his having to deliver it while swallowing his own blood?
14. Why is the school superintendent confident that the narrator will "lead his people in the proper paths"?
15. Why does the narrator stand in front of his grandfather's picture holding his briefcase? Who gets the better of this confrontation?

Topics for Writing

1. Make a study of seeing and understanding in "Battle Royal."
2. Analyze the role of sex, violence, and power in Ellison's "Battle Royal."
3. Write an essay exploring the battle royal and black experience in America.
4. Describe the "permanent interest" of "Battle Royal." (See Ellison's Commentary in Part Two, p. 864.)
5. Examine the blonde, the gold coins, and the calfskin briefcase in "Battle Royal."
6. Select a passage of twenty lines or less from this story for detailed explication. Relate as many of its images as possible to others in the story and to the general ideas that the story develops. To what extent does the passage you chose reflect the meaning of the story as a whole?
7. **RESPONDING CREATIVELY** Recall an experience in which you were humiliated or embarrassed. What motives of your own and of those before whom you were embarrassed put you in such a position? Narrate the incident so these underlying purposes become evident to the reader.
8. **RESPONDING CREATIVELY** Write a description of a game or ceremony with which you are familiar. What set of principles or relationships (not necessarily malign) does it express?

Related Commentary

Ralph Ellison, The Influence of Folklore on "Battle Royal," p. 864.

Suggested Readings

Blake, Susan L. "Ritual and Rationalization: Black Folklore in the Works of Ralph Ellison." *PMLA* 94 (1979): 121–26, esp. 122–23.
Horowitz, Ellin. "The Rebirth of the Artist." *Twentieth-Century Interpretations of Invisible Man.* Ed. John M. Reilly. Englewood Cliffs, NJ: Prentice, 1970. 80–88, esp. 81. (Originally published in 1964.)
O'Meally, Robert G. *The Craft of Ralph Ellison.* Cambridge, MA: Harvard UP, 1980. 12–14.
Vogler, Thomas A. "*Invisible Man:* Somebody's Protest Novel." *Ralph Ellison: A Collection of Critical Essays.* Ed. John Hersey. Englewood Cliffs, NJ: Prentice, 1974. 127–50, esp. 143–44.

LOUISE ERDRICH

The Red Convertible (p. 277)

The story takes place in 1974, when Henry Junior comes back to the Chippewa Indian reservation after more than three years as a soldier in Vietnam. He is mentally disturbed by his experiences in the war, and, as his brother Lyman (who narrates the story) says laconically, "the change was no good."

Erdrich has structured her story in a traditional manner. It is narrated in the first person by Lyman, who uses the past tense to describe the finality of what happened to his brother and the red Oldsmobile convertible they once shared. The plot moves conventionally, after a lengthy introduction giving the background of the two brothers and their pleasure in the car. They are Indians who work hard for what they earn, but they also enjoy their money. As Lyman says, "We went places in that car, me and Henry." An atmosphere of innocence pervades this part of the story. They enjoy sightseeing along the western highways, going when and where they please, spending an entire summer in Alaska after they drive a female hitchhiker with long, beautiful hair home.

The story moves forward chronologically (although it is told as a flashback after the opening frame of four paragraphs), organized in sections usually several paragraphs long. Its structure is as loose and comfortable as the brothers' relationship. Then, midway, the story darkens when Henry goes off to Vietnam. For three sections, Lyman describes Henry's disorientation after the war. Then Henry fixes the convertible, the boys get back behind the wheel, and it seems briefly as if the good times are again starting to roll. But Henry feels internal turmoil similar to that of the flooded river they park alongside. The story reaches its climax when Henry suddenly goes wild after drinking several beers, deteriorating into what he calls a "crazy Indian." Lyman stares after him as he jumps into the river, shouting, "Got to cool me off!" His last words are quieter, "My boots are filling," and then he is gone.

The last paragraph of the story is its final section, Lyman describing how he drove the car into the river after he couldn't rescue Henry. It has gotten dark, and he is left alone with the sound of the rush of the water "going and running and running." This brings the story full circle, back to the beginning, where Lyman told us that now he "walks everywhere he goes." His grief for his brother is as understated as the rest of his personality. Erdrich has invented a natural story-teller in Lyman. We feel his emotional loss as if it were our own.

Questions for Discussion

1. In the opening paragraph, Lyman says that he and Henry owned the red convertible "together until his boots filled with water on a windy night and he bought out my share." When does the meaning of this sentence become clear to you? What is the effect of putting this sentence in the first para-graph?

2. Also in the opening paragraph, Erdrich writes: "his youngest brother Lyman (that's myself), Lyman walks everywhere he goes." If Lyman is nar-rating this story, why does he name himself? Does speaking of himself in the third person create any particular effect?

3. What is the function of the third section of the story? Why does the narra-tor tell us about their wandering, about meeting Susy? What associations does the red convertible carry?

4. Watching Henry watching television, Lyman says, "He sat in his chair grip-ping the armrests with all his might, as if the chair itself was moving at a high speed and if he let go at all he would rocket forward and maybe crash right through the set." How would you describe the diction in this sen-tence? What effect does the sentence's length — and its syntax — create? What is the tone? What does this line, and the paragraphs around it, tell you about Lyman's reaction to Henry's change?

5. Where do Lyman and Henry speak directly to each other in this story? Where do they speak indirectly? How do they communicate without speech? Describe how Erdrich presents the moments of emotion in this story.

6. Why is Lyman upset by the picture of himself and his brother? When does the picture begin to bother him? Do we know if it's before or after Henry's death? Does it make a difference to our interpretation of the story? What burden of memory does this picture carry?

7. Consider the tone of the final paragraph, in which Lyman is describing how he felt when he gave his car to his dead brother. Look at the diction sur-rounding the red convertible here: It plows into the water; the headlights "reach in . . . go down, searching"; they are "still lighted. . . ." What attrib-ute does the diction give the car? How is the car different now from the way it's been in the rest of the story? Does this transformation of the car invoke a sense of closure in the story?

8. The closing sentence says, "And then there is only the water, the sound of it going and running and going and running and running." How does this statement comment on the relationship between the two brothers?

Topics for Writing

1. Write an essay considering brotherhood in "The Red Convertible."
2. Discuss Erdrich's use of setting to determine tone.
3. **RESPONDING CREATIVELY** Rewrite the story from the third-person point of view.
4. **CONNECTIONS** Compare and discuss Lyman's initiation into maturity with that of Julian in Flannery O'Connor's "Everything That Rises Must Converge."

Suggested Readings

Erdrich, Louise. "Excellence Has Always Made Me Fill with Fright When It Is Demanded by Other People, but Fills Me with Pleasure When I Am Left to Practice It Alone." *Ms.* 13 (1985): 84.

———. "Where I Ought to Be: A Writer's Sense of Place." *New York Times Book Review* 28 (July 1985): 1+.

Howard, J. "Louise Erdrich." *Life* 8 (1985): 27+.

WILLIAM FAULKNER

A Rose for Emily (p. 286)

Few stories, surely, differ more on a second reading than does "A Rose for Emily," which yields to the initiate some detail or circumstance anticipating the ending in nearly every paragraph. But Faulkner sets the pieces of his puzzle in place so coolly that the first-time reader hardly suspects them to fit together into a picture at all, until the curtain is finally swept aside and the shocking secret of Miss Emily's upstairs room is revealed. Faulkner makes it easy to write off the episodes of the smell, Miss Emily's denial of her father's death, the arsenic, and the aborted wedding (note the shuffled chronology) as the simple eccentricities of a pathetic old maid, to be pitied and indulged. The impact of the final scene drives home the realization that the passions of a former generation and its experience of life are no less real or profound for all their being in the past — whether we view them through the haze of sentimental nostalgia, as the Confederate veterans near the end of the story do, or place them at an aesthetic distance, as the townspeople do in the romantic tableau imagined in section II.

In his interviews with students at the University of Virginia (excerpted in Part Two, p. 866), Faulkner stressed Miss Emily's being "kept down" by her father as an important factor in driving her to violate the code of her society by taking a lover, and he expressed a deep human sympathy for her long expiation for that sin. In the narrative consciousness of the story, however — the impersonal "we" that speaks for the communal mind of Jefferson — Miss Emily Grierson is a town relic, a monument to the local past to be shown to strangers, like the graves of the men slain at the battle of Jefferson or the big houses on what long ago, before they put the sidewalks in, was the "most select street." Because all relics are to a degree symbolic, one should not hesitate to take up the challenge found in Faulkner's ambiguous claim quoted in the headnote, that "the writer is too busy . . . to have time to be conscious of all the symbolism that he may put into what he does or what people may read into it." Miss Emily, for example, may be understood to express the part of southern culture that is paralyzed in the present by its inability to let go of the past, even though that past is as dead as Homer Barron, and even though its reality differed from the treasured memory as greatly as the Yankee paving contractor — "not a marrying man" — differs from the husband of Miss Emily's desperate longings. Other details in Faulkner's economical narration fit this reading: the prominence of Miss Emily's iconic portrait of her father; her refusal to acknowledge changing laws and customs; her insistence that the privilege of paying no taxes, bestowed on her by the chivalrous Colonel Sartoris, is an inalienable right; her dependence on the labors of her Negro servant, whose patient silence renders him an accomplice in her strange crime; and, not least, her relationship of mutual exploitation with Homer, the representative of the North — a relationship that ends in a morbid and grotesque parody of marriage. In this context, the smell of death that reeks from Miss Emily's house tells how the story judges what she stands for, and the dust that falls on everything brings the welcome promise of relief.

But Faulkner will not let it lie. Seen for what she is, neither romanticized nor trivialized, Miss Emily has a forthright dignity and a singleness of purpose that contrast sharply with those representatives of propriety and progress who sneak around her foundation in the dark spreading lime or knock on her door in the ineffectual effort to collect her taxes. And as the speechless townsfolk tiptoe aghast about her bridal chamber, it is Miss Emily's iron will, speaking through the strand of iron-gray hair that lies where she has lain, that has the final word.

WILLIAM E. SHEIDLEY

Questions for Discussion

1. The story begins and ends with Miss Emily's funeral. Trace the chronology of the intervening sections.
2. Emily is called "a fallen monument" and "a tradition." Explain.
3. Why does the narrator label Miss Emily's house "an eyesore among eyesores"?
4. Define the opposing forces in the confrontation that occupies most of section I. How does Miss Emily "vanquish them"?
5. Discuss the transition between sections I and II. In what ways are the two episodes parallel?
6. Apart from her black servant, Miss Emily has three men in her life. What similarities are there in her attitudes toward them?
7. Why is Homer Barron considered an inappropriate companion for Miss Emily?
8. Consider Faulkner's introduction of the rat poison into the story in section III. What is the narrator's avowed reason for bringing it up?
9. At the beginning of section IV, the townspeople think Emily will commit suicide, and they think "it would be the best thing." Why? What is the basis of their error regarding her intentions?
10. Why do you think Miss Emily gets fat and develops gray hair when she does?
11. Why does Miss Emily's servant disappear after her death?

12. Describe Miss Emily's funeral before the upstairs room is opened. In what way does that scene serve as a foil to what follows?
13. Discuss the role of dust in the last few paragraphs of the story.
14. Why does Faulkner end the story with "a long strand of iron-gray hair"?

Topics for Writing

1. Contrast the various attitudes toward the past in "A Rose for Emily."
2. Discuss the meaning of time and Faulkner's handling of chronology in "A Rose for Emily."
3. Construct a profile of Emily Grierson: Is she a criminal, a lunatic, or a heroine?
4. Explain the title of "A Rose for Emily."
5. Consider the relationship between "A Rose for Emily" and the history of the South.
6. What can you discern about the narrator of "A Rose for Emily"?
7. Were you surprised by the story's ending? On a second reading, mark all the passages that foreshadow it.
8. **RESPONDING CREATIVELY** Imitate Faulkner by telling the events that lead up to a climax out of chronological order. What new effects do you find it possible to achieve? What problems in continuity do you encounter?

Related Commentary

William Faulkner, The Meaning of "A Rose for Emily," p. 866.

Suggested Readings

See page 54.

WILLIAM FAULKNER

That Evening Sun (p. 293)

"That Evening Sun" is one of a handful of American short stories that have been so frequently anthologized and discussed that they almost define the style and the method of American short fiction. For the instructor the question may not be so much presenting the story for its literary qualities, but in seeing how well the story still relates to the political and social attitudes of students today, more than seventy years since it was first published. It isn't as acceptable now for a white writer to deal with themes of African American life, and for many feminists there can be questions about a white male author's presentation of a black woman's experience. Does the story still have the powerful effect on its readers that it had in the harsh years of the Great Depression and the cruelest decades of legalized segregation?

The answer is that the narrative device that gave the story so much of its first impact still is as effective today. By weaving through the story the uncomprehending chorus of children's voices, Faulkner succeeds in making the brutal violence of the story frighteningly real. There is no more desperate moment in American literature than when Nancy's attempt to keep the children amused in her lonely cabin ends with the broken popcorn popper. The reader's realization that the children don't understand what is happening only sharpens the effect. For women readers the story perhaps will reflect some of their own emotions and responses as the society is ready now to listen to the stories of battered wives and of women threatened by lovers or friends. The terror that is stalking Nancy is no different from the fear that a woman feels when she knows that a restraining order issued by a distant judge won't protect her from the rage of a disturbed ex-husband.

From the perspective of seventy years, it is also possible to see the racial dimensions of the story in a different way. Perhaps part of what gave Faulkner his great international reputation — and his Nobel Prize — was an understanding that what he was describing was the bitter reality of life for any underclass. The black underclass outside the white neighborhoods of this southern town has been forced into the way of life of the peasants of the older European societies. Faulkner's Nancy could have been a servant in a renter's cottage outside the manor walls in nineteenth-century England, or a woman forced outside the social framework — as she would be by her unwed pregnancy — in any European small town before World War I. Faulkner's story still forces us to face this very real inhumanity in a world we realize has not left this legacy of violence behind.

Questions for Discussion

1.   Compare the ages of the children with the responses to Nancy's fear. How much more awareness do the older children have?
2.   How does Faulkner describe the small town's ability to help someone like Nancy?
3.   Why is Jesus still able to go free, despite the awareness of the children's father of what is happening?

Topics for Writing

1.   Faulkner describes the uneasy boundary where the white and the black societies of this small town meet. What are the real effects of this boundary?
2.   Compare the situation Nancy faces with a similar situation today.
3.   The children's father acts in a way that he would consider sympathetic and protective but would be considered paternalistic today. Discuss his character and role in the story.

Suggested Readings

Basset, John E. *Vision and Revisions: Essays on Faulkner.* West Cornwall, CT: Locust Hill, 1989.

Bloom, Harold. *William Faulkner.* New York: Chelsea House, 1986.

Blotner, Joseph. *Faulkner: A Biography.* New York: Random, 1991.

Brooks, Cleanth. *A Shaping Joy.* New York: Harcourt, 1971.

Gwynn, Frederick, and Joseph Blotner, eds. *Faulkner in the University.* Charlottesville: U of Virginia P, 1959.

Hall, Donald. *To Read Literature: Fiction, Poetry, Drama.* New York: Holt, 1981. 10–16.

Heller, Terry. "The Telltale Hair: A Critical Study of William Faulkner's 'A Rose for Emily.'" *Arizona Quarterly* 28 (1972): 301–18.

Hoffman, Frederick J. *William Faulkner, Revised.* Boston: Twayne, 1990.

Howe, Irving. *William Faulkner: A Critical Study.* 2nd ed. New York: Vintage, 1962. 265.

Leary, Lewis. *William Faulkner of Yoknapatawpha County.* Twentieth-Century American Writers. New York: Crowell, 1973. 136.

Millgate, Michael. *The Achievement of William Faulkner.* New York: Random, 1966.

Gabriel García Márquez

A Very Old Man with Enormous Wings (p. 307)

The word *allegories* in the headnote presents a challenge to readers of this story, and the inevitable failure of any simple scheme of interpretation to grasp fully the mystery at its heart reflects García Márquez's central theme exactly. Like the crabs, which come into the human world from an alien realm, the "flesh-and-blood angel" constitutes an intrusion of something strange and unfathomable into the comfortable world of reality as we choose to define it. Everybody, from the "wise" woman next door to the pope, takes a turn at trying to find a slot in which to file the winged visitor, but no definition seems satisfactory, and even Pelayo and Elisenda, whom the angel's presence has made wealthy, spend their money on a house "with iron bars on the windows so that angels wouldn't get in." When at last the old man flies away, Elisenda feels relief, "because then he was no longer an annoyance in her life but an imaginary dot on the horizon of the sea."

In discussing how he receives artistic inspiration, García Márquez says, "There's nothing deliberate or predictable in all this, nor do I know when it's going to happen to me. I'm at the mercy of my imagination." Without intending to limit the story's implications, one might associate the angel with this sort of unpredictable intrusion of the visionary and wonderful into everyday life. As an old man with wings, the angel recalls the mythical symbol of the artist, Daedalus, except that his wings are "so natural on that completely human organism that [the doctor] couldn't understand why other men didn't have them too." Bogged down in the mud, the angel seems less an allusion to Daedalus's son, the overreacher Icarus, than a representation of the difficulty of the artistic imagination in sustaining its flight through the unpleasant circumstances of this "sad" world. True artists are often misunderstood, ill treated, and rejected in favor of more practical concerns or of the creators of ersatz works that flatter established prejudices. Just so, nobody can understand the angel's "hermetic" language, and when he performs his aggressively unpractical miracles, no one is delighted. Exploited by his keepers, to whom he brings vast wealth, the angel receives as royalties only his quarters in the chicken coop and the flat side of the broom when underfoot. Popular for a time as a sideshow attraction, the angel is soon passed over in favor of the horrible "woman who had been changed into a spider for having disobeyed her parents," a grotesque and slapdash creation of the lowest order of imaginative synthesis, whose "human truth" gratifies both sentimentality and narrow-mindedness. But the artistic imagination lives happily on eggplant mush, possesses a supernatural patience, and though functionally blind to the bumping posts of ordinary reality, ever again takes wing. The angel has, perhaps rightly, appeared to his human observers "a cataclysm in repose," but near the end, as he sings his sea chanteys under the stars, he definitely comes to resemble "a hero taking his ease," preparing to navigate the high seas beyond the horizon.

WILLIAM E. SHEIDLEY

Questions for Discussion

1. Why are there crabs in the house? Is it for the same reason the old man with enormous wings has fallen in the courtyard? What other associations does the story make between the old man and the crabs?
2. Pelayo first thinks the old man is a nightmare. What other attempts are made to put this prodigy into a familiar category?
3. How does the old man differ from our usual conceptions of angels? What is the essential difference?
4. Explain Father Gonzaga's approach to the angel. What implications — about the angel and about the church — may be derived from his failure to communicate with him effectively?
5. Comment on the angel's career as a sideshow freak. Who receives the benefit of his success? Why does he fall? Compare what he has to offer with what the spider-woman has. What reasons might people have to prefer the latter?
6. Why do you think the angel tolerates the child patiently?
7. What are the implications of the angel's examination by the doctor?
8. How do we feel as the angel finally flaps away at the end? Does Elisenda's response adequately express the reader's?

Topics for Writing

1. Consider the ordinary and the enormous in "A Very Old Man with Enormous Wings." (Consider the etymological meaning of "enormous.")
2. Is García Márquez's fallen angel a fairy tale, a myth, or an allegory?
3. Recharging the sense of wonder: How does García Márquez make the reader believe in his angel?
4. Read the story aloud to a selected spectrum of people (at least three) of various ages and educational levels. Tabulate their responses and opinions, perhaps in an interview. Combining this evidence with your own response to the story, try to define the basis of its appeal.
5. **RESPONDING CREATIVELY**   Select a supernatural being from a fairy tale or other familiar source (the cartoons involving talking animals that wear clothes and drive cars might be worth considering), and imagine the being as a physical reality in your own ordinary surroundings. Write a sketch about what happens.

6. **CONNECTIONS** Compare "A Very Old Man with Enormous Wings" with other presentations of the supernatural (Hawthorne's, for example).

Suggested Readings

Bell-Villada, Gene H. *García Márquez: The Man and His Work.* Chapel Hill: U of North Carolina P, 1990.

Byk, John. "From Fact to Fiction: Gabriel García Márquez and the Short Story." *Mid-American Review* 6.2 (1986): 111–16.

Fau, Margaret Eustella. *Bibliographic Guide to Gabriel García Márquez 1979–1985.* Westport, CT: Greenwood, 1986.

García Márquez, Gabriel. *Collected Stories.* New York: Harper, 1984.

———. *Strange Pilgrims: Twelve Stories.* New York: Knopf, 1993.

McMurray, George R. *Gabriel García Márquez.* New York: Ungar, 1977. 116–19.

McNerney, Kathleen. *Understanding Gabriel García Márquez.* Columbia: U of South Carolina P, 1989.

Morello Frosch, Marta. "The Common Wonders of García Márquez's Recent Fiction." *Books Abroad* 47 (1973): 496–501.

Oberhelman, Harley D., ed. *Gabriel García Márquez: A Study of the Short Fiction.* Boston: Twayne, 1991.

Ortega, Julio. Gabriel *García Márquez and the Powers of Fiction.* Austin: U of Texas P, 1988.

Williams, Raymond L. *Gabriel García Márquez.* Boston: Twayne, 1984.

Zhu, Jingdong. "García Márquez and His Writing of Short Stories." *Foreign Literatures* 1 (1987): 77–80.

CHARLOTTE PERKINS GILMAN

The Yellow Wallpaper (p. 313)

Gilman wrote "The Yellow Wallpaper" between 1890 and 1894, during what she later recalled were the hardest years of her life. She had left her first husband and child to live alone in California after a nervous breakdown, and she was beginning to give lectures on socialism and freedom for women while she kept a boardinghouse, taught school, and edited newspapers. During this time, her husband married her best friend, to whom Gilman relinquished her child. The emotional pressures and economic uncertainties under which Gilman lived contributed to the desperate tone of this story.

Early readers of "The Yellow Wallpaper" compared it with the horror stories of Edgar Allan Poe (William Dean Howells said it was a story to "freeze our . . . blood" when he reprinted it in 1920 in *Great Modern American Stories*). Like Poe's homicidal narrators, Gilman's heroine tells her story in a state of neurotic compulsion. But she is no homicidal maniac. Unlike Poe, Gilman suggests that a specific social malady has driven her heroine to the brink of madness: the bondage of conventional marriage.

Her husband is her physician and keeper, the father of her beloved but absent child, the money earner who pays the rent on the mansion where she is held captive for her "own good." When she begs to get away, he replies practically, "Our lease will be up in three weeks, and I can't see how to leave before." Insisting that he knows what is best for her, he believes that the cure for her mysterious "weakness" is total rest. The husband is supported in his view by the opinion of the foremost medical authority on the treatment of mental illness, Dr. S. Weir Mitchell, a name explicitly mentioned in the story. Gilman had spent a month in Dr. Mitchell's sanitorium five years before. In her autobiography she later reported that she almost lost her mind there and would often "crawl into remote closets and under beds — to hide from the grinding pressure of that profound distress."

Gilman transferred the memory of her physical debilitation and "absolute incapacity" for normal (read "conventional") married life into her heroine's state in "The Yellow Wallpaper." The story dramatizes Gilman's fear while living with her first husband that marriage and motherhood might incapacitate her (as it apparently had Gilman's mother) for what she called "work in the world." She felt imprisoned within her marriage, a victim of her desire to please, trapped by her wedding ring. Gilman left her husband, but in "The Yellow Wallpaper" her heroine is sacrificed to the emotional turmoil she experiences.

As a symbolic projection of psychological stress, "The Yellow Wallpaper" has resemblances to Kafka's "The Metamorphosis," although it is more specific in its focus on social injustice to women. Like Gregor Samsa, Gilman's heroine is victimized by the people she loves. The yellow wallpaper surrounding her is "like a bad dream." It furnishes the central images in the story. The reader can use it like a Rorschach test to understand the heroine's experience of entrapment, confinement, and sacrifice for other family members. Like Gregor Samsa, she regresses to subhuman behavior as a self-inflicted punishment following her psychological rebellion — the wallpaper's bad smell, its bars and grid, its fungus and toadstools, and its images of the creeping (dependent, inferior) woman. But unlike Gregor Samsa, Gilman's heroine thinks she is freed from the "bad dream" by telling her story, not to a "living soul," but to what she calls (nonjudgmentally) "dead paper."

Telling her story enables her to achieve her greatest desire — the symbolic death of her husband. The story ends, "Now why should that man have fainted? But he did, and right across my path by the wall, so that I had to creep over him every time!" The central irony of the story, however, is that by the time she realizes the twisted ambition fostered by obediently following "like a good girl" her passive role as a conventional member of the "weaker sex," she has been driven insane.

Questions for Discussion

1.   Why have the narrator and her husband, John, rented the "colonial mansion"? What is its history, and what is the reaction of the heroine to this estate? Does she feel comfortable living in the house?

2.   Give a description of John. Why does the heroine say that his profession is *"perhaps . . . one reason I do not get well faster"?* How does the narrator view her husband? Does she agree with John's diagnosis and treatment? Who else supports John's diagnosis? What effect does this have on the heroine?

3.   What clue does the narrator's repeated lament, "what can one do?" give us about her personality? Describe other aspects of the woman's personality

that are revealed in the opening of the story. What conflicting emotions is she having toward her husband, her condition, and the mansion?

4. How would you characterize the narrator's initial reaction to, and description of, the wallpaper?

5. Describe the narrator's state after the first two weeks of residence. Has John's relationship with his wife changed at all?

6. Who is Jennie? What is her relationship to the narrator, and what is her function in the story?

7. How has the narrator changed in her description of the wallpaper? Is it fair to say that the wallpaper has become more dominant in her day-to-day routine? Explain.

8. By the Fourth of July, what does the narrator admit about the wallpaper? What clues does Gilman give us about the education of the narrator and her increasingly agitated state? Is she finding it more and more difficult to communicate? Explain.

9. As the summer continues, describe the narrator's thoughts. What is her physical condition? Is there a link between her symptoms and psychological illness?

10. How does the narrator try to reach out to her husband? What is his reaction? Is this her last contact with sanity? Do you think John really has no comprehension of the seriousness of her illness?

11. Why do you think Gilman briefly changes the point of view from first person singular to the second person as the narrator describes the pattern of the wallpaper? What effect does the narrator say light has on the wallpaper?

12. Who does the narrator see in the wallpaper? How have her perceptions of John and Jennie changed from the beginning of the story?

13. Abruptly the narrator switches mood from boredom and frustration to excitement. To what does she attribute this change? How does John react to this? What new aspects of the wallpaper does she discuss?

14. By the final section of the story, what is the narrator's relationship to her husband? to Jennie? to the wallpaper? How has the narrator's perspective changed from the start of the story? What change do we see in her actions?

15. Identify what has driven the narrator to the brink of madness. How does she try to free herself from this element? What is her greatest desire? What is the central irony of the story?

Topics for Writing

1. Compare and contrast the husband-wife relationship and its outcome in Gilman's "The Yellow Wallpaper" and Henrik Ibsen's play "A Doll's House."

2. **CONNECTIONS** Compare and contrast the monologue in Gilman's "The Yellow Wallpaper" with that in Poe's "The Cask of Amontillado" or "The Tell-Tale Heart."

3. **CONNECTIONS** Compare and discuss the concept of marriage in Gilman's "The Yellow Wallpaper" and Carver's "What We Talk About When We Talk About Love."

Related Commentaries

Sandra M. Gilbert and Susan Gubar, A Feminist Reading of Gilman's "The Yellow
    Wallpaper," p. 867.
Charlotte Perkins Gilman, Undergoing the Cure for Nervous Prostration, p. 870.
Charlotte Perkins Gilman, Why I Wrote "The Yellow Wallpaper," p. 872.

Suggested Readings

Bader, J. "The Dissolving Vision: Realism in Jewett, Freeman and Gilman."
    American Realism: New Essays. Ed. Eric J. Sundquist. Baltimore: Johns
    Hopkins UP, 1982. 176–98.
Delaney, Sheila. *Writing Women: Women Writers and Women in Literature, Medieval
    to Modern.* New York: Schocken, 1983.
Feminist Papers: From Adams to de Beauvoir. Ed. Alice S. Rossi. New York: Columbia
    UP, 1973.
Hanley-Peritz, J. "Monumental Feminism and Literature's Ancestral House:
    Another Look at 'The Yellow Wallpaper.'" *Women's Studies* 12.2 (1986):
    113–28.
Hill, Mary A. "Charlotte Perkins Gilman: A Feminist's Struggle with
    Womanhood." *Massachusetts Review* 21 (1980): 503–26.
————. *Charlotte Perkins Gilman: The Making of a Radical Feminist, 1860–1896.*
    Philadelphia: Temple UP, 1980.
Lane, Ann J. "Charlotte Perkins Gilman: The Personal Is Political." *Feminist
    Theorists.* Ed. Dale Spender. New York: Pantheon, 1983.
Nies, Judith. *Seven Women.* New York: Viking, 1977. 127–45.
Shumaker, C. "'Too Terribly Good to Be Printed': Charlotte Gilman's 'The Yellow
    Wallpaper.'" *American Literature* 57 (1985): 588–99.

Nadine Gordimer

Some Are Born to Sweet Delight (p. 327)

The opening paragraphs of Gordimer's chilling story foreshadow the plot
to come. Vera, the seventeen-year-old girl who will unknowingly carry the bomb
in her hand baggage onto the airliner that explodes in midair, is the daughter of
a man who is highly conscious "of the danger of bombs affixed under the cars of
members of parliament and financiers." But these car bombs, set by radical IRA
members fighting their guerrilla battles against the British who control Northern
Ireland, are only a forerunner to the much more widespread terrorist battle
against Western nations fought by the radicalized Muslims in Pakistan and other
countries. "Some Are Born to Sweet Delight" was published in Gordimer's 1991
collection *Jump,* a decade before the events of September 11 in the United States.
The story is a terrible omen of the things that will continue to happen in the world
in the years after its publication.

Rad, the foreign lodger who becomes Vera's lover and uses her as a carrier
for the explosive devise that will destroy the airplane, remains a mysterious

stranger throughout the story. Gordimer describes him through Vera's innocent eyes as possessing "the strange expression of a caged animal, far from wherever it belonged." When she asks him if he wants to go home, he says "No," looking at her "with the distant expression of an adult before the innocence of a child." When she tries to draw him out about his family, "He was not to be drawn; he was never to be drawn." Gordimer's words are weighted with irony, referring to Rad's ultimate plan to annihilate as many Westerners as possible. In England he might have encountered "the disadvantages young men like him had in an unwelcoming country," but he is revealed as a completely heartless enemy agent by the end of the story.

The theme of "Some Are Born to Sweet Delight" is suggested in the epigraph Gordimer has placed at the beginning, the two-line quotation from William Blake's *Auguries of Innocence:* "Some are Born to sweet delight, / Some are Born to Endless Night." The story brings together the world's politically innocent "haves" (like Vera) and the radicalized, initiated "have-nots" (like Rad) in an explosive mixture. In effect, the darkness is striking back against the light, using terrorism as the only weapon available to them in the unequal struggle: "a faction of the world's wronged, claiming the destruction . . . in some complication of vengeance for holy wars, land annexation, invasions, imprisonments, cross-border raids, territorial disputes, bombings, sinkings, kidnappings no one outside the initiated could understand."

Questions for Discussion

1. Why has Gordimer made Vera only seventeen years old? Is she a sympathetic character, or do you consider her too stupid and vapid to be the protagonist?
2. How does Gordimer make you aware of Vera's sexual interest in Rad in the scene where she offers him a slice of her mother's homemade gingerbread?
3. What do Vera's parents think of Rad? In what ways do they possess the typical prejudices of their social class? Why do the owners of the house celebrate Vera's engagement with a bottle of champagne?
4. From Rad's point of view, does Vera behave like a well-brought-up young woman at any time of their involvement? Considering his strict Muslim background, how does he regard her behavior? What do his friends think about Vera?

Topics for Writing

1. Write a short paper in which you analyze the opening paragraphs of the story, discussing how Gordimer foreshadows the characters and events to come.
2. Compare and contrast Gordimer's story with the stories by Lahiri and Mukherjee in the anthology.

Suggested Readings

Clayton, Cherry, ed. *Women and Writing in South Africa: A Critical Anthology.* Marshalltown: Heinemann Southern Africa, 1989, 183ff.

Cooke, J. "African Landscapes: The World of Nadine Gordimer." *World Literature Today* 52 (1978): 533–38.

Eckstein, B. "Pleasure and Joy: Political Activism in Nadine Gordimer's Short Stories." *World Literature Today* 59 (1985): 343–46.

Gordimer, Nadine. *Jump and Other Stories.* New York: Farrar, 1991.

Gray, S. "Interview with Nadine Gordimer." *Contemporary Literature* 22 (1981): 263–71.

Heywood, Christopher. *Nadine Gordimer.* Windsor, ONT: Profile, 1983.

Hurwitt, J. "Art of Fiction: Nadine Gordimer." *Paris Review* 25 (1983): 83–127.

Jacobs, J. U. "Living Space and Narrative Space in Nadine Gordimer's 'Something Out There.'" *English in Africa* 14.2 (Oct. 1987): 31–43.

Lazar, Karen. "Feminism as 'Piffling'? Ambiguities in Some of Nadine Gordimer's Short Stories." *Current Writing* 2.1 (Oct. 1990): 101–16.

Mazurek, Raymond A. "Nadine Gordimer's 'Something Out There' and Ndebele's 'Fools' and Other Stories: The Politics of Literary Form." *Studies in Short Fiction* 26.1 (Winter 1989): 71–79.

Newman, Judie. *Nadine Gordimer.* New York: Routledge, 1988.

Ross, Robert L., ed. *International Literature on Major Writers.* New York: Garland, 1991. 762ff.

Smith, Rowland. *Critical Essays on Nadine Gordimer.* Boston: G. K. Hall, 1990.

Smyer, R. I. "Africa in the Fiction of Nadine Gordimer." *Ariel* 16 (1985): 15–29.

Trump, Martin. "The Short Fiction of Nadine Gordimer." *Research in African Literature* 17.3 (Fall 1968): 341–69.

NATHANIEL HAWTHORNE

Young Goodman Brown (p. 339)

Teaching "Young Goodman Brown," you should encourage students to read Appendix 2, "The Elements of Fiction" (p. 1044), carefully, since different aspects of Hawthorne's story are analyzed throughout the discussion of the elements of short fiction. Appendix 4, "Writing about Short Stories" (p. 1070), also has student essays developing different ideas about "Young Goodman Brown."

Students often need help recognizing stories that are not intended to be read as realistic narrative. Some readers tend to take every word in the story literally; Hawthorne, however, meant "Young Goodman Brown" to be a moral allegory, not a realistic story. While most students will be able to recognize the use of symbolism, you might have to introduce them to the idea of allegory, in which the entire story is an extended metaphor representing one thing in the guise of another.

An allegory is a story that has a dual meaning — one in the events, characters, and setting; and the other in the ideas they are intended to convey. At first, "Young Goodman Brown" holds our interest on the level of the surface narrative. But the story also has a second meaning, which must be read beneath, and concurrent with, the surface narrative. This second meaning is not to be confused with the theme of the story — all stories have themes, but not all stories are allegories. In an allegory, the characters are usually personifications of abstract qualities (faith) and the setting is representative of the relations among the abstractions (Goodman Brown takes leave of his "Faith" at the beginning of the story).

A story is an allegory only if the characters, events, and setting are presented in a logical pattern so that they represent meanings independent of the action described in the surface story. Most writers of allegorical fiction are moralists. In this moral allegory, Hawthorne is suggesting the ethical principle that should govern human life. The *unpardonable sin* for Hawthorne is a "want of love and reverence for the Human Soul" and is typified by the person who searches the depths of the heart with "a cold philosophical curiosity." The result is a separation of the intellect from the heart, which is fatal in relationships among human beings, as shown in what happens to Goodman Brown when he returns to Salem village at the end of the story.

Questions for Discussion

1. When is a careful reader first aware that Hawthorne intends this story to be read as a moral allegory?
2. One of the characters in a Hawthorne story says, "You know that I can never separate the idea from the symbol in which it manifests itself." Hawthorne's flat characters — such as Deacon Gookin, Goody Cloyse, and the minister — represent social institutions. Why does Hawthorne include them in the story?
3. On page 340, Hawthorne writes, "But the only thing about him that could be fixed upon as remarkable was his staff, which bore the likeness of a great black snake, so curiously wrought that it might almost be seen to twist and wriggle itself like a living serpent. This, of course, must have been an ocular deception, assisted by the uncertain light." What is the assertion contained in the first sentence? What effect do the words "might almost" have on that assertion? Why does Hawthorne immediately qualify the first sentence in the second? On page 345, Hawthorne writes: "Either the sudden gleams of light flashing over the obscure field bedazzled Goodman Brown, or he recognized a score of the church members of Salem village famous for their especial sanctity." Discuss the function of this sentence and find others like it throughout the story. What is their cumulative effect?
4. Why is it important that most of the action in this story takes place in the forest? Looking through Hawthorne's story, isolate the particular words that are associated with the woods. Consider the paragraph on page 344 that begins "And, maddened with despair." List the characteristics of forests that are responsible for this long literary tradition. Consider, too, whether the idea of wilderness remains static throughout history. In the late nineteenth century, with industrialization such a potent force, would people have conceived of the forest in the same way the early settlers did? Why or why not?
5. Where does this story take place (besides in the forest)? On page 340 a man addresses the protagonist, saying, "You are late, Goodman Brown. . . . The clock of the Old South was striking as I came through Boston, and that is full fifteen minutes agone." What does this detail — that the traveler was in Boston fifteen minutes ago — mean to our interpretation of the story?
6. On page 346, "the dark figure" welcomes his listeners to "the communion of your race." What is usually meant by the word "communion"? How is it

meant here? What does the speaker mean by the phrase in which he uses it? What kinds of powers does the "sable form" promise the crowd? Discuss the kinds of knowledge that will henceforth be accessible to his listeners' senses. Who is speaking in this passage on page 347: "Herein did the shape of evil dip his hand and prepare to lay the mark of baptism upon their foreheads, that they might be partakers of the mystery of sin, more conscious of the secret guilt of others, both in deed and thought, than they could now be of their own"? How does this sentence guide your judgment of Young Goodman Brown in the closing paragraph of the story? How does the sable figure's sermon comment on the closing paragraph?

7.   How much time does this story cover? Where do the first seven paragraphs take place? How many paragraphs are set in the forest? What do the final three paragraphs address? What might be some reasons for the story to be built this way?

Topic for Writing

1.   Show how a knowledge of seventeenth-century New England history and Puritan theology can enhance a reading of the story.

Related Commentaries

Herman Melville, Blackness in Hawthorne's "Young Goodman Brown," p. 889.
Edgar Allan Poe, The Importance of the Single Effect in a Prose Tale, p. 907.

Suggested Readings

Arvin, Newton. *Hawthorne.* New York: Russell and Russell, 1961.

Bloom, Harold. *Nathaniel Hawthorne.* New York: Chelsea House, 1990.

Cowley, Malcolm, ed. *Portable Hawthorne.* New York: Penguin, 1977.

Crowley, J. Donald, ed. *Centenary Edition of the Works of Nathaniel Hawthorne.* Columbus: Ohio State UP, 1974. Vol IX, *Twice-Told Tales;* Vol. X, *Mosses from an Old Manse;* Vol. XI, The Snow Image and Uncollected Tales.

Ferguson, J. M., Jr. "Hawthorne's 'Young Goodman Brown.'" *Explicator* 28 (1969): Item 32.

Fetterley, Judith. *The Resisting Reader.* Bloomington: Indiana UP, 1978.

Gallagher, Edward J. "The Concluding Paragraph of 'Young Goodman Brown.'" *Studies in Short Fiction* 12 (1975): 29–30.

McIntosh, James, ed. *Nathaniel Hawthorne's Tales.* New York: Norton, 1987.

Newman, Lea Bertani. *A Reader's Guide to the Short Stories of Nathaniel Hawthorne.* Boston: G. K. Hall, 1979.

Robinson, E. Arthur. "The Vision of Goodman Brown: A Source and Interpretation." *American Literature* 35 (1963): 218–25.

Von Frank, Albert J., ed. *Critical Essays on Hawthorne's Short Stories.* Boston: G. K. Hall, 1991.

Whelan, Robert E. "Hawthorne Interprets 'Young Goodman Brown.'" *Emerson Society Quarterly* 62 (1971): 3–6.

ERNEST HEMINGWAY

Hills Like White Elephants (p. 350)

Hemingway wrote this story in May 1927, while on his honeymoon in the Rhône delta with his second wife, Pauline. According to his biographer Kenneth Lynn, the story was a dramatization of a fantasy he had about his first wife, Hadley: "[I]f only the two of them had not allowed a child to enter their lives they would never have parted." Throughout his biography, Lynn interprets the fiction in terms of Hemingway's relationships. How much this approach sheds light on the fiction each reader must judge.

This story is an early example of a minimalist technique. Characterization and plot are mere suggestions, and it is possible for some young readers to finish the story for the first time with no idea that the couple are discussing an abortion. The setting Hemingway chooses for the couple's conversation is more richly developed. The symbolism of the "two lines of rails" at the station (the choice either to end the pregnancy or have the child); the fields of grain and trees along the Ebro River, which the girl sees on the other side of the station (fertility, a settled life) compared with the barren hills, long and white like white elephants (something considered unlucky, unwanted, and rejected); the bar and the station building (the temporary escape offered by alcohol, the sense of people in transit) — one can interpret these details in perfect harmony with the couple's emotional and physical dilemma.

The man's bullying of the girl drives the story. His ignorance about abortion and his insensitivity to what she is feeling or will have to endure physically ("It's not really anything. It's just to let the air in") are not presented as weakness. They are simply part of his insistence on persuading Jig to do what he wants her to do. The girl is also worthy of discussion. Her vulnerability is idealized, yet she is not stupid. Without the suggestion of her intelligence, there would be no story.

Hemingway regarded "Hills Like White Elephants" as one of his best stories, reserving a prominent place for it in his second collection, *Men Without Women*, published in the fall of 1927. Lynn states that in choosing this title for the book, Hemingway meant to suggest "that the alienation of women from men (as well as vice versa) was one of his themes."

Questions for Discussion

1. In what ways could you categorize this story as a minimalist work?
2. What do we know about the man? About the girl? Why isn't Jig called "a woman" in the story?
3. What is a "white elephant"? How does this expression suit the story?
4. What do you think will happen to this couple after the story ends?
5. Read the story aloud in class, assigning two students the roles of the man and the girl. Is the story as effective read as dialogue as it is on the page as a literary text?

Topic for Writing

1.   **RESPONDING CREATIVELY**   Rewrite the story in a different setting to discover the importance of the railroad station and the Spanish landscape in "Hills Like White Elephants."

Related Story

Russell Banks, Black Man and White Woman in Dark Green Rowboat, p. 68.

Suggested Readings

Baker, Carlos, ed. *Ernest Hemingway: A Life Story.* New York: Macmillan, 1976.
———. *Ernest Hemingway: Selected Letters 1917–1961.* Scribner's, 1981.
Beegel, Susan F., ed. *Hemingway's Neglected Short Fiction: New Perspectives.* Ann Arbor: UMI Research Press, 1989.
Benson, Jackson. *The Short Stories of Ernest Hemingway: Critical Essays.* Durham, NC: Duke UP, 1975.
———, ed. *New Critical Approaches to the Short Stories of Ernest Hemingway.* Durham, NC: Duke UP, 1990.
Brenner, Gerry, and Earl Rovit. *Ernest Hemingway.* Rev. ed. Boston: Twayne, 1986.
Flora, Joseph M. *Ernest Hemingway: A Study of the Short Fiction.* Boston: Twayne, 1989.
Hays, Peter L. *Ernest Hemingway.* New York: Continuum, 1990.
Lynn, Kenneth S. *Hemingway.* New York: Simon, 1987.
Reynolds, Michael S., ed. *Critical Essays on Ernest Hemingway's* In Our Time. Boston: G. K. Hall, 1983.

ZORA NEALE HURSTON

Sweat (p. 355)

"Sweat" is interesting for the modern reader on many levels. For the student familiar with the regional authors of the previous generation — writers such as Sarah Orne Jewett and Kate Chopin — the style of the story will be familiar. The story is set in a small, isolated community; the central figure is an older woman; and the story is concerned with her personal tragedy. As in most regional stories, the line of the horizon is the boundary of the action. In "Sweat" there is no suggestion that there is a world beyond the limits of the small town and the woman's cabin on a dirt road just on the outskirts. The carefully rendered dialogue is written in the colloquial speech favored by the regionalists, and, as in their work, the descriptions of the house and the dirt roads set the scene with precise detail.

For the student who has read such contemporary black women writers as Alice Walker and Toni Morrison, the theme of the story will also be familiar.

Hurston presents the same bitter anger and despair between black men and women in the rural South that Walker and Morrison present later. Hurston is perhaps even more important as a precursor of current openness than she is as a writer who is simply continuing an older, regional literary style.

In reading a story like "Sweat" it is useful to forget Hurston's studies in black folklore, which in fact were done *after* the story was published. At this point in her career she was part of a very sophisticated and socially conscious movement that was attempting to give the black minority in the United States a literary voice. Unlike many of the writers of a generation before who modeled their work on Maupassant, Hurston is much closer to the French realist Émile Zola, whose grim novels of small-town life in the French provinces were widely read in the United States at this time. There is in his work, as in Hurston's, an uncompromising hardness, and he would have approved of Hurston's heroine as she creeps back in the shadows to let her husband die of the rattlesnake bite he had intended for her. It is a description that Alice Walker would appreciate.

Questions for Discussion

1. Why doesn't Delia go to the sheriff when her husband terrorizes her with the snake?
2. Why is it this "other" woman of Sykes's who finally drives Delia to try to do something to save what is left of her life?
3. What will happen to Delia now that her husband is dead?
4. Why didn't people in the community try to help Delia when they learned of her husband's open infidelities?
5. Why does Delia decide to go to a different church?
6. Why is her husband still permitted to take part in church services, even though he is not trying to hide his "sinful ways"?
7. Will there be any investigation into the circumstances of Delia's husband's death?

Topics for Writing

1. Discuss the role of the white families in the small town in making it possible for Delia to eke out her hard living. What could the community have done to make her life better?
2. Discuss the social attitudes that accept Delia's husband's right to brutalize her physically and emotionally.
3. **CONNECTIONS** Compare the description of Delia's situation in "Sweat" with Nancy's situation in Faulkner's "That Evening Sun." How do the different authors resolve their plots?

Related Commentaries

Zora Neale Hurston, How It Feels to Be Colored Me, p. 873.
Alice Walker, Zora Neale Hurston: A Cautionary Tale and a Partisan View, p. 930.

Suggested Readings

Edwards, Lee R. *Psyche as Hero: Female Heroism and Fictional Form.* Middletown, CT: Wesleyan, 1984.

Gates, Henry Louis, ed. *Black Literature and Literary Theory.* New York: Methuen, 1984.

Hemenway, Robert. *Zora Neale Hurston: A Literary Biography.* Urbana: U of Illinois P, 1977.

Howard, Lillie P. *Zora Neale Hurston.* Boston: Twayne, 1980.

Hull, Gloria T. *Color, Sex, and Poetry: Three Women Writers of the Harlem Renaissance.* Bloomington: Indiana UP, 1987.

Hurston, Zora Neale. *The Gilded Six-Bits.* Minneapolis: Redpath, 1986.

———. *I Love Myself When I Am Laughing . . . and Then Again When I Am Looking Mean and Impressive.* Ed. Alice Walker. Old Westbury, NY: Feminist, 1979.

———. *Mules and Men.* Westport, CT: Greenwood, 1969.

Lupton, Mary Jane. "Zora Neale Hurston and the Survival of the Female." *Southern Literary Journal* 15.1 (Fall 1982): 45–54.

Washington, Mary Helen, ed. *Invented Lives: Narratives of Black Women, 1860–1960.* Garden City, NY: Anchor, 1987.

Yates, Janelle. *Zora Neale Hurston: A Storyteller's Life.* Staten Island, NY: Ward Hill, 1991.

SHIRLEY JACKSON

The Lottery (p. 365)

The interpretive suggestions in the headnote should guide students toward a recognition of the main themes of "The Lottery." The near universality of the ritual sacrifice of year gods and scapegoats in primitive cultures to ensure fertility, the continuation of life, and the purgation of society has been a common assumption since the publication of James G. Frazer's The Golden Bough. Jackson does not explore the transmutations of these old ceremonies in the accepted religious practices and psychological mechanisms of modern humanity; rather, she attempts to shock her readers into an awareness of the presence of raw, brutal, and superstitious impulses within us all. A fruitful approach for class discussion might involve exploring how the story achieves its impact. Jackson's comments (included in Part Two, p. 877) provide incontrovertible documentation of the power of "The Lottery" to stir the dark instincts dwelling below the surface of the civilized psyche, perhaps the same regions from which the story emerged fully formed — as Jackson claims — in the mind of the writer. No wonder readers, from the author's agent on, have found "The Lottery" disturbing.

But they have also found it compelling, fascinating, and irresistible, and the reason may have partly to do with Jackson's technical skill. For the inattentive first reader, the natural suspense of any drawing, contest, or lottery provides strong motivation to hurry through to the ending, and when the realization of what is at stake comes, it strikes with redoubled force because of the reader's increased velocity. For the more careful reader, or for the reader already aware of the ending, the subtle foreshadowing — the boys are gathering stones, the box is black, Tessie Hutchinson "clean forgot what day it was" — triggers an uncomfortable double awareness that also urges haste, a haste like that which spurs Mr. Summers's final, horrible remark, "All right, folks. . . . Let's finish quickly," and the cries of "Come on" and "Hurry up" by other villagers.

For Jackson has succeeded in gaining the reader's vicarious participation in the lottery. Even the backwoods New England quaintness of the setting draws not the kind of condescending laughter that would distance the reader but the warm sentimental indulgence we reserve for the cutest Norman Rockwell illustrations. Little boys are being little boys as they pick up the stones, the villagers are walking clichés, and even Tessie Hutchinson, singled out from the rest by her tardiness, is tardy for the most housewifely of reasons. (How different the story would be if she appeared nervous and flustered, a few moments ahead of, say, a disheveled Steve Adams!) The reader is drawn to sink into this warm bath of comfortable stereotypes, illusions intact. Totally off guard against the possibility that the good hearts of these neighborly folks might beat in time with an ancient and brutal rhythm, that superstitious fears of hunger and death might easily outweigh feelings of friendliness and compassion, the reader may well recoil from any previous fascination and, in an effort to deny involvement, recoil from the story, too. Except that we do not reject it; "The Lottery" continues to exert such power over the imagination of its readers that it clearly must be providing a catharsis for instincts similar to those that move the villagers to pick up stones.

WILLIAM E. SHEIDLEY

Questions for Discussion

1. What associations does the word *lottery* have for you? Are they relevant to the story?
2. Comment on the ending of the first paragraph.
3. On what other occasions might the people of the village gather in the way they do for the lottery? Mr. Summers is in charge of "civic activities." Is the lottery one of these? Explain.
4. Discuss the degree to which the tradition of the lottery has been kept. Why does no one want to make a new box? Why is the whole institution not abandoned?
5. Examine the character of Tessie Hutchinson. She claims that her fate is not *fair.* Is there any reason why she should be singled out? Is she a tragic heroine? Consider her cry, "There's Don and Eva. . . . Make them take their chance!"
6. On your first reading, when did you begin to suspect what happens at the end of the story? How soon might it become evident? What are the most important hints?
7. One reason the ending can surprise a reader is that the villagers never speak directly of what they are about. Why not? Are they ashamed? afraid?
8. Comment on the conversation between the Adamses and Old Man Warner. What is the implication of Steve Adams's last appearance in the story?
9. Does the rhyme "Lottery in June, corn be heavy soon" adequately explain the institution of the lottery? What other reasons might people have for such behavior? What is the social function of a scapegoat?
10. After her family has received the black spot, Tessie complains, but Mrs. Delacroix tells her, "Be a good sport, Tessie." Comment on this choice of words.

11. Discuss the reaction of the Hutchinson family. Why does the lottery single out a family first, then a victim?
12. Old Man Warner says, "People ain't the way they used to be." Are they? What does he mean?
13. Why are the people in such a hurry to "finish"?
14. What is the implication of "someone gave little Davy Hutchinson a few pebbles"?

Topics for Writing

1. Discuss Jackson's techniques for building suspense in "The Lottery."
2. Write an essay exploring the usefulness of stereotypes in "The Lottery."
3. Examine the behavior of groups of people with which you are familiar. Can you find actual instances of formal or informal practices similar to the one described in "The Lottery" — even though they may not lead to such a brutal finale? Have you or has anyone you know been made a scapegoat? Write an essay showing how one such case reflects and confirms the implications of Jackson's story.

Related Commentary

Shirley Jackson, The Morning of June 28, 1948, and "The Lottery," p. 877.

Suggested Reading

Freidman, Lenemaja. *Shirley Jackson.* Twayne's United States Authors Series 253. Boston: G. K. Hall, 1975. 63–67.

GISH JEN

Who's Irish? (p. 373)

Although this troubling story is presented as a painful moment in the experience of an elderly Chinese woman attempting to adjust to life in the United States, it could have been a story of any older person who finds herself in an unfamiliar situation that she can neither understand nor accept. Attempts to solve the new problem with answers from an older life experience can lead to unfortunate consequences, as it does here, and the life of the woman in the story is left empty and confused.

Gish Jen, who is herself a child of Chinese immigrants to the United States, structures the story around the polarities of the child's parentage — her Chinese American mother and her Irish American father. The older woman says that the Chinese traits she hopes to develop in the girl are obedience and self-control, since the Irish side, the Shea family, is "wild." In an interview, Jen was asked about her use of humor in her stories, in contrast to other Asian American writers who express considerable anger in their portrayal of their American experience. She responded, "Maybe humor is one way of expressing anger." Certainly the woman's problems with her daughter's life lead her into confrontations with her Irish son-in-law and his family. When the family has talked at some length about the baby's brown color the woman grows tired of the conversation, which she compares to a Christmas tree train that goes around and around in an unending circle.

"Maybe John is not her father, I say one day, to stop the train. And sure enough, train wreck."

The woman seems too unaware of the consequences of her suggestion that her daughter has been unfaithful to her husband, but we suspect that she is conscious of the consequences of her actions. When she begins to spank the daughter, and when finally she loses control and hurts the daughter after the little girl has defied her by crawling into a hole in a sand pile, we realize that the strongest element in the woman's character is anger. She is angry at a life that excludes her, a life in which the role she once played in the restaurant she owned with her husband has been taken from her. She is a woman who struggled to achieve the economic success she and her husband enjoyed, and she is contemptuous of her son-in-law and his brothers for their inability to find jobs. She rails at them: "They say they cannot find work, this is not the economy of the fifties, but I say, Even the black people doing better these days, some of them live so fancy, you'd be surprised. Why the Shea family have so much trouble? They are white people, they speak English."

And her anger finally overwhelms her. As she attacks the three-year-old girl who has hidden in the sand with a long stick, the reader is afraid that the woman may kill her. In the confrontation with her daughter and her husband that follows, the woman justifies what she has done by saying, "She is not like any Chinese girl I ever saw."

It is necessary for the daughter to move her mother away from the family before her husband divorces her. At the end of the story it is clear that the older woman is unrepentant, and the experience of living with the Irish mother of her son-in-law has not endeared her to the woman or to the Irish. She feels that the woman's words, "Permanent resident. Not going anywhere," which echo the legal term for a resident alien, strike her like the stick she used against her granddaughter. "I don't know how Bess Shea learn to use her words, but I hear what she say a long time later." There are aspects of the story the woman's telling that have elements of humor, but the reader's final impression is that Jen has used the humor, as she said, to express a deep and continuing anger.

Questions for Discussion

1. The woman's description of herself is "fierce." What confirms the reader in this impression of her? Does she seem conscious of the implications of the word?
2. What is her opinion of the Irish? Would you describe her as prejudiced?
3. What does the daughter mean when she tells her mother not to say "Irish this, Irish that"?
4. Are the mother's attitudes representative of newly arrived immigrant groups?

5. What is the difference between her and her daughter in their understanding of words like "supportive" and "creative"? Is the mother making an effort to understand these differences? Is the daughter sympathetic to her mother's attitudes?
6. Are the differences between the two women only a misunderstanding of certain words, or do their differences reflect their new life experience in the United States?
7. What does the woman's statement that "Chinese people don't think a daughter is so great" tell us about her?
8. Do the two old women in the story have any deeper understanding of each other? Has their age made them any closer?

Topics for Writing

1. The old woman feels justified in her physical punishment of her granddaughter. Discuss her attitudes toward child rearing, in contrast to what she perceives as the American attitudes toward discipline and obedience.
2. Some of the woman's strong temperament must be a necessary element of a new immigrant's character if the individual is to survive the wrenching changes in her life. Discuss this statement and relate it to the woman's memories of her life in the restaurant with her husband.
3. Relate the comments the woman makes about the Irish, and her comparisons with African Americans, to the larger problems of immigrant assimilation, using one additional group as an example.
4. Many of the woman's comments about her granddaughter's behavior reflect differences between generations as much as they characterize the Chinese attitude toward childrearing. Discuss the unrealistic expectations that some older people have toward newer ideas as you have experienced them.

Suggested Readings

Chin, Marilyn. *Dwarf Bamboo*. Greenfield Center, NY: Greenfield Review Press, 1987.

———. *The Phoenix Gone, the Terrace Empty*. Minneapolis: Milkweed Editions, 1994.

Hagedorn, Jessica, ed. *Charlie Chan Is Dead: An Anthology of Contemporary Asian American Fiction*. New York: Penguin, 1993.

SARAH ORNE JEWETT

A White Heron (p. 382)

Jewett portrays Sylvia, whose very name associates her with the woodland, as torn between the natural world in which she is so fully at home and the first stirrings of the "great power" of love in her "woman's heart." Her project of pleasing the young hunter and winning the treasure of his gratitude, in the form of ten dollars, leads her out of her shyness and into the heroic adventure of climbing the great pine tree. As a result of her efforts, Sylvia grows within herself. The reader worries that she may be tempted into betraying the white heron and thus into surrendering something essential to her own integrity, but Sylvia, in her vision from the top of the tree and her face-to-face meeting with the heron, has gained the perspective necessary to hold firm.

Jewett's rich evocation of the landscape and the emotional intensity with which she narrates the climactic action contribute to the story's deeper resonances. If Sylvia recalls the woodland goddess Diana — and similarly guards her chastity — she also resembles those heroes and heroines of myth and folklore who must go to some symbolic world-navel or towering height in quest of wisdom, or who must suffer an initiation that involves mastering their fear of the (sometimes phallic) *other* and reintegrating their identities in order to cope with it. Sylvia rejects the destructive gun and mounts the pine tree, "a great main-mast to the voyaging earth," electing the fecund life of a natural world she is still discovering over the destructive promises of the "ornithologist," whose grounds are populated with dead, stuffed birds. While the narrator ends fretting over Sylvia's having consigned herself to loneliness and love-longing, nothing in the story suggests that she would be better off having sold herself for ten dollars and a whistle.

Students may find it easier to approach the story through its autobiographical dimensions. According to Eugene Hillhouse Pool, who builds on F. O. Matthiessen's early study, Jewett remained childlike and single all her life, treasuring the love of her father, who used to take her on long rambles through the countryside when she was a girl. "As Sylvia elects to keep her private and meaningful secret, so is she choosing for Miss Jewett too. . . . She chooses, psychologically, to remain a child, with Sylvia." But if Jewett chose to remain a child, it is a child in terms she met in reading Wordsworth, whom she admired: as one privy to the indwelling spirit of the natural world.

The imagery that surrounds Sylvia is uniformly associated with mother nature until she ventures up the tree and meets the heron. Her adventure enables her to reject assertively the young man and the advancing modern world of science and machinery with which he is associated. This is a step forward from her original strategies of withdrawal and concealment. The antinomy, however, is not resolved. The only perfect marriage in the story is between the nesting herons; and Jewett offers no key to a satisfactory union between the world of nature and the civilization that threatens to despoil it.

WILLIAM E. SHEIDLEY

Questions for Discussion

1. Jewett is known as a local colorist. To what extent is the locale of this story its subject? To what extent does the story transcend its specific Maine setting?
2. Discuss the presentation of the cow Sylvia is driving as the story opens. What does her "loud moo by way of explanation" actually explain?
3. Comment on the men, apart from the hunter, mentioned in the story. Is the absence of men from Sylvia's world a significant factor in the story?
4. As a child in town, Sylvia has the reputation of being "afraid of folks." Is she? Does she have reason?

5. Explain Sylvia's reaction when she hears the hunter's whistle. Why does Jewett briefly switch to the present tense here? Does she do so elsewhere?
6. Comment on the omniscient-narrative point of view in this story. How is it controlled? What does the narrative voice contribute?
7. Describe the character and appurtenances of the young hunter, and contrast them with those of Sylvia. How important are his evident gentleness and good intentions?
8. How does Jewett charge the pine tree and Sylvia's climb to the top of it with special meaning? What does Sylvia see up there that she has never seen before?
9. What do Sylvia and the heron have in common?
10. Analyze the last paragraph. What has Sylvia lost? What has she preserved? What has she gained?

Topics for Writing

1. Research elements of folk and fairy tale in "A White Heron."
2. Analyze Sylvia's nighttime excursion as a journey into the self.
3. Examine maternal and sexual imagery in "A White Heron."
4. Consider "A White Heron" as a rejection of modern industrial society.

Related Commentary

Sarah Orne Jewett, Looking Back on Girlhood, p. 880.

Suggested Readings

Brenzo, Richard. "Free Heron or Dead Sparrow: Sylvia's Choice in Sarah Orne Jewett's 'A White Heron.' " *Colby Library Quarterly* 14 (1978): 36–41.

Cary, Richard. *Sarah Orne Jewett.* Albany, NY: New Collections UP, 1962.

Donovan, Josephine L. *Sarah Orne Jewett.* New York: Ungar, 1980.

Hovet, Theodore R. "America's 'Lonely Country Child': The Theme of Separation in Sarah Orne Jewett's 'A White Heron.'" *Colby Library Quarterly* 14 (1978): 166–71.

———. "'Once Upon a Time': Sarah Orne Jewett's 'A White Heron' as a Fairy Tale." *Studies in Short Fiction* 15 (1978): 63–68.

Keyworth, Cynthia, et al. *Master Smart Women: A Portrait of Sarah Orne Jewett.* Belfast, ME: North Country, 1988.

Nagel, Gwen. *Critical Essays on Sarah Orne Jewett.* Boston: G. K. Hall, 1984.

Pool, Eugene Hillhouse. "The Child in Sarah Orne Jewett." Appreciation of Sarah Orne Jewett. Ed. Richard Cary. Waterville, ME: Colby College P, 1973. 223–28, esp. 225. Originally published in *Colby Library Quarterly* 7 (1967): 503–09.

Westbrook, Perry D. *Acres of Flint: Sarah Orne Jewett and Her Contemporaries.* Rev. ed. Metuchen, NJ: Scarecrow, 1981.

HA JIN

Saboteur (p. 391)

This sad tale about the Chinese lecturer Mr. Chiu will probably be unclear to students who read it too quickly, but Ha Jin is playing fair with his readers. In the fourth paragraph we are told that Mr. Chiu has just recently recovered from acute hepatitis and is afraid he might have a relapse, despite the fact that he's feeling "on the course of recovery" after his two-week honeymoon. Illness hovers close by, however. His bride tells him that she has a headache and didn't sleep well on their last night together. Reading the exposition closely, the alert student will sense that poor health is in the story to stay.

The third-person narrator makes it very clear that Mr. Chiu is a victim of police harassment after the couple finish eating their lunch and the rising action of the story begins. Mr. Chiu is tough, and his treatment at the Railroad Police Station doesn't humiliate him, though he is shocked to discover he has been set up for the crime of sabotage by the police informers at the station restaurant, who have signed statements against him describing behavior that the reader knows never happened. The torture of his colleague Fenjin, the lawyer who comes to help him and is handcuffed to the trunk of the pine tree in the prison courtyard outside Mr. Chiu's window, adds another, even worse dimension to the police department's crime — they will stop at nothing to force a confession from an innocent man. Powerless to help his friend unless he confesses to the crime he didn't commit, Mr. Chiu finally signs his name to the sheet containing the false charges against him. This is the climax of the story, but Ha Jin appends falling action and a powerful conclusion straight out of Maupassant's "surprise ending" technique.

For the first time Ha Jin describes Mr. Chiu ingenuously when we read that he dragged his lawyer from restaurant to restaurant near the police station "as if dying of hunger." Before he boards his train to get out of town, Mr. Chiu deliberately sets out to infect as many people as possible with acute hepatitis. Leaving most of his soup untouched at the last restaurant, he knows that the personnel will merely pour it back into the common pot, and it will sicken the patrons who eat there later that day. After an epidemic of acute hepatitis infects the townspeople, Mr. Chiu gets his revenge against the policemen who treated him so unfairly.

Questions for Discussion

1. Is Mr. Chiu a sympathetic or an unsympathetic character? He's on his honeymoon, but why are we told that he didn't miss his bride and enjoyed sleeping alone in prison?
2. Why are we given the detail that the fleas in the mattress don't bother him?
3. Why does Mr. Chiu blame his bride for sending Fenjin to defend him at the prison?
4. Mr. Chiu tells the police that he will report them to the Provincial Administration. What makes him change his mind and infect the food in the nearby restaurants instead?

Topic for Writing

1.   Write a book review of the stories in Ha Jin's *The Bridegroom* (2000), the collection in which "Saboteur" appears. In what different ways is Ha Jin critical of Communist China in his stories?

Suggested Readings

Jin, Ha. *Between Silences: A Voice from China.* Chicago: U of Chicago P, 1990.
———. *The Bridegroom: Stories.* New York: Pantheon, 2000.
———. *Under the Red Flag: Stories.* Athens: U of Georgia P, 1997.

JAMES JOYCE

Araby (p. 400)

The rich texture of imagery and allusion that Joyce weaves into "Araby" may delight the sophisticated reader, but for the classroom instructor it represents a temptation comparable to the temptation that may be brought to mind by the apple tree in the "wild garden" mentioned in the second paragraph. Students should not be asked to contemplate the story's symbolism until they grasp its plot. To begin class discussion of "Araby" with the question What happens? may well be to discover that, for a novice reader, no meaningful action seems to have been completed. When the confusion arising from this sense of anticlimax is compounded by the difficulties presented by the unfamiliarity of florins, bazaars, hallstands, and other things old and Irish, "Araby" may strike students as pointless and unnecessarily obscure.

Once it is seen, however, that the narrator's disappointment at the bazaar resolves the tension built up by his attraction to Mangan's sister and his quest to fetch her a symbol of his love, the many specific contrasts between the sensuous and romantic world of the narrator's imagination and the banal and tawdry world of actual experience become meaningful keys to understanding what has happened. The opposition between fantasy and reality continues throughout: "Her image accompanied me even in places the most hostile to romance." The story's pivotal paragraph ends with the narrator cooling his forehead against the window in one of the empty upper rooms, staring out not really at Mangan's sister but at "the brown-clad figure cast by my imagination." Before this moment, his excited fancy has transformed the "decent" and somewhat dilapidated neighborhood of North Richmond Street into a fitting backdrop for such a tale as one might find in a yellow-leaved romance. Mangan's sister, kissed by lamplight, becomes in his view a work of art like a painting by Rossetti. The narrator's soul luxuriates in a dream of exotic beauty soon to be possessed by means of a journey to Araby: "I imagined that I bore my chalice safely through a throng of foes." But after the protracted visit from the tedious Mrs. Mercer and the even longer delayed return of the narrator's uncle with the necessary coin, the limitations of the romantic imagination begin to emerge. The "chalice" is replaced by a florin, held "tightly in my hand"; the quest is made by "third-class carriage"; and the bazaar itself, its potential visionary qualities defeated by failing illumination, turns out to be an ordinary market populated by ordinary shop girls from no farther east than England. At Araby, what matters is not purity of heart but hard cash.

The pitiful inadequacy of the narrator's two pennies and sixpence to master "the great jars that stood like eastern guards" at the door of the bazaar stall completes his painful disillusionment, but Joyce allows his hero one last Byronic vision of himself "as a creature driven and derided by vanity." When the lights go out in Araby, its delusive magic collapses, and the bazaar becomes as "blind" as North Richmond Street. Well might the narrator's eyes burn, for they have been working hard to create out of intractable materials a much more beautiful illusion than Araby. This imaginative power cannot be entirely vain, however, since in the mind that tells the story it is capable of evoking experiences like those described in the story's third paragraph, against which even the hoped-for transports of Araby would have paled.

WILLIAM E. SHEIDLEY

Questions for Discussion

1. Why does the narrator want to go to the bazaar?
2. Why does he arrive so late?
3. Why doesn't he buy anything for Mangan's sister?
4. Enumerate the activities taking place at Araby. To what extent do they sustain its "magical name"?
5. What had the narrator expected to find at Araby? What was the basis of his expectation?
6. Define the narrator's feelings for Mangan's sister. To what extent is she the cause of those feelings? What, as they say, does he see in her?
7. What purpose might Joyce have had in choosing not to mention the object of the narrator's affections until the middle of the third paragraph? Describe the context into which she is introduced. In what ways is she part of the world of North Richmond Street?
8. What is the role of the narrator's uncle in the story? What values and attitudes does he represent? Are they preferable to those of the narrator?

Topics for Writing

1. Make a study of light, vision, and beauty in "Araby."
2. Compare "Araby" and the quest for the Holy Grail.
3. Analyze the function of nonvisual sense imagery in "Araby."
4. Explore Joyce's control of tone in "Araby."
5. On a second reading of the story, keep two lists. In the first record ideas, images, and allusions that suggest contexts remote from the immediate situation, jotting down associations that they bring to mind. In the second list note anything mentioned in the story with which you are unfamiliar. Look up some of these items. Then write an informal paragraph or two showing to what extent tracking Joyce's mind in this fashion helped you to understand and enjoy the story.

6. **RESPONDING CREATIVELY** Using the first three paragraphs of "Araby" as a model, write a recollection of the way you spent your evenings at some memorable period of your childhood. Use specific sensory images to evoke the locale, the activities, and the way you felt at the time.
7. **RESPONDING CREATIVELY** Narrate an experience in which you were disappointed. First show how your erroneous expectations were generated; then describe what you actually encountered in such a way that its contrast with your expectations is clear.

Suggested Readings

See page 81.

JAMES JOYCE

The Dead (p. 404)

"The Dead" is an apprehension of mortality. Joyce's carefully detailed scrutiny of the party, with all its apparent vivacity, serves only to reveal the triviality, transience, and emptiness of what passes for life in Dublin. The story involves a series of supersessions. Miss Ivors's friendliness is superseded by rigid politics, and she departs. Her kind of fervor is superseded by the "hospitality" of the dinner table that Gabriel feels so good about and that he celebrates in his speech. That conviviality, however, is exposed as mostly hypocritical, as each person reveals a selfish preoccupation — including Gabriel, who uses his oration to reassure himself after his self-esteem has been wounded by Miss Ivors. The long evening, however, generates in the heart of Gabriel a strong surge of love for Gretta that supersedes his selfishness. It is edged with jealousy and self-contempt, Gabriel's habitual weaknesses; nonetheless, the reader feels for a while that out of the waste of the soiree at least this rejuvenation has been salvaged. But Gabriel is longing for something just as dead as Michael Furey, and Gretta's devastating disclosure of a dead lover's power over her mind brings the "thought-tormented" Gabriel to his final recognition of the predominance of death. Like the monks of Mount Melleray, all people in Ireland, dead or alive — from the aged Aunt Julia on down — seem to be sleeping in their coffins.

While Gabriel's vision is triggered by the revelation of a dead man's sway over the emotions of his wife and of his consequent power to thwart Gabriel's desire, it is supported by the pervasive imagery of snow, chill, and death that comes to fulfillment in the last paragraph. The snow has been falling intermittently throughout the story. Gabriel is blanketed with it when he arrives on the scene, and images of cold and dampness pervade the narration. Last year "Gretta caught a dreadful cold"; Bartell D'Arcy has one this year. The girl in the song he sings holds her death-cold infant in a soaking rain. Not only are the physical descriptions of some characters so vivid that one almost sees the skulls beneath the flesh; even the warm, lively, cheerful elements of the story contribute to the final impression of morbidity. The Misses Morkan are giving what may be their final dance. The alcoholic antics of Mr. Browne and Freddy Malins consist only of ersatz good humor. And Gabriel himself, on whom everyone depends, can barely sustain his nerve and perform his function as master of the revels, keeper of order, and sustainer of life.

In the moribund and sterile world presided over by his three spinster aunts, Gabriel is called upon to play a role not unlike that of a year god at this Christmas season. (The party probably takes place on Epiphany, January 6.) From the outset he is willing, but in three sequential encounters he fails. Each failure strikes a blow at his naiveté, his self-confidence, and his sense of superiority. His first two defeats are followed by accomplishments (handling Freddy, his performance at dinner), but their effect on him is cumulative. Gabriel's cheerful banter with the pale, pale Lily does not suit her, as one who has been hurt in love, and his Christmas gift of a coin can do little to ease her "great bitterness." Afterward, his pretensions to take care of people are subjected to merciless ridicule in the "goloshes" passage. With Miss Ivors, Gabriel is more circumspect than with Lily, but that does not prevent him from being whipsawed between her political hostility and her personal affection. This confusing interaction not only causes Miss Ivors to abandon the company and Gabriel in his speech to reject the entire younger generation of Ireland, it also sets the stage for his ultimate failure with Gretta. Gretta's favorable response to Miss Ivors's plan for a trip to Galway now seems to Gabriel a betrayal, and the association of this trip with Gretta's love for the long-dead Michael compounds the feelings of alienation and self-contempt that Miss Ivors's disapproval fosters in him.

Gabriel's failures and self-doubts should not diminish him unduly in the reader's eyes: Joyce portrays him as aesthetically sensitive, charitable, and loving. The "generous tears" he sheds out of sympathy for Gretta's sorrow may not redeem anyone in a world devoted to death, but they are the distillation of a compassion quite opposite to the self-serving hypocrisy that has passed for friendly conversation at the Misses Morkan's ball. By the end of the story Gabriel no longer feels superior to his compatriots. He recognizes that when Aunt Julia dies his speechifying will be useless. He turns his mind away from the past and toward a future in which, as he feels his old identity fade and dissolve, at least the theoretical possibility of growth and change exists. The ambiguity of Gabriel's much-debated "journey westward" reflects the uncertainty of any future, but Gabriel's readiness to embrace it represents a major step forward from his rejection of Miss Ivors's proposition in favor of cycling the European continent again.

WILLIAM E. SHEIDLEY

Questions for Discussion

1. Contrast the mood of the first paragraph with that of the second. Why does Joyce move from anticipation to rigidity?
2. Why are the Misses Morkan so eager for Gabriel to arrive?
3. What is the basis of Gabriel's error with Lily?
4. Explain Gabriel's hesitation to quote Browning.
5. What does Gabriel's interest in galoshes reveal about him?
6. Comment on the men present at the dance besides Gabriel. Why does Joyce limit his cast so narrowly?
7. Discuss the reception of Mary Jane's "Academy piece."

8.   What does Miss Ivors want from Gabriel? Why is he so upset by his conversation with her? Why does she leave early? Figuratively, what does she take with her when she goes?

9.   Explain Gabriel's longing to be out in the snow. Is Gabriel "thought-tormented"?

10.   Explain the irony of Julia's singing "Arrayed for the Bridal" to Mary Jane's accompaniment. What, in this regard, is the effect of the subsequent conversation?

11.   Comment on the relevance of the dinner-table conversation to the themes of the story.

12.   Why is Gabriel so cheerful when carving and when proposing his toast? Is he justified? Why does he imagine people standing in the snow before he begins to speak?

13.   What is the effect of Joyce's ending the tribute to the Misses Morkan with a glimpse of Freddy conducting the singers with his fork?

14.   Comment on Gabriel's anecdote about "the never-to-be-forgotten Johnny." Can it be read as a summation in a minor key of the party now ending? of the life of the Morkan family? of their society?

15.   Discuss the scene in which Gabriel watches Gretta listening to D'Arcy. What is Gabriel responding to? What is Gretta responding to? What do they have in common? Trace their moods as they proceed to the hotel.

16.   Why is Gabriel so humiliated when he learns that Michael Furey is dead? What other effects does this revelation have on him? Explain what he realizes in the last section of the story.

17.   Discuss the final paragraph. What does its poetic beauty contribute to the story? What is our final attitude toward Gabriel?

Topics for Writing

1.   Discuss the relationship between Gabriel Conroy and women in general.
2.   Would you say "The Dead" is a Christmas story? Why or why not?
3.   Comment upon Gabriel Conroy's death wish.
4.   Consider Gabriel Conroy as a failed redeemer.
5.   Explore habit and hypocrisy in "The Dead."
6.   After your first reading of the story, scan it again, marking the following: all references to cold, dampness, and snow; all references to death, illness, or people dead at the time of the story; all references to warmth, light, fire, and the like; all references to youth, young people, children, and the like. Catalog your findings and write a paragraph on the importance of these elements in the story.
7.   **RESPONDING CREATIVELY**   For a specific occasion, plan and compose an after-dinner speech with several headings like Gabriel's. Then analyze your speech, explaining what you were trying to accomplish for your audience — and for yourself. Compare your intentions with Gabriel's.

Related Commentary

Frank O'Connor, Style and Form in Joyce's "The Dead," p. 901.

Suggested Readings

Anderson, Chester G. *James Joyce*. New York: Thames Hudson, 1986.
Attridge, Derek, ed. *The Cambridge Companion to James Joyce*. New York: Cambridge UP, 1990.
Beck, Warren. Joyce's *"Dubliners": Substance, Vision, and Art*. Durham, NC: Duke UP, 1969. 303–60.
Beckett, Samuel, et al. *An Examination of James Joyce*. Brooklyn: Haskell, 1974.
Benstock, Bernard, ed. *Critical Essays on James Joyce*. Boston: G. K. Hall, 1985.
Brugaletta, J. J., and M. H. Hayden. "Motivation for Anguish in Joyce's 'Araby.'" *Studies in Short Fiction* 15 (1978): 11–17.
Cronin, E. J. "James Joyce's Trilogy and Epilogue: 'The Sisters,' 'An Encounter,' 'Araby,' and 'The Dead.'" *Renascence* 31 (1979): 229–48.
Ellmann, Richard. *James Joyce*. New and rev. ed. New York: Oxford UP, 1982.
Levin, Harry. *James Joyce: A Critical Introduction*. New York: New Directions, 1960.
Loomis, C. C., Jr. "Structure and Sympathy in 'The Dead.'" *Twentieth Century Interpretations of "Dubliners."* Ed. Peter K. Garrett. Englewood Cliffs, NJ: Prentice, 1968. 110–14. Originally published in PMLA 75 (1960): 149–51.
Mason, Ellsworth, and Richard Ellmann, eds. *The Critical Writings of James Joyce*. Ithaca, NY: Cornell UP, 1989.
Morrissey, L. J. "Joyce's Narrative Struggles in 'Araby.'" *Modern Fiction Studies* 28 (1982): 45–52.
Riqueline, John P. *Teller and Tale in Joyce's Fiction: Oscillating Perspectives*. Baltimore: Johns Hopkins UP, 1983.
Roberts, R. P. "'Araby' and the Palimpsest of Criticism, or Through a Glass Eye Darkly." *Antioch Review* 26 (1966–67): 469–89.
San Juan, Epifanio, Jr. *James Joyce and the Craft of Fiction: An Interpretation of "Dubliners."* Rutherford, NJ: Fairleigh Dickinson UP, 1972, 209–23.
Scott, Bonnie. *James Joyce*. Atlantic Highlands, NJ: Humanities P International, 1987.
Stone, H. "'Araby' and the Writings of James Joyce." *Antioch Review* 25 (1965): 375–410.

FRANZ KAFKA

A Hunger Artist (p. 435)

This "brief but striking parable of alienation" (to quote Kafka biographer Ernst Pawel) was probably written in February 1922, shortly before Kafka began *The Castle*. He had just returned to Prague after a four-week winter vacation prescribed by his doctor as a sort of "shock treatment" to arrest his advancing tuberculosis and deepening depression. Back at his desk, in his room in his parents' apartment, Kafka described his activities in a letter to a friend: "In order to save myself from what is commonly referred to as 'nerves,' I have lately begun to write a little. From about seven at night I sit at my desk, but it doesn't amount to much. It is like trying to dig a foxhole with one's fingernails in the midst of battle."

"A Hunger Artist" was among the few works Kafka allowed to be published in his lifetime. Ironically, he read the galley proofs only a few days before his death. Pawel describes the scene:

On May 11, [his friend Max] Brod came for what he knew would be his last visit, pretending merely to have stopped off on his way to a lecture in Vienna so as not to alarm his friend. Kafka, by then quite unable to eat, was wasting away, dying of starvation [because of throat lesions] and immersed in the galley proofs of "A Hunger Artist." Fate lacked the subtle touch of Kafka's art.

The effort drained him. "Kafka's physical condition at this point," Klopstock [a medical student] later wrote, "and the whole situation of his literally starving to death, were truly ghastly. Reading the proofs must have been not only a tremendous emotional strain but also a shattering kind of spiritual encounter with his former self, and when he had finished, the tears kept flowing for a long time. It was the first time I ever saw him overtly expressing his emotions this way. Kafka had always shown an almost superhuman self-control."

As a parable, "A Hunger Artist" may be interpreted in as many ways as there are readers finding words to describe their response to the text. Kafka created in his fiction a metaphorical language akin to music, touching emotions at a level beyond the denotations of the words he used to dramatize his imaginary characters' situations. The title is significant: "A Hunger Artist," not *The* Hunger Artist." There are many kinds of hungers, and many kinds of artists expressing different needs for substance. Students may define the "hunger" as a desire for religious certainty and the "fasting" as the stubborn abstention from a faith without God. Or the key to the parable may lie in the Hunger Artist's statement at the end of the story: "I have to fast. I can't help it. . . . Because I couldn't find the food I liked. If I had found it, believe me, I should have made no fuss and stuffed myself like you or anyone else." Kafka was tormented by a failure of nourishment — from his faith, his family, his talent, his art.

Questions for Discussion

1. What is a parable? Is "A Hunger Artist" a parable?
2. Is it possible to read Kafka's story literally, as a realistic tale? What gives you the sense that there is more to "A Hunger Artist" than its plot and characters?
3. Is Kafka describing an unimaginable situation? Explain.
4. Gaping spectators, butchers, theatrical managers, circus people — the world of the Hunger Artist is mercenary and materialistic. He is described as a "martyr." A martyr to what?
5. As the Hunger Artist loses his popularity, he joins the circus, and his cage is put on display near the animal cages. What does this symbolize? What does this action foreshadow?
6. Explicate the last paragraph of the story. Analyze the function of the panther and his "noble body."

Topics for Writing

1. **RESPONDING CREATIVELY**   Write a parable of your own.
2. Agree or disagree with this statement by Primo Levi, the Italian author who translated Kafka's *The Trial*:

Now I love and admire Kafka because he writes in a way that is totally unavailable to me. In my writing, for good or evil, knowingly or not, I've always strived to pass from the darkness into the light. . . . Kafka forges his path in the opposite direction: he endlessly unravels the hallucinations that he draws from incredibly profound layers, and he never filters them. The reader . . . never receives any help in tearing through the veil or circumventing it to go and see what it conceals. Kafka never touches ground, he never condescends to giving you the end of Ariadne's thread.

But this love of mine is ambivalent, close to fear and rejection: it is similar to the emotion we feel for someone dear who suffers and asks us for help we cannot give. . . . His suffering is genuine and continuous, it assails you and does not let you go.

3. **CONNECTIONS** "It was not the hunger artist who was cheating, he was working honestly, but the world was cheating him of his reward." Compare and contrast "A Hunger Artist" and "The Metamorphosis," taking this statement as the theme of both stories.

Related Commentaries

Ann Charters, Translating Kafka, p. 851.
R. Crumb & David Zane Mairowitz, A Hunger Artist, p. 996.
John Updike, Kafka and "The Metamorphosis," p. 927.

Suggested Readings

See page 85.

FRANZ KAFKA

The Metamorphosis (p. 441)

This story admits the broadest range of explications — biographical, psychoanalytical, religious, philosophical. Here is one way it might be read: As the sole supporter of his family after the collapse of his father's business, Gregor Samsa has selflessly devoted himself to serving others. Bringing home "hard cash that could be plunked down on the table at home in front of his astonished and delighted family" has given him great satisfaction, and his only ambition has been to send his sister, "who, unlike him, loved music," to study at the Conservatory. After his metamorphosis, Gregor can no longer justify his existence by serving others. Instead, he must come to terms with himself as himself, an alien being whose own nature and needs are perhaps only by a degree more strange to Gregor than those of the human Gregor Samsa would have been, if somehow he had confronted them rather than deferring to the version of himself projected by the supposed needs of his family.

Kafka simultaneously traces Gregor's painful growth to self-willed individuality and the family's liberation from dependence upon him, for the relationship of dependence and exploitation has been crippling to both parties. Gregor learns what food he likes, stakes his sticky claim to the sexually suggestive picture of the woman with the fur muff (which may represent an objectification of his libido), and, no longer "considerate," at last comes out, intruding his obscene existence upon the world out of a purely self-assertive desire to enjoy his sister's music and to be united with its beauty. With this act Gregor has become fully himself; his death soon after simply releases him from the misery of his existence.

It is also a final release of the family from dependence and from the shame and incompetence that it entails. As an insect, Gregor becomes quite obviously the embarrassment to the family that they allowed him to be when he was human. Step by step they discover their ability to support themselves — taking jobs, coping with what is now merely the troublesome burden of Gregor, and learning finally the necessity of escaping from the prison that his solicitousness has placed them in. Gregor's battle with his father strangely transmutes the Oedipal conflict. It is triggered by Gregor's becoming a being for whom there is no longer room in the family, just as if he were a youth growing to sexual maturity, but the result is that the father, who has previously been reduced to a state of supine inertia by Gregor's diligent exertions, returns to claim his full manhood as husband and paterfamilias.

Emerging from their apartment, "which Gregor had picked for them," the family members grow into an independent purposiveness that Gregor himself is never able to attain. The story may be said to end with a second metamorphosis, focused in the image of Grete stretching her young body — almost like a butterfly newly emerged from her cocoon. Gregor, left behind like the caterpillar whose demise releases her, is denied all but a premonitory glimpse of the sexual and reproductive fulfillment for which his sister seems destined.

WILLIAM E. SHEIDLEY

Questions for Discussion

1. Describe the effect of Kafka's matter-of-fact assertion of the bizarre incident with which the story begins. Are you very interested in how it came to pass? How does Kafka keep that from becoming an issue in the story?

2. What are Gregor's concerns in section I? To what degree do they differ from what would matter to him if he had not been transformed into an insect?

3. When Gregor is trying to get out of bed, he considers calling for help but then dismisses the idea. Why?

4. What seems most important to the members of Gregor's family as he lies in bed? his health?

5. Describe the reaction of Gregor's parents to their first view of the metamorphosed Gregor. What circumstances in ordinary life might elicit a similar response?

6. Discuss the view from Gregor's window.

7. Trace Gregor's adaptation to his new body. In what ways do the satisfactions of his life as an insect differ from the satisfactions of his life as a traveling salesman?

8. When Gregor's father pushes him back into his room at the end of section I, Kafka calls it "truly his salvation." Comment on the possible implications of that description.

9. Describe Grete's treatment of Gregor in section II. Is Gregor ill?
10. What are Gregor's hopes for the future? Is there anything wrong with those hopes?
11. For a time, Gregor is ashamed of his condition and tries to hide from everyone. In what way might this be called a step forward for him?
12. Discuss the conflicting feelings Gregor has about the furniture's being taken out of his room. Why does he try to save the picture? What might Kafka's intention be in stressing that it is on this occasion that Grete calls Gregor by his name for the first time since his metamorphosis?
13. "Gregor's broken out." What does Gregor's father do? Why? Explain the situation that has developed by the end of section II.
14. How does the charwoman relate to Gregor? Why is she the one who presides over his "funeral"?
15. Compare the role of the lodgers in the family with that of Gregor. Have they supplanted him? Why does Gregor's father send them away in the morning?
16. Why does Gregor, who previously did not like music, feel so attracted to his sister's playing? What change has taken place in his attitude toward himself? What might Kafka mean by "the unknown nourishment he longed for"?
17. Comment on Grete's use of the neuter pronoun "it" to refer to Gregor.
18. What is the mood of the final passages of the story?

Topics for Writing

1. Write an essay describing how Kafka gains the reader's "willing suspension of disbelief."
2. Consider Gregor Samsa's metamorphosis as a triumph of the self.
3. Analyze Kafka's "The Metamorphosis" as a study of sublimated incest.
4. **RESPONDING CREATIVELY** Consider Kafka's use of apparently symbolic images whose complete meaning seems impossible to state in abstract terms — the apples, the fur muff, or the hospital beyond the window, for example. Write a vignette in which symbolic objects play a role without becoming counters in a paraphrasable allegory. Some examples of symbols: a candle, a cup, the sea, broken glass, ants.
5. **CONNECTIONS** Compare and discuss Tolstoy's "The Death of Ivan Ilych" and Kafka's "The Metamorphosis" as two studies of dying.

Related Commentaries

Ann Charters, Translating Kafka, p. 851.
John Updike, Kafka and "The Metamorphosis," p. 927.

Suggested Readings

Anderson, Mark. *Reading Kafka.* New York: Schocken, 1990.
Canetti, Elias. *Kafka's Other Trial: Letters to Felice.* New York: Schocken, 1988.
Greenberg, Martin. "Kafka's 'Metamorphosis' and Modern Spirituality." *Tri-Quarterly* 6 (1966): 5–20.

Gross, Ruth V. *Critical Essays on Franz Kafka.* Boston: G. K. Hall, 1990.

Kafka, Franz. *The Diaries of Franz Kafka.* New York: Schocken, 1988.

———. *The Metamorphosis.* Trans. and ed. Stanley Corngold. New York: Bantam, 1972. (Contains notes, documents, and ten critical essays.)

Levi, Primo. "Translating Kafka." *The Mirror Maker.* New York: Schocken, 1989.

Moss, Leonard. "A Key to the Door Image in 'The Metamorphosis.'" *Modern Fiction Studies* 17 (1971): 37–42.

Nabokov, Vladimir. *Lectures on Literature.* New York: Harcourt, 1980. 250–83.

Pascal, Roy. *Kafka's Narrators: A Study of His Stories and Sketches.* New York: Cambridge UP, 1984.

Pawel, Ernst. *The Nightmare of Reason: A Life of Franz Kafka.* New York: Farrar, 1984.

Spann, Meno. *Franz Kafka.* Boston: G. K. Hall, 1976.

Tauber, Herbert. *Franz Kafka: An Interpretation of His Works.* Brooklyn: Haskell, 1969.

Taylor, Alexander. "The Waking: The Theme of Kafka's 'Metamorphosis.'" *Studies in Short Fiction* 2 (1965): 337–42.

Wolkenfeld, Suzanne. "Christian Symbolism in Kafka's 'The Metamorphosis.'" *Studies in Short Fiction* 10 (1973): 205–07.

JAMAICA KINCAID

Girl (p. 477)

Kincaid's one-paragraph story is a dialogue between a mother and a daughter, consisting mostly of the mother's litany of advice about how to act in a ladylike manner. Students might enjoy reading it aloud. The West Indian prose rhythms are subtly beautiful, and the humor of the mother's advice is revealed in the audible reading process for anyone who has missed it by scanning too quickly. The conflict between the girl and her mother is evident in the mother's fears that her daughter will grow up to be a "slut." Everything the mother says is twisted in light of that fear. The daughter wonders, "But what if the baker won't let me feel the bread?" And the mother replies, "You mean to say that after all you are really going to be the kind of woman who the baker won't let near the bread?" The speech rhythm is reminiscent of James Joyce's interior monologues. In fact, we are not amiss to ask whether the mother is actually speaking to her daughter in the story, or whether the daughter has internalized her mother's voice and written it down for us to read to the accompaniment of our own laughter.

Questions for Discussion

1. What are the major subjects in this litany of advice? What kind of life do they describe?
2. The title of the story is "Girl," yet the girl seems to have only two lines of her own, one a protest and the other a question. Why might the author have decided to call the story "Girl" rather than "Mother" or "Woman" or "Advice" or "Memory"?
3. Identify and discuss Kincaid's use of humor in "Girl." What contribution does it make to the story?

4. What is the effect of fairly precise household rules alternating with comments such as "on Sundays try to walk like a lady and not like the slut you are so bent on becoming." String together the lines that admonish the potential slut. What do we think of the mother? What connection is there between the subjects the mother is speaking of and the idea of a slut? Why does it keep popping up from the most innocuous of items? What does this refrain make us think of the daughter? Is the slut refrain a joke or is the author making a suggestion about the construction of self?

5. Some of the advice seems like it could never have been spoken, but only inferred: "this is how you smile to someone you don't like too much; this is how you smile to someone you don't like at all; this is how you smile to someone you like completely." Throughout the whole piece, do you think the mother is speaking to her daughter? What other possibilities could underlie the story's composition?

6. On page 477 the kind of advice changes: "this is how to make a good medicine to throw away a child before it even becomes a child," says the mother. Surely she's not speaking to a young girl here. In the final line, the mother calls her a "woman," the only direct address in the story; earlier the listener has been addressed as a potential slut and been told she's "not a boy." What's the difference between the advice that precedes and follows the reference to aborting a child? Which is more concrete? More abstract? Why does the advice change because of the listener's age? What kinds of knowledge is her mother able to offer?

Topics for Writing

1. Analyze Kincaid's use of humor to indicate conflict in "Girl."
2. **RESPONDING CREATIVELY** Expand the story through the use of descriptive prose. Is the result more or less effective than Kincaid's original?
3. **RESPONDING CREATIVELY** Write a short story in which you use only dialogue.

Related Commentary

Jamaica Kincaid, On "Girl," p. 884.

Suggested Readings

Kincaid, Jamaica. *At the Bottom of the River.* New York: Vintage, 1985.
———. Interview. *New York Times Book Review* 7 Apr. 1985: 6+.

Jhumpa Lahiri

When Mr. Pirzada Came to Dine (p. 480)

Lahiri's opening sentence summarizes the plot of her story: "In the autumn of 1971 a man used to come to our house, bearing confections in his pocket and hopes of ascertaining the life or death of his family." The man is Mr. Pirzada, a Pakistani professor of botany who is living in a university town north of Boston for a year on an academic grant, studying the foliage of New England and writing a book on what he has found there. His innocent research project — and we must assume it is innocent and that he is not an enemy agent or a CIA spy — is literally a world away from the devastation of the war between India and Pakistan that began in his homeland while he is in the United States. From September to the end of December 1971, he is unable to get any news of the welfare of his wife and seven daughters in Dacca, except from the dire accounts he hears every evening on the American television news programs he watches at the home of the narrator's parents.

The narrator tells us that she was only ten years old when Mr. Pirzada became a dinner guest at her home, but she tells the story from the first-person point of view of an adult, writing nearly thirty years later. By describing her memories as an unsophisticated ten year old, Lahiri emphasizes the essential irrationality and inexplicable nature of national conflict and war. The most important event for the ten-year-old girl was the candy Mr. Pirzada brought as a gift for her when he visited her parents, not his anxiety about the growing conflict in Pakistan. Although her parents were Indian immigrants to the United States, she had been born in America and had no knowledge of their homeland's history since her lessons at school were single-mindedly concentrated on early American history, an uncontroversial subject — unlike the chaotic events in Asia being televised into her living room each evening. (In 1971 the United States was still fighting the unpopular war in Vietnam.)

Lahiri's narrator is older and more sophisticated than her earlier ten-year-old self. Her vocabulary and diction show her to be intelligent and well educated, as evidenced by her use of words like "bearing confections" and "hopes of ascertaining the life or death of his family" in the opening paragraph. As narrator, she avoids sentimentality and easy generalizations about the complex political situation that has trapped Mr. Pirzada into the harrowing end of his year in America. We share her distance from Mr. Pirzada's plight, but we also feel empathy for what he must be feeling in her skillful presentation of his behavior during his dinners with his American hosts.

Questions for Discussion

1. Do you think this is an autobiographical story? Does it matter if the events in it actually happened to Lahiri when she was ten years old?
2. Why did Lahiri spend so much time describing the girl's Halloween activities of carving the pumpkin and trick or treating with her friend in the neighborhood?
3. What was the relationship between Mr. Pirzada and the ten year old? What was his relationship with her parents?

4. Why aren't we given more information about what happened to Mr. Pirzada and his family when he returned to Pakistan?

Topic for Writing

1. Write a book report about Lahiri's collection *The Interpreter of Maladies* (1999).

Suggested Reading

Lahiri, Jhumpa. *Interpreter of Maladies: Stories.* Boston: Houghton Mifflin, 1999.

D. H. LAWRENCE

The Rocking-Horse Winner (p. 493)

Lawrence's masterful technical control wins the reader's assent to the fantastic premise on which the story is built; without that assent, the thematic statement the story propounds would lack cogency. Rather than confronting us boldly with his improbable donnée, as Kafka does in "The Metamorphosis," Lawrence edges up to it. The whispering voices in the house that drive Paul to his furious rocking begin as a thought in the mother's mind and then become a figure of speech that crystallizes imperceptibly into a literal fact — or rather, into an auditory hallucination heard by the children that expresses their perception of their mother's unquenchable need for funds. Paul's ability to pick a winner by riding his rocking horse to where he is lucky requires even more circumspect handling. Like the family members, we learn about it after the fact, putting together bits of information to explain a set of peculiar but at first not at all implausible circumstances — Paul's claim, "Well, I got there!", his familiarity with race horses, Bassett's reluctance "to give him away" to Oscar, Paul's giving Oscar a tip on a long shot that comes in a winner, and only then, with Oscar's skepticism always preempting that of the reader, the revelation of how much he has won. It is not until the very end that we, with his astonished mother, actually witness Paul in the act of receiving revelation — just as he slips beyond the world of everyday probability for good and into the uncharted supernatural realm from whence his "luck" seems to emanate.

Although no explanation, supernatural or otherwise, is necessary to account for good fortune at the race track, Lawrence persuades the reader that Paul's success is caused by his exertions and therefore has a moral meaning. In Paul's household the lack of love is perceived as a lack of money and the lack of money is attributed to a lack of luck. Since luck is by definition something that happens to one, to blame one's troubles on luck is to deny responsibility for them and to abandon any effort to overcome them. As the event makes clear, Paul's mother will never be satisfied, no matter how much money falls her way, because no amount of money can fill the emptiness left by the absence of love. The "hard little place" in her heart at the beginning of the story has expanded until, at the end, she feels that her whole heart has "turned actually into a stone." Paul sets out by the force of will to redefine luck as something one can acquire. He places belief before evidence and asserts, "I'm a lucky person. . . . God told me," and then makes good on his promise by riding his rocking horse to where luck comes from. "'It's as if he had it from heaven,'" Bassett says, "in a secret, religious voice."

In his single-minded devotion to winning money for his mother at the racetrack by riding his rocking horse (which W. D. Snodgrass has likened to masturbation as Lawrence understood it), Paul diverts his spiritual and emotional forces to material aims, and Lawrence symbolically represents the effect of this materialization in the process of petrification by which the mother's heart and Paul's blue eyes, which have throughout the story served as an emblem of his obsession, turn to stone. At the end Oscar states the case with epigrammatic precision: Hester's son has been transformed into eighty-odd thousand pounds — a tidy sum, but of course it will not be enough.

WILLIAM E. SHEIDLEY

Questions for Discussion

1. How is Paul's mother portrayed at the outset? Does Lawrence suggest that she is blameworthy? Why or why not?
2. Explain the family's "grinding sense of the shortage of money." Why do the voices get even louder when some money becomes available? What would it take to still the voices?
3. Discuss the implications of Paul's confusing luck with lucre. How accurate is his mother's definition of luck? What would constitute true good luck for him?
4. Explain Paul's claim to be lucky. In what sense is he justified? In what sense is he very unlucky?
5. What function do Oscar and Bassett play in the story, beyond providing Paul with practical access to the racetrack and the lawyer?
6. "Bassett was serious as a church." Is this a humorous line? Does it suggest anything beyond the comic?
7. What is the effect on the reader of the episode in which Oscar takes Paul to the track and Paul's horse Daffodil wins the race?
8. Explain the mother's response to her birthday gift. What is its effect on Paul? Why?
9. Before the Derby, Paul does not "know" for several races. Can this dry spell be explained? What brings it to an end?
10. Analyze Paul's last words in the story. What does he mean by "get there"? Where, in fact, does he go? Is *absolute* certainty possible? How? Why is Paul so proud to proclaim that he is lucky to his mother? Finally, comment on her reaction.
11. Evaluate Oscar's remarks, which end the story. Was Paul a "poor devil"? In what senses?

Topics for Writing

1. Describe the handling of the supernatural in Lawrence's "The Rocking-Horse Winner."

2. Explore the religious theme of "The Rocking-Horse Winner."
3. Consider luck, will, and faith in "The Rocking-Horse Winner."
4. Analyze the realistic elements and the social theme of Lawrence's supernatural tale.
5. **RESPONDING CREATIVELY** Consider luck, lucre, and love in "The Rocking-Horse Winner."
6. **RESPONDING CREATIVELY** Look up a newspaper story about some unexplained phenomenon, ghost, or poltergeist, and work it into a narrative whose meaning is finally not dependent on an interest in the supernatural.

Suggested Readings

Boulton, J. T., ed. *The Letters of D. H. Lawrence*. New York: Cambridge UP, 1989.

Clayton, J. J. "D. H. Lawrence: Psychic Wholeness through Rebirth." *Massachusetts Review* 25 (1984): 200–21.

Harris, Janice. *The Short Fiction of D. H. Lawrence*. New Brunswick, NJ: Rutgers UP, 1984.

Hyde, G. M. *D. H. Lawrence*. New York: St. Martin's, 1990.

Jackson, Dennis, and Felda Jackson. *Critical Essays on D. H. Lawrence*. Boston: G. K. Hall, 1988.

Kalnins, M. "D. H. Lawrence's 'Odour of Chrysanthemums': The Three Endings." *Studies in Short Fiction* 13 (1976): 471–79.

Lawrence, D. H. *Portable D. H. Lawrence*. New York: Penguin, 1977.

Meyers, Jeffry. *D. H. Lawrence: A Biography*. New York: Knopf, 1990.

Olson, Charles. *D. H. Lawrence and the High Temptation of the Mind*. Santa Barbara, CA: Black Sparrow, 1980.

Rice, Thomas Jackson. *D. H. Lawrence: A Guide to Research*. New York: Garland, 1983.

Rose, S. "Physical Trauma in D. H. Lawrence's Short Fiction." *Contemporary Literature* 16 (1975): 73–83.

Sager, Keith. *D. H. Lawrence: Life into Art*. Athens: U of Georgia P, 1985.

San Juan, E., Jr. "Theme versus Imitation: D. H. Lawrence's 'The Rocking-Horse Winner,'" *D. H. Lawrence Review* 3 (1970): 136–40.

Schneider, Daniel J. *The Consciousness of D. H. Lawrence: An Intellectual Biography*. Lawrence: UP of Kansas, 1986.

———. *D. H. Lawrence: The Artist as Psychologist*. Lawrence: UP of Kansas, 1984.

Shaw, M. "Lawrence and Feminism." *Critical Quarterly* 25 (1983): 23–27.

Snodgrass, W. D. "A Rocking Horse: The Symbol, the Pattern, the Way to Live." *D. H. Lawrence: A Collection of Critical Essays*. Ed. Mark Spilka. *Twentieth Century Views*. Englewood Cliffs, NJ: Prentice, 1963. Originally published in Hudson Review 11 (1958).

Squires, Michael, and Keith Cushman. *The Challenge of D. H. Lawrence*. Madison: U of Wisconsin P, 1990.

Widmer, Kingsley. *The Art of Perversity: D. H. Lawrence's Shorter Fictions*. Seattle: U of Washington P, 1962. 92–95, 213.

KATHERINE MANSFIELD

The Fly (p. 506)

The fly character in this story is called by several pet names ("the little beg-gar," "a plucky little devil," "you artful little b[astard]," "the draggled fly"). Its determined efforts to clean itself of the ink on its "small sodden body" are com-pared to a stone going over and under a scythe and a "minute cat" cleaning its face. This is a totally admirable fly, valiant in its energetic attempts to rid itself of the ink, industrious in its labors, heroic in its persistence to survive despite repeated ink attacks by "the boss."

Despite the realistic descriptions, the fly is also a symbol. Young, heroic English soldiers "died like flies" on Flanders Field and other World War I battle-grounds, and the boss's only son was among them. Yet Mansfield isn't writing a sentimental story about the horrors of war. Her focus is the horrors of humankind in times of peace and prosperity. The boss should be merciful, having suffered the loss of his beloved son. Instead, he is as void of wisdom and pity as a small boy torturing flies.

All the characters in "The Fly" are old men. Mr. Woodifield is five years younger than the boss, yet he is made weak by a stroke and his retirement, kept like a baby at home by his wife and daughters. "Old Macey," the office assistant, is gray-haired and subservient, waiting expectantly on the boss "like a dog that expects to be taken for a run." The only "man" in the group is the boss, and he is described as fat and healthy, a lover of whiskey and cigars, electric heaters and massive desks "with legs like twisted treacle" (a molasseslike substance made into candy and baked sweet goods). He is beginning not to see the photograph of his son in uniform over the table near Mr. Woodifield.

Mansfield's sympathy for the victims of overbearing bullies is seen in this story. Her technique, like Chekhov's, is transparent, lulling you into a sense of repose and then, before you know it, submerging you in a scene gone wrong. Her description of the sadistic torture of the fly is a brilliant exposure of the torturer's emotional duplicity; he seems to sympathize with the "plucky little devil," yet compulsively compounds its struggle to the point of the insect's exhaustion and death.

There is no comforting moral at the end of this story. If anything, the boss is more of a bully than before. Mansfield seems to be saying that suffering does not ennoble most people; even if the boss was not consciously thinking of the flies buzzing around the bodies of slain soldiers on Flanders Field, he is out for revenge in whatever fashion he can take it.

Questions for Discussion

1. Why does Mansfield give Mr. Woodifield daughters ("the girls") in this story? Does Mr. Woodifield feel toward his daughters the way the boss felt toward his only son?
2. Why does Mansfield take such pains to describe the comfort of the boss's office?

3.   What is the significance of the pot of jam the daughters took home as a souvenir of their trip to Belgium? How does it prepare the reader for the boss's treatment of the fly?

4.   Explain the boss's image of his son in his grave in Belgium. Is it more clear than his memory of his son's perfection during the year he worked in the office?

5.   The boss feels there is something wrong with him when he decides to get up to look at his son's photogrpah. What do you think is "wrong" with him? How do his subsequent actions with the fly follow naturally from his state of mind?

Topic for Writing

1.   Rewrite the story so that the fly survives the third blot of ink the boss drips on him.

Related Commentary

Willa Cather, The Stories of Katherine Mansfield, p. 847.

Suggested Readings

Boddy, Gill. *Katherine Mansfield: The Woman and the Writer.* New York: Penguin, 1988.

Fullbrook, Kate. *Katherine Mansfield.* Muskogee: Indiana UP, 1986.

Hanson, Clare, ed. *The Critical Writings of Katherine Mansfield.* New York: St. Martin's, 1987.

Kobler, Jasper F. *Katherine Mansfield: A Study of the Short Fiction.* Boston: G. K. Hall, 1990.

Mansfield, Katherine. *Journal of Katherine Mansfield.* New York: Ecco, 1983.

O'Sullivan, Vincent, and Margaret Scott. *The Collected Letters of Katherine Mansfield.* New York: Oxford UP, 1987.

Rohrberger, Mary H. *The Art of Katherine Mansfield.* Ann Arbor, MI: University Microfilms, 1977.

BOBBIE ANN MASON

Shiloh (p. 511)

The trip to Shiloh is supposed to be a second honeymoon for Leroy and Norma Jean Moffitt, a chance for them to start their marriage all over again, as Leroy says, "right back at the beginning." The trouble is, as Norma Jean is quick to point out to her husband, they had already started all over again after his tractor-trailer accident brought him home for good, and "this is how it turned out."

It's a topsy-turvy world in Mason's story. Husbands are hurt so they take up needlepoint; housewives are self-reliant so they study composition at community college when they aren't working at the drugstore. Thirty-four-year-old "girls" like Norma Jean irrationally turn on their mothers after years of obedience just because their mothers catch them smoking cigarettes. And yet it's a familiar world to readers of fiction by women authors about women's domestic rebellion these past fifteen years: Erica Jong's *Fear of Flying,* Sue Kauffman's *Diary of a Mad Housewife,* and Lisa Alther's *Kinflicks,* for example. Norma Jean might scoff at her husband's suggestion that she has been influenced by the feminist movement — he asks her, "Is this one of those women's lib things?" — but he's no fool. She probably wouldn't have told him she was going to leave him if Betty Friedan hadn't published *The Feminine Mystique* and helped bring a feminist consciousness back to America about the time Norma Jean married her high school sweetheart, Leroy Moffitt.

The old patriarchal consciousness still permeates the story, of course, since this consciousness has a tight hold on the mate and the older fictional characters. Norma Jean is introduced in the first sentence as "Leroy Moffitt's wife, Norma Jean." The story is told in the present tense, making the reader aware of the slow passage of time for the characters caught in a static way of life, as mother Mabel says, "just waiting for time to pass." But Norma Jean feels the need for change. The opening of "Shiloh" is one of the most exhilarating first sentences in contemporary American short fiction. "Leroy Moffitt's wife, Norma Jean, is working on her pectorals." Used to be only boys lifted weights to build up their muscles. Now opportunity beckons even for a thirty-four-year-old married woman who bakes cream-of-mushroom casseroles. She doesn't want to be known as somebody's wife, a hackneyed first name between two commas evoking the more famous "real" name of a departed sex goddess from an era before Betty Friedan.

We don't know much about what she's thinking, this fictional Norma Jean, because Mason has structured the story so that her husband's consciousness and feelings are in the forefront. Through his confusion about what's happening with his wife, the reader senses that probably at this point Norma Jean doesn't know exactly what she wants herself, beyond wanting to break free. On their trip to Shiloh she walks rapidly away from Leroy to stand alone on a bluff by the river. He sees her waving her arms, and he can't tell if she's beckoning him or doing another exercise for her pectorals. One thing they both know is that she won't be needing the dust ruffle his mother-in-law made for their marital bed. If this Wonder Woman has her way, she won't be pushing her jogging shoes under her husband's couch or hiding the dust under his bed one day longer than she has to.

Questions for Discussion

1. After reading the story, look back at the first five paragraphs. What do they say about Norma Jean and Leroy's relationship? Does the rest of the story bear out the opening moment?

2. On the first page we discover that, through building an array of kits, "Leroy has grown to appreciate how things are put together." How does his fascination with building comment on Leroy's marriage? What is the impulse behind building the log cabin? How would you compare Leroy's hobby with Norma Jean's interests?

3. In this passage Mason introduces the background of the Moffitts' marriage: "Perhaps he reminds her too much of the early days of their marriage, before he went on the road. They had a child who died as an infant, years

ago. They never speak about their memories of Randy, which have almost faded, but now that Leroy is home all the time, they sometimes feel awkward around each other, and Leroy wonders if one of them should mention the child. He has the feeling that they are waking up out of a dream together — that they must create a new marriage, start afresh. They are lucky they are still married. Leroy has read that for most people losing a child destroys the marriage." The figure of a dead child might be expected to haunt the couple in this story. Does the child control their present actions? We discover later that Randy would be sixteen now, so Leroy has been away from home, basically, for sixteen years. What difference does his sudden presence make to the marriage?

4. "When the first movie ended, the baby was dead. . . . A dead baby feels like a sack of flour." Usually, a subject like the death of infants evokes a particular kind of rhetoric, laden with sentimentality and tragedy. How would you describe these two sentences? Why doesn't the narrator use some euphemisms for death? What effect do these perceptions create? How do these sentences influence your assessment of Leroy's character?

5. Although the title emphasizes the importance of "Shiloh," we don't hear anything about it until page 514, when Mabel Beasley says, "I still think before you get tied down y'all ought to take a little run to Shiloh." What does Shiloh represent for Mabel? What does history itself mean to Leroy and Norma Jean? Can they articulate their shared history? Consider the passage about the baby on page 513.

6. When Norma Jean tells Leroy she's leaving him, he asks her, "Is this one of those women's lib things?" Is this a story about feminism? Consider the point of view; discuss the ideology apparent in the opening line of the story. What do we know about Norma Jean's feelings? Consider how a descriptive sentence such as "She is doing goose steps" gives us some access into her emotional life. How would you describe Mabel Beasley within a feminist framework?

7. How does Leroy's opinion that "nobody knows anything. . . . The answers are always changing" comment on the themes of this story?

8. Leroy concludes that "the real inner workings of a marriage, like most of history, have escaped him." This seems like a poignant realization in the face of Norma Jean's departure. Does Leroy assign blame for the dissolution of his marriage? Does this knowledge imply that he will be able to forge a new, vital marriage with Norma Jean? Is the final paragraph hopeful? What do you make of Leroy's inability to distinguish between Norma Jean's exercise and her signals?

Topics for Writing

1. In an interview Mason gave to Lila Havens, she said she's more interested in the male characters in her stories than in the females. How has she selected the details of "Shiloh" to portray Norma Jean's husband, Leroy Moffitt, with compassion?

2. Discuss Mason's use of details to enrich the story's reality.

Related Commentary

Bobbie Ann Mason, On Tim O'Brien's "The Things They Carried," p. 885.

Suggested Readings

Reed, J. D. "Postfeminism: Playing for Keeps." *Time* 10 Jan. 1983: 61.
Ryan, Maureen. "Stopping Places: Bobbie Ann Mason's Short Stories." *Women Writers of the Contemporary South.* Ed. Peggy Whitman Prenshaw. Jackson: UP of Mississippi, 1984. 283–94.
Smith, W. "Publisher's Weekly Interviews." *Publisher's Weekly* 30 Aug. 1985: 424–25.

GUY DE MAUPASSANT

The Necklace (p. 523)

"The Necklace" has long been one of the most popular of Maupassant's stories, and one of the most interesting aspects of the story is this popularity, since artistically it is far from his best. The story is little more than an anecdote. Mme. Loisel, a woman from the lower middle class, is deeply dissatisfied with her station in life. As she sits down to dinner with her husband — a "little clerk at the Ministry of Public Instructions" — she thinks of "dainty dinners, of shining silverware, of tapestry which peopled the walls with ancient personages and with strange birds in the middle of a fairy forest."

Her husband, sensing her unhappiness, gets a ticket for a grand ball, and, when she is miserable at not having a fine dress, he gives her money he has been saving for a gun and a shooting holiday with his friends. When she is still unhappy at not having jewels, he suggests she borrow some from a wealthy friend, Mme. Forestier. Mme. Loisel borrows what she thinks is a diamond necklace, is a great success at the ball, but loses the necklace on the way home.

Too ashamed to tell the friend what has happened, the couple borrow money to buy a diamond necklace like the one that was lost. They return the necklace and slowly repay the loan. After ten years, during which the wife has become "the woman of impoverished households — strong and hard and rough," she accidentally meets Mme. Forestier and learns that she had lent her only a paste copy of a diamond necklace. Mme. Loisel and her husband have destroyed their lives for nothing.

Unlike in his finest stories, Maupassant here stays on the surface of the characters. Mme. Forestier and Mme. Loisel's husband are only faintly sketched; they seem to exist merely to act out roles. The anecdote itself is so implausible that a single question — why didn't Mme. Forestier notice that a different necklace had been returned to her? why did M. Loisel allow his life to be destroyed without a protest? — would bring it to earth. But most readers are willing to suspend their disbelief.

When we place the story in the time it was written, its themes stand out even more sharply. On its most obvious level this is one of the tales of moral instruction that were so widespread in nineteenth-century popular literature. Mme. Loisel's dreams of clothes and jewels represent the sin of vanity, and someone who has such dreams must be punished. The punishment inflicted on the woman and her husband is memorably out of proportion to their sin, the better to serve as a warning to those reading the story for moral instruction.

A second theme, which may be less obvious to the contemporary reader, is that Mme. Loisel has dreamed of moving to a higher social level. French society was rigidly structured, and Mme. Loisel's ambitions represented a threat, however vague, to the story's privileged audience. They would, of course, want to see her punished for this ambition.

These facts help to explain why the story was so widely read when it was written — but for today's readers other factors seem to be at work. For example, to one young student the necklace became the symbol for everything the world of adults represents. Perhaps it is the story's weaknesses — its implausible simplicities, the lack of definition of its minor characters, the trite obviousness of Mme. Loisel's yearning, and the pious cruelty of her punishment — that make it possible for other generations to give "The Necklace" their own interpretation.

Questions for Discussion

1. Do we use anecdotes like "The Necklace" to point out moral lessons today? What other examples of this kind of moral instruction can you think of in popular literature?
2. How did an evening at a ball offer Mme. Loisel a chance to present herself in a new guise?
3. What do we learn from the story about the structure of French society at the time "The Necklace" was written?
4. What symbols for wealth and station could be used in a story like this written for today?

Topics for Writing

1. Analyze the symbolic implications of the necklace.
2. Consider the contrast between the lives of Mme. Loisel and her friend Mme. Forestier.

Related Commentaries

Kate Chopin, How I Stumbled upon Maupassant, p. 858.
Guy de Maupassant, The Writer's Goal, p. 887.

Suggested Readings

Fusco, Richard A. "Maupassant and the Turn of the Century American Short Story." *Dissertation Abstracts International* 51.5 (Nov. 1990): 1612A.

James, Henry. *Tales of Art and Life.* Schenectady, NY: Union College P, 1984.

Lohafer, Susan, ed. *Short Story Theory at a Crossroads.* Baton Rouge: Louisiana State UP, 1989. 276–98.

Los Angeles Public Library Staff. *Index to the Stories of Guy de Maupassant.* Boston: G. K. Hall, 1970.

McCrory, Donald. "Maupassant: Problems of Interpretation." *Modern Languages: Journal of the Modern Language Association* 70.1 (Mar. 1989): 39–43.

Poteau-Tralie, Mary L. "Voices of Authority: The Criminal Obsession in Guy de Maupassant's Short Works." *Dissertation Abstracts International* 52.4 (Oct. 1991): 1353A.

Traill, Nancy Helen. "The Fantastic for the Realist: The Paranormal Fictions of Dickens, Turgenev, and Maupassant." *Dissertation Abstracts International* 50.9 (Mar. 1990): 2891A.

Troyat, Henri. *Maupassant.* Paris: Flammarion, 1989.

HERMAN MELVILLE

Bartleby, the Scrivener (p. 531)

Many students have trouble reading this story because they cannot accept what they consider the weirdness of Bartleby's character. On first reading, the story seems to yield this interpretation. Shortly after it appeared in the November and December issues of *Putnam's Monthly Magazine* in 1853, for example, Richard Henry Dana Sr. wrote to Melville's friend Evert Duyckinck saying that he admired the skill involved in creating the character of Bartleby because "the secret power of such an inefficient and harmless creature over his employer, who all the while has a misgiving of it, shows no common insight." Dana's interpretation will probably also be the way 99 percent of present-day college students will respond to the story, sharing his lack of sympathy for Bartleby.

The question is: Did Melville intend the readers of his story to feel this way? Why did he conclude his tale with the lines "Ah, Bartleby! Ah, humanity!"?

Most sympathetic literary critics see this story as Melville's attempt to dramatize the complex question of an individual's obligation to society. Like the dead letters that Bartleby burned in his previous job after they were no longer needed, his life ends when he is no longer useful to his employer. What standards should we use to judge someone's worth? How should we view those who no longer accept the world they are offered?

Questions for Discussion

1. How does the narrator's viewpoint affect your feelings toward Bartleby? What details particularly influence you one way or the other?
2. Do your feelings toward Bartleby change when the narrator reveals Bartleby's previous job in the Dead Letter Office?
3. How does Melville's humorous description of the two other clerks in the law office relieve his heavy presentation of the Wall Street setting? How do these minor characters set off each other, the lawyer, and Bartleby?

4. Do you ever feel like saying "I would prefer not to" in reply to figures of authority? What do you do when you feel a bit of Bartleby in you?

Topics for Writing

1. Explicate the paragraph beginning "For the first time in my life a feeling of overpowering stinging melancholy seized me." A close reading of this passage may bring you closer to realizing the complexity of Melville's portrayal of the lawyer's relationship to Bartleby.
2. Analyze the conclusion of the story. How can Bartleby's life be compared to a dead letter?
3. This story has an unusually prolonged and discursive exposition before the title character is introduced. Also, Melville doesn't motivate his behavior until the end of the story, after he is dead and the lawyer finds out about his previous job. Breaking the customary rules of starting a short story with a brief exposition and motivating the characters as they are introduced, Melville might be accused of writing a poorly structured tale. Argue for or against this accusation, remembering that the short story genre was in its infancy when Melville wrote "Bartleby, the Scrivener."

Related Commentary

Herman Melville, Blackness in Hawthorne's "Young Goodman Brown," p. 889.

Suggested Readings

Boswell, Jeanetta. *Herman Melville and the Critics: A Checklist of Criticism.* Metuchen, NJ: Scarecrow, 1981.

Budd, Louis J., and Edwin H. Cady, eds. *On Melville.* Durham, NC: Duke UP, 1988.

Dillingham, W. B. *Melville's Short Fiction, 1853–1856.* Athens: U of Georgia P, 1977.

Fogle, R. H. *Melville's Shorter Tales.* Norman: U of Oklahoma P, 1960.

Freeman, John. *Herman Melville.* Brooklyn, NY: Haskell, 1974.

Higgins, Brian. *Herman Melville: A Reference Guide, 1931–1960.* Boston: G. K. Hall, 1987.

Inge, M. Thomas, ed. *Bartleby the Inscrutable: A Collection of Commentary on Herman Melville's Tale "Bartleby, the Scrivener."* Hamden, CT: Shoe String, 1979.

McCall, Dan. *The Silence of Bartleby.* Ithaca, NY: Cornell UP, 1989.

Melville, Herman. *Correspondence.* Evanston, IL: Northwestern UP, 1991.

———. *Pierre, The Piazza Tales and Uncollected Prose.* New York: Library of America, 1984.

Vincent, H. P., ed. *"Bartleby, the Scrivener": Melville Annual for 1965.* Kent, OH: Kent State UP, 1967. Includes Henry Murray's "Bartleby and I," 3–24.

Whitehead, Fred A. "Melville's 'Bartleby, the Scrivener': A Case Study." *New York State Journal of Medicine* 90 (Jan. 1990): 17–22.

Nicholasa Mohr

Tell the Truth (p. 559)

Mohr's story about Vickie, a Puerto Rican American, thirteen-year-old girl whose mother sells "la bolita," lottery tickets for an organization in New York City that also deals in street drugs, is a realistic account of the perils and pressures of life for the immigrants in the barrio. The police have found a suspicious packet of white powder in Vickie's mother's apartment in the Bronx, and she has been charged with a serious crime. The mother has never sold drugs and she is innocent of the crime, chosen by the "organization" to be the "fall guy" in a drug bust so that the real organizers can continue their operation. Their lawyer, Mr. Crane, has been told to get a confession out of Vickie by pressuring her to admit that she has seen the drugs. The last time Vickie has seen her mother, she was in handcuffs, surrounded by detectives, but she remembers her mother's last words before she was taken away — "Not a word. This is a frame-up! . . . Don't say anything."

Mr. Crane tries every trick in his possession to break Vickie's silence, but he is unsuccessful in his efforts to intimidate her. She remembers her mother's words and refuses to cooperate, even as the lawyer — claiming to be her friend — grows more furious with her. At the end of the story, when he allows Vickie to leave his office, the girl learns that her mother has already been released from prison on insufficient evidence. Vickie's testimony would have given this necessary evidence to the lawyer, and her mother would have faced a prison sentence. Mother and daughter walk toward the subway with their arms around each other, heading for home.

Questions for Discussion

1. Are Vickie and Mr. Crane round, dynamic characters? How typical are their social positions compared to other New Yorkers?
2. Why does Vickie have trouble swallowing the saliva in her mouth. Why does Mohr refer to her difficulty in swallowing throughout the story?
3. Why does Mr. Crane let Vickie leave his office after he receives his phone call? What do we learn from his replies to the person who has called him?
4. How does Mr. Crane feel about Vickie at the end of their conversation?
5. How does the ending of the story suggest the importance of family to American immigrants?

Bharati Mukherjee

The Management of Grief (p. 565)

Bharati Mukherjee cites Moghul miniature painting, with "its insistence that everything happens simultaneously, bound only by shape and color," as a model for her fiction. This "sense of the interpenetration of all things" informs

"The Management of Grief," which initially situates the reader among a rather bewildering array of characters and actions. Gradually we become aware that Shaila Bhave, who narrates the story, has recently lost her husband and two sons in a plane crash. The disoriented quality of her narrative ("A woman I don't know is boiling tea the Indian way in my kitchen") mirrors the state of her mind as she struggles to make sense of her loss, focusing on memories and odd details. The abruptness of our entry into the story suggests the abruptness of tragedy itself. Kusum, the similarly bereaved neighbor, voices the question that might occur to anyone afflicted with such loss: "Why does God give so much if all along He intends to take it away?"

Mukherjee asks us to consider the manner in which various characters cope with grief. The community looks toward Mrs. Bhave as "a pillar" because she has "taken it more calmly," but she is troubled by her inability to grieve outwardly, referring to herself as "a freak." Her equanimity, we learn, is due as much to Valium as to inner strength. With the help of the drug she is able to "manage" her grief in a way that may be ultimately less healthy than that of the relatives who express their grief more openly. While in Ireland waiting to identify bodies, she admits, "I haven't eaten in four days, haven't brushed my teeth." By the end of the story Shaila experiences a visitation on the streets of Toronto by her departed husband and sons, who urge her, "Go, be brave." While the experience may be interpreted in a positive light, a transition in her grieving process, it also may be seen as an aural hallucination, the result of her mixing tranquilizers in her distraught emotional state. Her dropping her package and directionless walking suggest purposelessness and lack of direction.

While personal tragedy commands center stage in this story, cultural vectors play out across the background. The crash may have been caused by a Sikh bomb. Judith Templeton, the culturally naive social worker, persuades Shaila to try to convince a grieving Sikh couple to take advantage of available aid. Templeton, while meaning well, has little sensitivity to the cultural and political complications of the situation, and she overlooks the difficulty of the position for which she recruits Shaila — that of helping a potential enemy. The plane crash pulls the relatives, now well assimilated into Canada, back to India and the old ways, which cling with more tenacity than they may have realized.

Questions for Discussion

1. At one point, Shaila observes, "Like my husband's spirit, I flutter between worlds." What does she mean?
2. Review the India section of the story. In what ways have the characters changed in moving from India to Canada?
3. Do you detect a pattern of inhibited emotional response in Shaila? If so, to what extent may this pattern be culturally induced?

Topic for Writing

1. Discuss the grieving processes and coping mechanisms of the various characters. Is Shaila as healthy and calm as she outwardly appears to be? What does Dr. Ranganathan mean when he says, "We've been melted down and

recast as a new tribe"? Do the relatives experience successive stages of grief?

Suggested Readings

Boxill, Anthony. "Women and Migration in Some Short Stories of Bharati Mukherjee and Neil Bissoondath." *Literary Half Yearly* 32.2 (July 1991): 43–50.

Mukherjee, Bharati. *The Middleman and Other Stories.* New York: Grove, 1988.

Nelson, Emmanuel S. *Bharati Mukherjee: Critical Perspectives.* New York: Garland, 1993.

———. "Kamala Markandaya, Bharati Mukherjee and the Indian Immigrant Experience." *Toronto South Asian Review* 9.2 (Winter 1991): 1–9.

ALICE MUNRO

Miles City, Montana (p. 578)

Munro begins her story with a long flashback to a time twenty years earlier, describing a drowning incident when she was six years old. Her opening sentence, "My father came across the field carrying the body of the boy who had been drowned," is a highly dramatic introduction to her tale. The eight-year-old drowned boy Steve Gauley had been the only child of a shiftless neighbor whose wife had run away; the first-person narrator tell us that she never liked Steve, who would never leave her alone. If this lack of sentimentality weren't enough, Munro's narrator tells us that she was wearing "disgustingly itchy" white ribbed stockings at the boy's funeral, which was held in her parents' home, and that when she watched her parents singing a hymn, she "felt a furious and sickening disgust" at them, though they weren't the guilty ones whose inattention had caused the death of the little boy. Her anger isn't explained until the end of the story, when she also finally tells us how Steve's father acted at his son's funeral.

So even before Munro begins the central story of what happened in Miles City, Montana, she has complicated our response to her narrative by setting up the double frame of the earlier death and the narrator's confusing words about it. Munro is considered one of the most accomplished short story writers of our time, and "Miles City, Montana" is a fine example of her work at its best. Her fondness for deepening the emotional resonance of her plots occurs here in an almost off-handed remark, midway in the story, about her husband Andrew after they have driven off in the summer of 1961 on their trip from Vancouver to Ontario with their two small daughters — Cynthia, six, and Meg, three and a half. After the narrator has described what we would consider the bumps in her marriage — her confused, unresolved emotional response to her husband — she casually tells us that they are now divorced: "I haven't seen Andrew for years, don't know if he is still thin, has gone completely grey, insists on lettuce, tells the truth, or is hearty and disappointed."

It's clear that the narrator is a survivor, and she has survived what she considered the constraints of her marriage which would have kept her from becoming a writer. At the start of the car trip with her family she is open about her independent spirit, telling us that "I loved taking off. . . . [At home] I wanted to hide so that I could get busy at my real work, which was a sort of wooing of distant parts of myself." She wants to be "a watcher" of the lives around her, "not a keeper."

Yet, ironically, she is the "keeper" of lives. After she and Andrew have left their two children at the municipal swimming pool under the care of the teenage lifeguard and her boyfriend, it is the narrator who asks herself *"Where are the children?"* and alerts Andrew that Meg has fallen into deep water in time to rescue the little girl. She may feel as distant from her children as Steve Gauley's father had felt toward his son, but she nevertheless feels a deep connection and a responsibility to them. At the end of the story, instead of feeling smug and self-congratulatory about herself, the narrator tells us that she shares the guilt for inflicting the necessary condition of mortality into her children's lives along with all caring parents, including her own parents, whom she blamed even as a child for Steve Gauley's accidental drowning.

Questions for Discussion

1. In what ways does the title of the story serve to guide us in reading Munro's narrative?
2. Is the opening paragraph of "Miles City, Montana" melodramatic, or is it emotionally consistent with the rest of the story?
3. With what details does Munro create round characters of the narrator, her husband, and their children during their car trip?
4. Why do the narrator and her husband feel obligated to make the long trip from Vancouver to Ontario? What really awaits them there?
5. Why does the narrator return to the drowning of Steve Gauley near the end of her story? Why doesn't she make it the conclusion of her story?
6. What is the theme of "Miles City, Montana"? How is the character of Munro's narrator shaped by this theme?

Topics for Writing

1. Analyze the sense of time in "Miles City, Montana." Munro has created a sense of different time frames in her description of the two drowning incidents twenty years apart, as well as a third sense of the present time in her narrator's ruminations about the role of parents in their children's lives. What has Munro gained by this strategy? What has she lost?
2. Write a book report on Munro's collection *The Progress of Love* (1986), in which this story appeared.

Related Commentary

Alice Munro, How I Write Short Stories, p. 893.

Suggested Readings

Bardolph, Jacqueline, ed. *Short Fiction in the New Literature in English: Proceedings of the Nice Conference of the European Association for the Common Wealth Literature and Language Studies.* Nice: Faculté des Lettres et Sciences Humaines de Nice, 1989. 141–51.

Blodgett, E. D. *Alice Munro.* Boston: Twayne, 1988.

Carrington, Ildiko de Papp. *Controlling the Uncontrollable: The Fiction of Alice Munro.* DeKalb: Northern Illinois UP, 1989.

Hanson, Clare, ed. *Rereading the Short Story.* New York: St. Martin's, 1989. 65–85.

Jansen, Reamy. "Being Lonely: Dimensions of the Short Story." *Crosscurrents* 39.4 (Winter 1989–90): 391–401, 419.

MacKendrick, Louis K., ed. *Probable Fictions: Alice Munro's Narrative Acts.* Downsview, ONT: ECW, 1983.

Martin, W. R. *Alice Munro: Paradox and Parallel.* Edmonton: U of Alberta P, 1987.

Miller, Judith. *The Art of Alice Munro: Saying the Unsayable: Papers from the Waterloo Conference.* Madison: U of Wisconsin P, 1984.

Munro, Alice. *Selected Stories.* New York: Knopf, 1996.

Nischik, Reingard M., ed. *Modes of Narrative: Approaches to American, Canadian, and British Fiction.* Wurzburg: Konigshausen, 1990. 110–18, 141–52.

Rasporich, Beverly J. *Dance of the Sexes: Art and Gender in the Fiction of Alice Munro.* Edmonton: U of Alberta P, 1990.

Stich, K. P., ed. *Reflections: Autobiography and Canadian Literature.* Ottawa: U of Ottawa P, 1988. 176.

JOYCE CAROL OATES

Where Are You Going, Where Have You Been? (p. 595)

Pointing to Oates's remark that she usually writes "about real people in a real society" should help to keep discussion away from premature allegorization or mythologizing, which — for all its eventual value and interest — smothers the story's impact by diverting attention from its realism. Her further observation that she understands Connie to be "struggling heroically to define personal identity in the face of incredible opposition, even in the face of death itself," may suggest how to go about answering the main question the story poses when considered in naturalistic terms: Why does Connie go out to Arnold Friend?

Connie's life as Oates depicts it takes place in two realms. Within her home and family Connie feels condemned and rejected, and she returns the disapproval. Outside these familiar precincts lies a world defined by movies, the drive-in restaurant, and the ever-present popular music. It is *not* the music of Bob Dylan, as Tom Quirk assures us, but the comparatively mindless, sentimental, and romantic music against which in the early 1960s Dylan stood out in such bold contrast. Connie's idea of the world into which, at the age of fifteen, she is beginning to make her first tentative forays is shaped by these songs and occupied by *boys:* boys who can be snubbed with impunity, boys who merge into one undifferentiated and safe blur in her mind, boys who offer hamburgers and "the caresses of love." And that love is "not the way someone like June would suppose but sweet, gentle, the way it was in movies and promised in songs." To these boys Connie presents herself as undifferentiated *girl,* and she is concerned that she look attractive to them.

The world, however, is occupied not only by frank and tentative boys but also by determined and deceitful men, by evil as well as by innocence, by hypocrisy, perversion, and violence — an exponent of all of which Connie attracts in Arnold Friend. Although in the course of their interview Connie sees through his disguise, the impoverishment of her world provides her no way to resist his advances. Her home offers no refuge, her father does not come when she needs him (he has always been essentially absent anyway), and she is unable to manipulate the telephone because of her panic. Meanwhile, Arnold, who presents himself in the guise of a movie hero, a teenage "boy," and her lover, offers to take charge of her. He places his mark upon her and gives her a role to play in a world of his devising. Because she is cut off from her past and has no idea of a future, she is at his mercy in determining what to do in the present. Like her cultural cousin, Vladimir Nabokov's Lolita, sobbing in Humbert's arms, she simply has nowhere else to go. Not only does Arnold show Connie that she is desired, he also provides her a way to be "good": By going with him she will save her undeserving family from getting hurt. Connie does not so much decide to go out to Arnold as she watches an alien being that Arnold has called into existence in her body respond to his desires. The final ironic horror, of course, is that she will be raped and murdered and buried in the desert not as brown-eyed Connie but as the imaginary "sweet little blue-eyed girl" of Arnold's sick imagination.

Oates acknowledges that her inspiration for the story came in part from reading about an actual case, and Tom Quirk has demonstrated at length the degree to which the circumstances of "Where Are You Going, Where Have You Been?" seem to be derived from an article in *Life* (4 Mar. 1955) by Don Moser titled (in a reference to some lyrics from a popular song) "The Pied Piper of Tucson." Even some of the most apparently allegorical details, such as Arnold's trouble with his boots, which has been attributed to his having cloven hooves or wolf paws, reflect the facts about Charles Schmid, a wiry gymnast of twenty-three who stuffed things in his boots, wore makeup, and drove around Tucson in a gold car playing the hero to a group of high-school kids until he was arrested for raping and murdering three young girls. Quirk's argument that Oates followed the magazine article's theme in relating this horror in the "golden west" to the emptiness of "the American dream" points out an important dimension of the story, and his emphasis keeps the real horror of the incident in focus.

Gretchen Schulz and R. J. R. Rockwood are aware of the Life article, but they focus instead on another acknowledged source of Oates's inspiration, the folktale. Their discussion of the story's allusions to and affinities with "The Pied Piper of Hamelin," "Cinderella," "Little Red Riding Hood," and other tales suggests why "Where Are You Going, Where Have You Been?" is such a disturbing work. Their article offers detailed interpretations of the psychological crises Connie passes through, based on psychoanalytic interpretations of the meaning and developmental function of the analogous tales. (They use Bruno Bettelheim as their chief authority.) But whereas folktales most often smooth the passage of their readers through Oedipal conflicts and reintegration of the childhood identity into the adult by working through to a happy ending, "Where Are You Going, Where Have You Been?" taps these powerful psychic forces in the reader only to pour them out on the sand.

WILLIAM E. SHEIDLEY

Questions for Discussion

1. Define Connie's relationships with her mother, sister, and father. What is missing from this family? Why does Connie wish "her mother was dead and she herself was dead and it was all over"?

2. What are Connie's "two sides"? In your opinion, is Connie's case unusual for a girl her age in our society? In what ways is she atypical? What about June?

3. The girls enter the drive-in with "faces pleased and expectant as if they were entering a sacred building," and the popular music in the background seems "like music at a church service." Explore the drive-in religion further. What are its creeds, its mysteries? Is it a true religion? a guide to the good life? Does Connie believe in anything else?

4. Discuss the similarities between Eddie, who rotates on a counter stool and offers "something to eat," and the emblem of the drive-in on its bottle-top roof. What else does Eddie offer? Compare Eddie with Arnold Friend as we first see him at the drive-in.

5. What does Oates accomplish by returning briefly to Connie's relationship with her family before narrating what happens "one Sunday"?

6. Discuss Connie's daydreams, in which "all the boys fell back and dissolved into a single face that was not even a face, but an idea, a feeling, mixed up with the urgent insistent pounding of the music," and in which she associates sunbathing with the "sweet, gentle" lovemaking "in movies and promised in song." What is the source of the sexual desire reflected in these dreams? What is its object?

7. Asbestos was formerly used as a noninflammable insulating material. Trace the images of heat and fire associated with it in the story.

8. Compare Connie's gentle breathing as she listens to the "XYZ Sunday Jamboree" with her breath "jerking back and forth in her lungs" when she tries to use the telephone at the climax of the story.

9. Why does Connie whisper "Christ. Christ" when she hears a car coming up the driveway? Does the effort to see Arnold Friend as a Christ figure find further substantiation in the text? Does it yield any meaningful insights?

10. Where does Connie stand during the first part of her conversation with Arnold? Is Oates's blocking of the scene realistic? symbolic?

11. Describe Arnold's car and clothing. What purpose is served by his transparent disguise? Why does it take Connie so long to penetrate the disguise?

12. Does Arnold have supernatural knowledge about Connie, her family, and her friends? Can his apparent clairvoyance about the barbecue be explained in naturalistic terms?

13. Account for Connie's idea that Arnold "had driven up the driveway all right but had come from nowhere before that and belonged nowhere and that everything about him and even the music that was so familiar to her was only half real." Explain the importance of that idea for understanding what happens to Connie.

14. Why does Connie's kitchen seem "like a place she had never seen before"? How has Arnold succeeded in making Connie feel cut off from her past and unprotected in her home? What is the implication of "the echo of a song from last year" in this context?

15. What is the role of Ellie in Arnold's assault on Connie?

16. Arnold implies that Connie can protect her family from harm by coming with him. How important a factor is this in his winning her over to his will?

17. Examine the passage in which Connie tries to telephone her mother and then collapses in panic and hysteria. Notice its associations with sex and birth. What is taking place in Connie at this moment?
18. Arnold asks rhetorically, "What else is there for a girl like you but to be sweet and pretty and give in?" In what sense is this true?
19. Explain Connie's feeling that she is watching herself go out the door. What has caused this split in her consciousness?

Topics for Writing

1. Discuss Arnold Friend's obvious masquerade, and why it succeeds.
2. Comment on popular music and religion in "Where Are You Going, Where Have You Been?"
3. Read the story once while bearing in mind that it is "based on fact" — something very much like this is known to have actually happened. After finishing the story, write a personal essay giving your reaction. What does this account imply about human nature? About the society reflected in the story?
4. Reread the story with an eye to its allusions to folktales and fairy tales with which you are familiar. Arnold's "coach" has a pumpkin on it; Connie is nearly asleep when he awakens her; he has big teeth; and so forth. What are the tales alluded to about? Is this story a fairy tale, too?
5. **RESPONDING CREATIVELY** Select an item from the news that grips your imagination, and ask yourself why it does. Does it have affinities with folktales or myths? Does it suggest disturbing ideas about human nature and society? Write a narrative of the event, perhaps from the point of view of one of the participants, that incorporates these larger implications.
6. **CONNECTIONS** Compare technique and theme in Oates's "Where Are You Going, Where Have You Been?" and Jackson's "The Lottery."
7. **CONNECTIONS** Compare and contrast Arnold Friend and Flannery O'Connor's Misfit.
8. **CONNECTIONS** Study the allusions to religion in the story. How would Flannery O'Connor have handled this material?

Related Commentaries

Joyce Carol Oates, From Stories That Define Me: The Making of a Writer, p. 895.
Joyce Carol Oates, *Smooth Talk: Short Story into Film,* p. 896.

Suggested Readings

Bloom, Harold. *Joyce Carol Oates.* New York: Chelsea House, 1981.
Friedman, Ellen G. "Joyce Carol Oates." *Modern American Women Writers.* Ed. Elaine Showalter. New York: Macmillan, 1991.
Gardner, John. *On Writers and Writing.* Reading, MA: Addison-Wesley, 1994. 75.
Gillis, Christina Marsden. " 'Where Are You Going, Where Have You Been?': Seduction, Space, and a Fictional Mode." *Studies in Short Fiction* 18 (1981): 65–70.
Johnson, Greg. *Understanding Joyce Carol Oates.* Columbia: U of South Carolina P, 1987.

Oates, Joyce Carol. *New Heaven, New Earth.* New York: Vanguard, 1974.

———. "(Woman) Writer." *First Person Singular: Writers On Their Craft.* Comp. Joyce Carol Oates. Princeton: Ontario Review P, 1983. 190–97.

———. *(Woman) Writer: Occasions and Opportunities.* New York: NAL-Dutton, 1989.

Milazzo, Lee. *Conversations with Joyce Carol Oates.* Jackson: UP of Mississippi, 1989.

Pearlman, Mickey, ed. *American Women Writing Fiction: Memory, Identity, Family, Space.* Lexington: U of Kentucky P, 1989. 9–44.

Phillips, Robert. "Interview with Joyce Carol Oates." *The Paris Review Interviews: Writers at Work.* Ed. George Plympton. 5th Series. New York: Penguin, 1981. 359–84.

Plimpton, George. *Women Writers at Work: The Paris Review Interviews.* New York: Penguin, 1989.

Quirk, Tom. "A Source for 'Where Are You Going, Where Have You Been?' " *Studies in Short Fiction* 18 (1981): 413–19.

Rozga, Margaret. "Threatening Places, Hiding Places: The Midwest in Selected Stories by Joyce Carol Oates." *Midwestern Miscellany* 18 (1990): 34–44.

Schulz, Gretchen, and R. J. R. Rockwood. "In Fairyland, without a Map: Connie's Exploration Inward in Joyce Carol Oates's 'Where Are You Going, Where Have You Been?' " *Literature and Psychology* 30 (1980): 155–67.

Urbanski, Marie Mitchell Olesen. "Existential Allegory: Joyce Carol Oates's 'Where Are You Going, Where Have You Been?'" *Studies in Short Fiction* 15 (1978): 200–03.

Wegs, Joyce M. " 'Don't You Know Who I Am?': The Grotesque in Oates's 'Where Are You Going, Where Have You Been?'" *Journal of Narrative Technique* 5 (1975): 66–72.

Wesley, Marilyn Clarke. "Transgression and Refusal: The Dynamic of Power in the Domestic Fiction of Joyce Carol Oates." *Dissertation Abstracts International* 49.11 (May 1989): 3365A.

Winslow, Joan D. "The Stranger Within: Two Stories by Oates and Hawthorne." *Studies in Short Fiction* 17 (1980): 263–68.

TIM O'BRIEN

The Things They Carried (p. 608)

In "The Things They Carried," O'Brien has found a brilliant solution to one of the most common problems a writer faces: how to find a new way to approach a subject that has been written about many times before. His subject is men at war, a topic that has occupied writers since remotest antiquity. The earliest epic in the European tradition is Homer's account of the siege of Troy, and the earliest griot narratives from the empires of Africa recount battles fought along the banks of the Niger River.

The Vietnam War has been treated in a stream of stories, books, articles, studies, and debates. O'Brien's innovation is to tell us directly not about the soldiers, or about the meaningless war they find themselves in, but about the things they are carrying on their shoulders and in their pockets. This simple device is startling and effective. The things his "grunts" are carrying are one way to identify them, to bring them to life, and the author also tells us about the things they carry under different circumstances.

This use of the small detail to illuminate the whole picture would not be as effective if it were limited to a simple description of what each of the men is carrying. But as he discusses the items — their use, their importance to the assignment the men are carrying out, and the significance of each thing to each man — O'Brien tells us about the war itself, and the soldiers' attitudes toward what they are doing. By presenting each of these objects as a microcosm of the reality of the war, the author makes the experience more comprehensible. He has found a dimension that shows us the soldiers as human beings, and that is the most important task for a writer who wants to make us face this cruel reality again.

Questions for Discussion

1. What is the effect of O'Brien's use of abbreviations and acronyms: R & R, SOP, M & Ms, USO, Psy Ops, KIA?
2. When the author writes, "Afterward they burned Than Khe," what is he telling us about the attitude of the men toward the people in the villages around them?
3. Why is it important to specify the weight of the equipment each man is carrying?
4. Does the language of the soldiers sound "real"? Do the descriptions of the weapons have the feeling of reality?
5. Why does the lieutenant burn the letters he has been carrying?

Topics for Writing

1. Soldiers from both sides are fighting the war, but the author only tells us about the men from one side. Why doesn't he describe the North Vietnamese soldiers?
2. Discuss the attitudes toward the war in the United States as they are reflected in the attitudes of the soldiers in "The Things They Carried."
3. Stories about men at war usually emphasize heroism and heroic acts; these are completely absent in this story. What has caused this change in attitude?

Related Commentaries

Bobbie Ann Mason, On Tim O'Brien's "The Things They Carried," p. 885.

Suggested Readings

Bonn, Maria S. "A Different World: The Vietnam Veteran Novel Comes Home." *Fourteen Landing Zones: Approaches to Vietnam War Literature.* Ed. Philip K. Jason. Iowa City: U of Iowa P, 1992.
Calloway, Catherine. "Pluralities of Vision: Going after Cacciato and Tim O'Brien's Short Fiction." *America Rediscovered: Critical Essays on Literature and Film of the Vietnam War.* Ed. Owen W. Gilman, Jr. New York: Garland, 1990.

————. "Tim O'Brien (1946–): A Primary and Secondary Bibliography." *Bulletin of Bibliography* 50.3 (Sept. 1993): 223–29.

Flannery O'Connor

Everything That Rises Must Converge (p. 623)

"Everything That Rises Must Converge" is one of O'Connor's most power-ful stories. Although they are emotionally linked as closely as Siamese twins, Julian and his mother are in such fundamental disagreement that only death can bring their souls together, since "everything that rises must converge." O'Connor goes to great lengths to spell out the differences between mother and son. They are so extreme that humor is the one thing that makes them bearable to the sensi-tive reader. Julian asserts that "true culture is in the mind." His mother says, "It's in the heart." He insists that "nobody in the damn bus cares who you are." She replies, "I care who I am." She always looks on the bright side of things. He glo-ries in scenting out impending disasters. He tells himself he isn't dominated by his mother. She knows he's both financially and emotionally dependent on her, and she gets him to do whatever she asks.

Contrasts and opposites rule this unlikely pair, but the world they inhabit is also in a state of opposition to their sense of themselves. Blacks no longer know their place in the back of the bus; mother and son are exiled from the destroyed family mansion; Julian wants to be a writer after his college education, but he's selling typewriters instead. The only constant is his mother's ridiculous hat. It reappears on the head of the black lady sitting with her little son next to Julian and his mother on the bus. This sight amuses his mother, who hasn't lost her sense of humor, her spirit refusing to be worn down by the remarks and behavior of her critical, hostile son. As a character she is partially redeemed (despite her racial bigotry) by her humor and her fundamental generosity. In contrast, Julian is damned by his sense of pride.

O'Connor makes certain of this damnation by subtly shifting the point of view to Julian's mental outlook during his journey on the bus, when he with-draws "into the inner compartment of his mind where he spent most of his time." He will be alone there, feeling smugly superior to his mother, until he realizes that he has lost her, at which time he will be forced to include her in his emotional state by entering "the world of guilt and sorrow."

Students may enjoy discussing the humor in this story as well as O'Connor's sublime ear for the ridiculous in her characters' speech. "Everything That Rises Must Converge" also lends itself well to different critical perspectives. Since O'Connor wrote from a Christian orientation, the religious implications of the narrative can be traced: the references to Saint Sebastian, or the Negro mother's threat to her little boy, "Quit yo' foolishness . . . before I knock the liv-ing Jesus out of you!" Or O'Connor's quiet comment about "guilt and sorrow" at the end. Students who are budding social historians, psychologists, or feminists can also find abundant material in this story to explore from their orientations.

Questions for Discussion

1. O'Connor writes that Julian's mother's eyes, "sky-blue, were as innocent and untouched by experience as they must have been when she was ten." Again, when she turns her eyes, now a "bruised purple," on Julian, he gets an "uncomfortable sense of her innocence." What are we to make of her innocence? How do we reconcile this attribute with her racism?

2. Julian seems to hate almost everything about his mother. Does she hate anything about her son? Why does he despise her? Why does she love him?

3. The idea of family mansion implies family ties. How do family ties appear in this story? Does the "decayed mansion" mean more to Julian or to his mother? What does it mean to him? to her?

4. What point of view controls "Everything That Rises Must Converge"? At which points in the story do we have the most intimate access to Julian's thoughts?

5. Describe Julian's relationships with people other than his mother. Consider the paragraphs beginning "He began to imagine" and "He imagined his mother." Who would he like to be friends with and why? Does his acknowledgment of his mother's racism imply positive things about Julian's own character?

6. On page 627 we discover that Julian's mother doesn't think Julian knows "a thing about 'life,' that he hadn't even entered the real world" yet. Does the narrator agree with her? Discuss this sentence and the closing sentence of the story together. What does this imply about the characteristics that belong to "real life"?

7. After his mother's stroke, Julian looks "into a face he had never seen before." What is different about her face now? What metaphor is O'Connor sustaining behind the description of the literal differences brought on by neurological devastation?

8. O'Connor, a devout Catholic, said her stories were meant to be more like parables than true to life. What elements of this story are Christian? Is the preoccupation central to this story available only to Christians?

Topics for Writing

1. Compare and contrast the two mothers and the two sons in the story.
2. Analyze the symbolism of the hat at the convergence of two apparent opposites — the two mothers.
3. Discuss the role of pride and the response to charity in Julian and the black mother.
4. Write an examination of the changing social order between the generations of Julian's mother and Julian.
5. Explore the role of irony in "Everything That Rises Must Converge."

Related Casebook

Flannery O'Connor, From "Letters 1954–55," p. 964.
Flannery O'Connor, Writing Short Stories, p. 967.
Flannery O'Connor, A Reasonable Use of the Unreasonable, p. 972.

Robert H. Brinkmeyer Jr., Flannery O'Connor and Her Readers, p. 975.

Dorothy Tuck McFarland, On "Good Country People," p. 980.

Wayne C. Booth, A Rhetorical Reading of O'Connor's "Everything That Rises Must Converge," p. 984.

Sally Fitzgerald, Southern Sources of "A Good Man Is Hard to Find," p. 987.

Suggested Readings

See page 117.

FLANNERY O'CONNOR

Good Country People (p. 634)

In the world of Flannery O'Connor's fiction, characters are seldom who we think they are or even who they think they are. "Good Country People" provides an intriguing twist on the archetypal theme: Events and people are seldom as simple as they seem.

O'Connor revels in the idiosyncrasies of personality, peopling this story with three strong characters in Joy (Hulga), Mrs. Hopewell, and Manley Pointer, as well as an interesting subsidiary character, Mrs. Freeman, with her "special fondness for the details of secret infections, hidden deformities," and "assaults upon children." O'Connor's choice of names figures prominently. Joy changes her name to Hulga to symbolize her sense of her own ugliness. Mrs. Hopewell continually hopes well of things, blathering a stream of banal platitudes that reveal her own lack of depth. The name Manley Pointer strikes the reader as almost humorously phallic and predatory-sounding, given the surprising turn of events in the storage barn.

We don't see how "right" the details of this story are until we reach its sardonic conclusion, Pointer going Hulga's intellectual atheism one better, disappearing with her leg in his "Bible" valise, Mrs. Hopewell in her ignorance commenting on "that nice dull young man." Looking back, we see the clever meticulousness of Pointer's con — the feigned heaviness of his satchel, his feigned simplicity (as in mistaking the name of the house for its owner), the rube suit. It turns out that this specimen of "good country people" reads people better than the highly educated Hulga or the self-aggrandizing Mrs. Hopewell.

The experience of losing her artificial limb to the perverted Manley Pointer is the loss of a certain kind of virginity for Hulga, and however harrowing the experience, we sense that it will be a valuable one. Prior to her victimization, we feel mainly revulsion for Joy/Hulga. We sympathize with her hunting accident, but O'Connor highlights the unpleasant abrasiveness of her personality; clearly Hulga's psyche, as well as her body, has been damaged. Hulga's low self-esteem is exacerbated by her mother's implications of Hulga's abnormality, which focus on her intellectualism as much as on her disfigurement. For all Mrs. Hopewell's assertions that "it takes all kinds to make the world go 'round," she resents her daughter's interest in philosophy (female education is for a "good time") as well as Hulga's individuation: "It seemed to Mrs. Hopewell that every year she grew less like other people and more like herself."

In this multifaceted story of moral blindness, Hulga experiences a physical intimacy with Pointer that forces her into a new mode of reacting and out of her customary detached intellectualism: "Without the leg she felt entirely dependent on him. Her brain seemed to have stopped thinking altogether and to be about some other function that it was not very good at." However dastardly Pointer's actions, he forces Hulga to feel and acknowledge her emotions for the first time. We go away from the story feeling that Hulga will be a changed — and humbled — person less presumptuous and closer to psychic wholeness.

Questions for Discussion

1. What does Mrs. Hopewell mean by "good country people"?
2. Why does Joy change her name to Hulga?
3. In what ways do you expect Joy/Hulga will change after her experience in the barn with Manley Pointer?
4. Discuss O'Connor's choice of names for the characters in this story.
5. Is Manley Pointer a believable character? Have you in your own experience encountered people who are entirely other than they seem? What is Pointer really interested in? Why does he carry off Hulga's leg?
6. Discuss the dramatic function of Mrs. Freeman and her two daughters.
7. Discuss the effects on characterization of O'Connor's choosing to give Joy a Ph.D. in philosophy and an artificial leg. How do these details predispose our expectations?

Topics for Writing

1. Discuss the function of Christianity in "Good Country People."
2. **CONNECTIONS** Compare "Good Country People" with "Everything That Rises Must Converge." What similarities and differences do you find among mother, son or daughter, and stranger in these stories? What can you infer from this comparison about O'Connor's attraction to certain types of characters?

Related Casebook

See page 111.

Suggested Readings

See page 117.

Flannery O'Connor

A Good Man Is Hard to Find (p. 648)

O'Connor's comments (included in Part Three, p. 964) direct attention to the climax of her story and suggest how she intended the central characters to be viewed and what she meant the story to imply. Students may benefit, however, from struggling at first to interpret the text unassisted by authorial explanation. The effort should reveal dimensions of O'Connor's art that might otherwise be overlooked.

The grandmother's reawakening to reality, which leads to her gesture of grace as she reaches out to The Misfit as one of her own children, may be triggered by the violence of the murders going on just offstage and the extremity of her own case, but her conversion has been carefully prepared for. Throughout the story this old woman longs in various ways to go back *home* — to Tennessee, to the days of her youth, to the mansion with the imaginary secret panel, which is as much in heaven as it is down a hilly back road in Georgia. Death is seldom far from her thoughts, though for a long time she does not apprehend its reality. Her initial worries about The Misfit are disingenuous, but encountering him or returning to east Tennessee come to the same thing in the end. On the road, the grandmother dresses up in nice clothes so that "anyone seeing her dead on the highway would know at once that she was a lady," observes a graveyard, and remembers her mansion at a town named Toombsboro. The Misfit and his men approach in a "hearse-like automobile"; the family awaits them in front of the woods that "gaped like a dark open mouth." The grandmother is at odds with present times. She squabbles with the children (whose behavior even the reader may find unusually improper), easily upstages the cabbage-headed, slacks-wearing woman who is their mother, joins Red Sammy in deploring the state of world affairs, and disastrously deludes Bailey by smuggling the cat into the car. But she loves the world as well, in a selfish, childish way. She *will* have the cat along; she admires the scenery (including a picturesque "pickaninny" for whose poverty she is not yet ready to feel compassion); she wishes she had married Mr. E. A. Teagarden, who courted her with watermelon and would have supplied all her worldly needs from the proceeds of his Coca-Cola stock; and she even makes a play for Red Sammy, the only tycoon in sight.

These desires may be misdirected, but just as it takes very little to upset the valise, release the cat, flip the car off the road, and carry the story into an entirely new set of circumstances, so, under the intensifying presence of death, it takes only a moment for the grandmother's selfish love for and alienation from the world to flip over into the selfless love that leads her to open her heart to The Misfit. After all, she at least rationalizes bringing the cat to protect it; she supportively asserts that Red Sammy is "a good man" in face of his own cynicism and despair; and she offers the same praise to The Misfit from the moment she recognizes him. Without a doubt the grandmother's motive in insisting that The Misfit is "a good man" and in urging him to pray is to divert him from his evident intention and so to save her skin. But as the bullets ring out in the background and the grandmother's maternal instincts burst forth in her repeated cries of "Bailey Boy!" she begins to act charitably in spite of herself. She offers The Misfit one of Bailey's shirts, listens to his confession (although she is the one who is about to die), and when he is wearing Bailey's shirt, she reaches out to him in his anguish.

A good man is hard to find; Jesus may have been the only one who was intrinsically good. But when she loves and pities the radically fallen Misfit, the grandmother becomes for the moment a good woman through her Christlike action, as The Misfit himself acerbically recognizes.

As O'Connor mentions in her commentary, The Misfit has evoked widely differing responses from readers and critics, who have associated him with the devil, the modern agnostic existentialist, or "the prophet he was meant to become," in O'Connor's own phrase. Perhaps The Misfit's daddy provides the best way of distinguishing him from the rest of the characters with his remark "It's some that can live their whole life out without asking about it and it's others has to know why it is, and this boy is one of the latters." Unlike O'Connor, whose vision of the world was grounded in *belief,* The Misfit wants to *know.* With Faustian presumption, he seeks to comprehend the divine mysteries in terms of his own intellect and demands a kind of justice in life that he can understand. When he cannot find the answers to his questions, but only the implication of inexplicable guilt (like Original Sin) in the punishment he receives, The Misfit sees the world not as the charming place it has appeared to the grandmother but as a prison whose empty sky resembles the blank walls of his cell in the penitentiary. In his own calculus of guilt, The Misfit feels he has been excessively punished, and he seems to be going about the world committing crimes in order to right the balance. His most perverse principle, "No pleasure but meanness," is sustained surprisingly well by the world O'Connor portrays. (Is *this* the reason for the story's lack of anything or anyone to admire and its unremittingly ironic tone?) But it gives way after he has been touched by the grandmother to his first true prophecy: "It's no real pleasure in life" — no *real* pleasure in *this* life, though true goodness sometimes appears in those made conscious of death.

WILLIAM E. SHEIDLEY

Questions for Discussion

1. What is the grandmother's reason for bringing up The Misfit at the beginning of the story?
2. Describe "the children's mother." Why does O'Connor make her such a nonentity?
3. What about John Wesley and June Star? What would have been the result had O'Connor characterized them as something other than totally obnoxious?
4. Discuss the grandmother's reasons for her fatal decision to bring Pitty Sing on the trip.
5. Why does the grandmother dress so nicely for the trip?
6. Compare the grandmother's response to the scenery and the trip with that of the children. What does O'Connor accomplish by means of this distinction?
7. Just before the stop at The Tower, the grandmother reminisces about her old suitor, Edgar Atkins Teagarden. Specify the connections between the two episodes.
8. What tower might O'Connor have had in mind in choosing the name for Red Sammy's establishment? Why is there a monkey in a chinaberry tree feasting on fleas posted outside The Tower? What do we learn about the world at Red Sammy's?

9.   Contrast The Tower with the mansion the grandmother awakens to remember "outside of Toombsboro."

10.   What factors cause the accident? Consider its meaning as a consequence of the grandmother's choices and desires.

11.   Describe the manner in which The Misfit arrives on the scene. What effect does his appearance have on the reader?

12.   The grandmother's response to The Misfit's remark "it would have been better for all of you, lady, if you hadn't of reckernized me," is "You wouldn't shoot a lady, would you?" Evaluate her question.

13.   To what extent is the grandmother correct in her praise of The Misfit? In what ways is he a gentleman?

14.   Describe the grandmother's reaction to Bailey's departure. Is her response consistent with her previous behavior?

15.   Define The Misfit's experience of the world. To what extent can his criminality be blamed on the conditions of his life? Does The Misfit feel any more free outside the penitentiary than in it?

16.   How can the logic of The Misfit's position that "the crime don't matter. . . . because sooner or later you're going to forget what it was you done and just be punished for it" be attacked? To what extent does The Misfit's description of himself apply to everyone? Bear in mind that the whole family is being punished with death for no ascertainable crime.

17.   Explain how, to The Misfit, "Jesus thown everything off balance."

18.   What is the effect of O'Connor's comparing the grandmother to "a parched old turkey hen crying for water"?

19.   Does The Misfit do or say anything to deserve the grandmother's gesture of concern?

20.   Explain The Misfit's final evaluation of the grandmother: "She would of been a good woman . . . if it had been somebody there to shoot her every minute of her life."

21.   Contrast The Misfit's remark "No pleasure but meanness" with his last words in the story.

Topics for Writing

1.   What is the function of tone in O'Connor's story?

2.   Describe techniques of characterization in "A Good Man Is Hard to Find."

3.   **RESPONDING CREATIVELY**   Write a parable or short tale designed to illustrate a religious or philosophical truth. Following O'Connor's example, portray your characters ruthlessly as embodiments of what you want them to represent.

4.   **CONNECTIONS**   Compare and contrast O'Connor's "A Good Man Is Hard to Find" and Tolstoy's "The Death of Ivan Ilych."

5.   **CONNECTIONS**   Comment upon the relationship between the grandmother and The Misfit in "A Good Man Is Hard to Find" and the relationship between Connie and Arnold Friend in Oates's "Where Are You Going, Where Have You Been?"

Related Casebook

See page 111.

Suggested Readings

Asals, Frederick. *Flannery O'Connor: The Imagination of Extremity.* Athens: U of Georgia P, 1982. 142–54.

Brinkmeyer, Robert H., Jr. *The Art and Vision of Flannery O'Connor.* Baton Rouge: Louisiana State UP, 1989.

Browning, Preston M., Jr. *Flannery O'Connor.* Crosscurrents/Modern Critiques. Carbondale: Southern Illinois UP, 1974. 54–59.

Burke, John J. "Convergence of Flannery O'Connor and Chardin." *Renascence* 19 (1966): 41–47, 52.

Church, Joseph. "An Abuse of the Imagination in Flannery O'Connor's 'A Good Man Is Hard to Find.'" *Notes on Contemporary Literature* 20.3 (May 1990): 8–10.

Clark, Beverly Lyon, and Melville J. Friedman. *Critical Essays on Flannery O'Connor.* Boston: G. K. Hall, 1985.

Esch, Robert M. "O'Connor's 'Everything That Rises Must Converge.' " *Explicator* 27 (1969): Item 58.

Feeley, Sister Kathleen. *Flannery O'Connor: Voice of the Peacock.* New Brunswick, NJ: Rutgers UP, 1972.

Gatta, John. "The Scarlet Letter as Pre-Text for Flannery O'Connor's 'Good Country People.'" *The Nathaniel Hawthorne Review* 16.2 (Fall 1990): 6–9.

Giannone, Richard. *Flannery O'Connor: A Study of the Short Fiction.* Boston: Twayne, 1988.

Grimshaw, James A. *The Flannery O'Connor Companion.* Westport, CT: Greenwood, 1981.

Hendin, Josephine. *The World of Flannery O'Connor.* Ann Arbor, MI: Books Demand UMI, 1986.

Kane, Patricia. "Flannery O'Connor's 'Everything That Rises Must Converge.'" *Critique: Studies in Short Fiction* 8 (1965): 85–91.

Maida, Patricia Dinneen. "Convergence in Flannery O'Connor's 'Everything That Rises Must Converge.'" *Studies in Short Fiction* 7 (1970): 549–55.

Martin, W. R. "The Apostate in Flannery O'Connor's 'Everything That Rises Must Converge.'" *American Notes and Queries* 23 (1985): 113–14.

McDermott, John V. "Julian's Journey into Hell: Flannery O'Connor's Allegory of Pride." *Mississippi Quarterly* 28 (1975): 171–79.

Nisly, P. W. "Prison of the Self: Isolation in Flannery O'Connor's Fiction." *Studies in Short Fiction* 17 (1980): 49–54.

Ochshorn, Kathleen G. "A Cloak of Grace: Contradictions in 'A Good Man Is Hard to Find.'" *Studies in American Fiction* 18.1 (Spring 1990): 113–17.

O'Connor, Flannery. *The Habit of Being.* Letters edited and with an introduction by Sally Fitzgerald. New York: Farrar, 1979.

———. *Mystery and Manners.* New York: Farrar, 1969.

Orvell, Miles. *Invisible Parade: The Fiction of Flannery O'Connor.* Philadelphia: Temple UP, 1972.

Paulson, Suzanne. *Flannery O'Connor.* Boston: G. K. Hall, 1988.

Petry, Alice Hall. "Miss O'Connor and Mrs. Mitchell: The Example of 'Everything That Rises.'" *The Southern Quarterly: A Journal of the Arts in the South* 27.4 (Summer 1989): 5–15.

Pyron, V. "'Strange Country': The Landscape of Flannery O'Connor's Short Stories." *Mississippi Quarterly* 36 (1983): 557–68.

Frank O'Connor

Guests of the Nation (p. 660)

O'Connor's story draws exceptional power from its concern with a betrayal of the most primitive basis of human society, the host-guest relationship. The English prisoners, billeted with their guards in a cottage so thoroughly rooted in the land that its occupant still bears traces of indigenous paganism, earn the status of guests and come to feel at home. Belcher's contributions to the household chores call attention to the simple satisfactions of the peaceful, cooperative labor that is disrupted by the war, and Hawkins's learning Irish dances implies the underlying brotherhood of men, in contrast to which the scruples of "our lads" who "at that time did not dance foreign dances on principle" seem absurd — and ominous. The futility of Hawkins's debates with Noble on theology calls further into question the reality of the issues that divide the English from the Irish, and his international socialist politics provide a hint that there are issues of at least equal importance that would not polarize the two pairs of men but unite them against a common enemy.

The inhumanity of the conflict that orders Belcher and Hawkins to be executed by their "chums," their brothers, appears clearer for O'Connor's skillful portrayal of the prisoners as distinct from each other, individualized and consistent in their personalities. Further, by opening the story with a plunge into what seems an ongoing state of affairs, O'Connor shows that it is the war that interrupts the natural friendly interaction among the men rather than their fellowship interrupting a "normal" condition of bitter hostility between the English and the Irish. Even Jeremiah Donovan, who eventually brings down the cruel warrant and carries it out, forms part of the circle around the card table and scolds Hawkins for poor play "as if he were one of our own."

Bonaparte, the narrator, embraces the Englishmen as comrades and chafes at his official duties as their guard. With Noble, he imagines that the brigade officers, who also "knew the Englishmen well," will treat them as men rather than as enemies. But when the moment of decision arrives, Noble's resistance only extends to accepting the secondary role of gravedigger, and Bonaparte, though he hopes the prisoners will run away, finds himself powerless to aid them. Belcher and Hawkins are most fully themselves at the moment of their deaths, Hawkins talking on about his larger cause, Belcher finally revealing the fullness of his loving and generous nature. To Bonaparte and Noble the execution conveys a shock of revelation that changes the world for them. As Noble prays with the old woman in the doorway of the cottage — now become a shrine to the communion that took place within it, the only holy place in a world that seems to Noble composed entirely of the grave of his friends — Bonaparte, made profane in the literal etymological sense ("outside the shrine") and figuratively as well by his participation in the killing, feels himself cast out, alone, cut off from all atonement.

William E. Sheidley

Questions for Discussion

1.   Describe and explain the pacing of the story. Contrast the movement of sections II and III with that of section IV.

2. What is the effect of the abrupt beginning of the story? Why does O'Connor introduce the characters before specifying that they are prisoners and guards in a war?
3. Why does O'Connor trouble to introduce the message from Mary Brigid O'Connell about her brother's socks?
4. Distinguish between the two Englishmen. Are they more different from the Irishmen or from each other?
5. Explore the significance of the old woman's superstitions about Jupiter Pluvius and "the hidden powers." Compare her interest in religion with that of Noble and Hawkins.
6. Why is Bonaparte so shocked when he learns what may happen to the hostages?
7. What is the relevance to the story of Hawkins's political beliefs? Do we think less of him when he volunteers to become a traitor and join the Irish cause?
8. What is the effect of Belcher's last-minute confidences? of his apparently sincere repetition of the word chum throughout his ordeal?
9. Discuss Bonaparte's role in the execution. Is he culpable? Does he feel guilty?
10. Define the symbolic implications of the final scene. Why do Noble and Bonaparte have contrasting visions? Do their visions have anything in common? Why does Bonaparte burst out of the cottage where Noble and the old woman are praying?

Topics for Writing

1. What is the meaning of the old woman and her cottage in "Guests of the Nation"?
2. Summarize the conflict and the action of this story on personal, public (national, historical, political), and eternal (philosophical, religious, mythical) levels. Could these levels be reconciled so that the polarities of value would be parallel?

Related Commentaries

Frank O'Connor, The Nearest Thing to Lyric Poetry Is the Short Story, p. 900.
Frank O'Connor, Style and Form in Joyce's "The Dead," p. 901.

Suggested Readings

Bordewyk, Gordon. "Quest for Meaning: The Stories of Frank O'Connor." *Illinois Quarterly* 41 (1978): 37–47, esp. 38–39.
Matthews, James. *Voices: A Life of Frank O'Connor.* New York: Atheneum, 1983.
O'Connor, Frank. *The Lonely Voice: A Study of the Short Story.* Cleveland: World, 1963.
Prosky, Murray. "The Pattern of Diminishing Certitude in the Stories of Frank O'Connor." *Colby Library Quarterly* 9 (1971): 311–21, esp. 311–14.
Steinman, Michael. *Frank O'Connor at Work.* Syracuse, NY: Syracuse UP, 1990.
Tomory, William. *Frank O'Connor.* Boston: Twayne, 1980.

TILLIE OLSEN

I Stand Here Ironing (p. 671)

One way to begin discussing this story is to look at the ending. "I will never total it all," the narrator affirms and then pronounces the summary whose inadequacy she has already proclaimed. The summarizing passage clarifies and organizes the impressions the reader may have gleaned from the preceding monologue. It is so clear that if it stood alone or came first in the story the validity of its interpretation of Emily could hardly be doubted. But since it follows her mother's "tormented" meditations, the summary seems incomplete in its clinical precision and must give way to a final paragraph of comparatively obscure and paradoxical requests focused in the startling but brilliantly adept image of the "dress on the ironing board, helpless before the iron," which links the story's end to its beginning and directs attention to the true central character.

What is mainly missing from the summary is the love and understanding that Emily's mother feels for her daughter as a result of living through the experiences bracketed by the orderly generalizations. Just as much as Emily, her mother has been the victim "of depression, of war, of fear." By virtue of having had to cope with those circumstances, she can respect Emily's response to them. Doing so enables her to counter the suggestion that "she's a youngster who needs help" with "Let her be." A good deal of the help Emily and her mother have received so far has put them in separate prisons — as when Emily was incarcerated at the convalescent home — and cut them off from love. To let Emily alone is at least to allow her some freedom to grow at her own slow pace.

Her mother is tempted to blame herself for the deficiencies in Emily's childhood, since she learned things about being a mother with her second family that she did not know with Emily. But her consideration of a characteristic incident early in the narrative suggests a crucial qualifying factor: When she parked Emily at nursery school at the age of two, she did not know what she was subjecting her daughter to, "except that it would have made no difference if I had known. . . . It was the only way we could be together, the only way I could hold a job." As much a victim of rigid and unfavorable economic and historic circumstances as her daughter, Emily's mother can speak her concluding line with feeling. In pleading that Emily somehow be made to know "that she is more than this dress on the ironing board, helpless before the iron," Emily's mother asks that her daughter be spared a condition to which she herself has been subjected. But Emily's mother, unlike Whistler's, does not sit for her portrait passively in a rocking chair; she stands there wielding the iron, controlling the very symbol of the circumstances that have not yet flattened her, painting her own self-portrait, and calling for help not in adjusting Emily to the world but in making the world a place in which Emily can thrive.

WILLIAM E. SHEIDLEY

Questions for Discussion

1. Who is "you" in the first sentence? What is the mother's first response to the request to unlock the mystery of Emily? Does her position change?

2. Does Emily's mother feel guilty about how she has cared for Emily? Why? What factors have affected her dealings with her daughter?
3. Why is the passage in which Emily throws the clock so effective?
4. Discuss the "help" Emily gets at the convalescent home. How does it compare with the help her mother calls for at the end?
5. Emily has suffered from the absence of her father, the exhaustion of her mother, poverty, asthma and other diseases, sibling rivalry, and unpopularity, among other complaints. What is the effect of these hardships on the young woman she has become? What is the effect of her discovery of a talent?
6. What has her mother learned from Emily?
7. Does Emily's mother love her daughter? How can we tell?

Topics for Writing

1. Compare and contrast Emily's talent and her mother's.
2. Discuss the function of the interruptions in "I Stand Here Ironing."
3. Consider "I will never total it all" — the importance of indeterminacy in Olsen's analysis of Emily.
4. Analyze the politics of "I Stand Here Ironing."
5. **RESPONDING CREATIVELY** Write a summary statement in general terms about the personality of a sibling, relative, or friend you have known closely for a long time. Put it aside and cast your memory back to three or four specific incidents involving your subject. Narrate them briefly but in specific and concrete terms. Read over your sketches and compare the personality of your subject as it emerges with what you wrote in your generalized summary. Do you still think your summary is accurate? What are its limitations?

Suggested Readings

Frye, Joanne S. " 'I Stand Here Ironing': Motherhood as Experience and Metaphor." *Studies in Short Fiction* 18 (1981): 287–92.
O'Connor, William Van. "The Short Stories of Tillie Olsen." *Studies in Short Fiction* 1 (1963): 21–25, esp. 21–22.

ZZ PACKER

Drinking Coffee Elsewhere (p. 678)

The title of Packer's story refers to a disclosure her narrator Dina makes near the end of the story, when she is talking to the Yale psychiatrist Mr. Raeburn who has been trying to counsel her for nearly a year, since she first arrived at the college. Mr. Raeburn accuses Dina of "pretending" and she corrects him, superior as always: "Pretending. I believe the professional name for it might be denial." Meanwhile, she thinks to herself about how important "pretending" has been to her:

> I remembered the morning of my mother's funeral. I'd been given milk to settle my stomach; I'd pretended it was coffee. I imagined I was drink-

ing coffee elsewhere. Some Arabic-speaking country where the thick coffee served in little cups was so strong it could keep you awake for days.

"Pretending" is what Packer is doing when she creates her stories. She makes it a necessary but barely functioning survival mechanism in this narrative as Dina struggles as a freshman to adjust to the affluent world of Yale College after her mother's death in an underclass black ghetto of Baltimore. Feeling herself orphaned at Yale — she blames her father for bringing on her mother's fatal cancer — Dina finds that the only person she can feel close to is another troubled student, Heidi, a young woman from Canada whose struggles with her own sexual identity are put into perspective when she learns that her mother has died in Vancouver.

At the end of "Drinking Coffee Elsewhere," Dina has dropped out of school and is living with an aunt she "barely knew" in Baltimore. Characteristically, at the conclusion of the story, she is imagining being somewhere else, this time in Vancouver with Heidi. Yet she ends her narrative with a minor psychological breakthrough, the climax of the story: She imagines Heidi coming to Baltimore to visit her, knocking on her door to say "Open up."

Questions for Discussion

1. Heidi introduces herself to Dina by quoting from a poem by Frank O'Hara titled "Autobiographia Literaria." Heidi's words beginning "When I was a child" and ending "I am an orphan" are taken directly from O'Hara's poem. The last lines of this poem are

   > And here I am, the
   > center of all beauty!
   > writing these poems!
   > Imagine!

   How do the words in this last stanza of "Autobiographia Literaria" suggest the theme of Packer's story?
2. Why does Heidi want people to call her Henrik?
3. Why does the narrator avoid going with Heidi to the campus meeting on "Coming Out Day"?
4. "Drinking Coffee Elsewhere" spans a time frame of several months during the academic year, in which many events take place. Does this weaken the unity of the story?
5. How are adults portrayed in the story? Why doesn't the narrator trust any of them?

Topics for Writing

1. Write a book review of Packer's debut collection, *Drinking Coffee Elsewhere* (2003).
2. Analyze whether Dina is a reliable narrator in the story.

Grace Paley

A Conversation with My Father (p. 694)

The story the narrator writes in response to her father's request is so interesting that it is easy to forget for a while that it is only an element within the larger story Paley has to tell. Confronted with the inescapable fact of the father's imminent death, the narrator and her father respond in differing ways because of their differing needs. Both use gallows humor to make the situation less intolerable, as when the father remarks, "It so happens I'm not going out this evening"; but the narrator seeks that refuge much more often, and her father chides her repeatedly for doing so. Things *matter* to a dying man, and it is not surprising that he should prefer the straight line of tragedy — in which failure and defeat are compensated for by a perception of the real value of what has been lost — to the idea of "the open destiny of life," which, by holding out hope of recovery from any disaster, implies that there is nothing indispensable, no absolute loss. A man on his deathbed knows better.

The narrator's first attempt to write a story that suits her father's taste reflects her discomfort with the assignment. Her "unadorned and miserable tale" remains so sketchy that it lacks verisimilitude and conviction, like meaningless statistics on highway deaths or counterinsurgency body counts. Challenged to try again, she partly confirms her father's complaint that "with you, it's all a joke" by writing a brilliantly comic and incontrovertibly realistic version of the story, whose merits even her father has to recognize: "Number One: You have a nice sense of humor." In a few deft strokes, Paley renders an incisive satiric portrait of two contemporary "life-styles," their hypocrisy, and their destructiveness, focused neatly in the competing periodical titles, *Oh! Golden Horse!* (heroin) and *Man Does Live by Bread Alone*. The narrator knows as well as her father how thorough a perversion of true spiritual values is embodied in each of these titles, and she dramatizes her understanding in the destruction of the mother in her story. But she cannot quite "look it in the face," and she ends her tale with one last grim joke: "terrible, face-scarring, time-consuming tears." Her father spies her desperate evasion: "Number Two: I see you can't tell a plain story. So don't waste time." Ironically, the clarity of his disillusioned vision enables the dying man to feel a purer sympathy for the mother in the story than does the narrator herself, although she claims to care so much about her characters that she wants to give them all a second chance. "Poor woman," he says. "Poor girl, born in a time of fools, to live among fools. The end. The end. You were right to put that down. The end." Not necessarily, the narrator argues, and goes on to invent the kind of future for her character that we always imagine for the dying, in the probably misguided effort to ease their anxiety. But her father, as usual, knows better: " 'How long will it be?' he asked. 'Tragedy! You too. When will you look it in the face?' "

William E. Sheidley

Questions for Discussion

1. Describe the medical condition of the narrator's father. How important is it to understanding his position in the conversation?

2. Explain the phrase "despite my metaphors" in the first paragraph. What other writerly tactics of the narrator does her father ignore?
3. The narrator says she *would* like to tell a story with the kind of plot she has always despised. Analyze her conflict.
4. What is the point of the first version of the story? What is wrong with it as a piece of fiction?
5. When her father asks for details, the narrator comes up with things he calls jokes. Are they? What makes them jokes rather than facts?
6. Why does the narrator's father consider that "it is of great consequence" whether the woman in the story is married? Is he simply old-fashioned?
7. What does the narrator add to her story in the second version? Does the point of the story remain the same? Does her father get the point?
8. The woman in the story "would rather be with the young." Consider that motivation and its results from the point of view of the narrator and of her father.
9. What techniques does Paley use to satirize the woman's son and his girl-friend?
10. Explain the term "time-consuming" at the end of the inset story.
11. The narrator's father makes three separate responses to the story. Account for each of them. Do they cohere?
12. What does the narrator's father mean by the statement he makes in various forms culminating in his final question?

Topics for Writing

1. Analyze "A Conversation with My Father" as a story about writing.
2. Evaluate the qualities of tragedy versus satire in "A Conversation with My Father."
3. **RESPONDING CREATIVELY** Write your own version of the narrator's story. Start from her first version and elaborate on it as you choose, without necessarily using the material the narrator includes in her second version and subsequent commentary.
4. **CONNECTIONS** Compare and contrast attitudes toward death and life in Paley's "A Conversation with My Father" and Tolstoy's "The Death of Ivan Ilych."

Related Story

Grace Paley, Samuel [Appendix 1], p. 1039.

Related Commentary

Grace Paley, A Conversation with Ann Charters, p. 903.

Suggested Readings

Aarons, Victoria. "Talking Lives: Storytelling and Renewal in Grace Paley's Short Fiction." *Studies in Jewish Literature* 9.1 (Spring 1990): 20–35.

Arcana, Judith. "Grace Paley: Life and Stories." *Dissertation Abstracts International* 50.7 (Jan. 1990): 2271A.

Baba, Minako. "Faith Darwin as Writer, Heroine: A Study of Grace Paley's Short Stories." *Studies in American Jewish Literature* 7.1 (Spring 1988): 40–54.

Halfman, Ulrich, and Philipp Gerlach. "Grace Paley: A Bibliography." *Tulsa Studies in Women's Literature* 8.2 (Fall 1989): 339–54.

Isaccs, Neil David. *Grace Paley: A Study of the Short Fiction.* Boston: Twayne, 1990.

Logsdon, Loren, and Charles W. Mayer, ed. Since *Flannery O'Connor: Essays on the Contemporary American Short Story.* Macomb: Western Illinois U, 1987. 93–100.

Lyons, Bonnie. "Grace Paley's Jewish Miniatures." *Studies in American Jewish Literature* 8.1 (Spring 1989): 26–33.

Paley, Grace. *Long Walks and Intimate Talks: Stories and Poems by Grace Paley.* New York: Feminist Press and the City U of New York, 1991.

Taylor, Jacqueline. *Grace Paley: Illuminating the Dark Lives.* Austin: U of Texas P, 1990.

———. "Grace Paley on Storytelling and Story Hearing." *Literature in Performance: A Journal of Literature and Performing Art* 7.2 (April 1987): 46–58.

Wilde, Alan. "Grace Paley's World, Investing Words." Wilde, *Middle Grounds.* Philadelphia: U of Pennsylvania P, 1987.

EDGAR ALLAN POE

The Cask of Amontillado (p. 699)

Poe is the great master of the contrived suspense story, and "The Cask of Amontillado" is a model of narrative compression toward a single effect. Students should understand that Poe had a theory on the short story; its essential points are suggested in his review of Hawthorne's tales in Part Two (p. 907).

Despite Poe's rational explanation of how a writer should compose a story, his own fiction is directed toward eliciting irrational emotions. Poe's literary style aims at using as many extravagances of character, setting, and plot as he could invent, exploiting the reader's emotional vulnerability to disturbing images of darkness and chaos. The hectic unpredictability of the carnival season, the creepy subterranean wine cellar, and the ancient family crypt with its molding skeletons all challenge us emotionally and make us want to read further.

In the reading, our own fears become the true subject matter. As in a nightmare, Fortunato finds himself being buried alive, one of the most basic human fears. On a more conscious level, we rely on a social contract to bind us together as a human family, and Montresor's lawlessness plays on our fear that any person can take the law into his or her own hands without being checked by conscience. Poe doesn't have to give us a great number of details about his characters; our imagination draws from the depths of the common human psyche to supply all that we need.

This story is a good example to use in stressing the importance of the students' close reading of a text. It's easy for readers to miss, in the last paragraph, the sentence "My heart grew sick — on account of the dampness of the catacombs." Yet upon this sentence rests the interpretation of Montresor's character: Can we excuse his action on grounds of insanity? Was he insane at the time he buried Fortunato alive, or did he go insane in the half century during which, he tells us, his crime has remained undetected? If the reader has not paid careful attention to that sentence, he or she will have missed an essential detail in understanding the story.

The book *Mysterious New England,* edited by A. N. Stevens (1971), suggests that Poe first heard the anecdote upon which he might have based this story when he was a private in the army in 1827. Supposedly, only ten years before, a popular young lieutenant named Robert F. Massie had also been stationed at Fort Independence in Boston Harbor; when Poe was serving there, he saw a gravestone erected to the memory of one Lieutenant Massie, who had been unfairly killed in a duel by a bully named Captain Green.

> Feeling against Captain Green ran high for many weeks, and then suddenly he vanished. Years went by without a sign of him, and Green was written off the army records as a deserter.
>
> According to the story that Poe finally gathered together, Captain Green had been so detested by his fellow officers that they decided to take a terrible revenge on him for Massie's death.
>
> Visiting Captain Green one moonless night, they pretended to be friendly and plied him with wine until he was helplessly intoxicated. Then, carrying the captain down to one of the ancient dungeons, the officers forced his body through a tiny opening that led into the subterranean casemate. His captors began to shackle him to the floor, using the heavy iron handcuffs and footcuffs fastened into the stone. Then they sealed the captain up alive inside the windowless casemate, using bricks and mortar that they had hidden close at hand.
>
> Captain Green shrieked in terror and begged for mercy, but his cries fell on deaf ears. The last brick was finally inserted, mortar applied, and the room closed off, the officers believed, forever. Captain Green undoubtedly died a horrible death within a few days.

> WILLIAM E. SHEIDLEY

Questions for Discussion

1. How does Poe motivate the behavior of Montresor? Does the story provide any hints as to the "thousand injuries" he has suffered? Are any hints necessary?
2. Why is the setting of the story appropriate?
3. What does Montresor's treatment of his house servants tell us about his knowledge of human psychology, and how does it prepare us for his treatment of Fortunato?
4. How does Poe increase the elements of suspense as Fortunato is gradually walled into the catacombs?

Topics for Writing

1. Montresor doesn't tell his story until a half century after the actual event. Analyze how Poe adapts the flashback technique to affect the reader of "The Cask of Amontillado."
2. Explicate the passage in the story in which Montresor entices Fortunato into the crypt.

Related Commentary

Edgar Allan Poe, The Importance of the Single Effect in a Prose Tale, p. 907.

Suggested Readings

See page 128.

EDGAR ALLAN POE

The Tell-Tale Heart (p. 705)

"The Tell-Tale Heart" is a story about what has been called "the demonic self" — a person who feels a compulsion to commit a gratuitous act of evil. Poe wrote explicitly about what he calls this "spirit of perverseness" in his story "The Black Cat," published in 1843, two years before "The Tell-Tale Heart":

> Of this spirit [of perverseness] philosophy takes no account. Yet I am not more sure that my soul lives, than I am that perverseness is one of the primitive impulses of the human heart — one of the indivisible primary faculties, or sentiments, which give direction to the character of Man. Who has not, a hundred times, found himself committing a vile or a silly action, for no other reason than because he knows he should not? Have we not a perpetual inclination, in the teeth of our best judgment, to violate that which is Law, merely because we understand it to be such?

According to the critic Eric W. Carlson, "The Tell-Tale Heart" was one of Poe's favorite stories. In addition to dramatizing the "spirit of perverseness" in his narrative, Poe combines other elements of the gothic tale (the evil eye, the curse), the psychorealistic (the narrator's paranoia), the dramatic (concentrated intensity of tone, gradually heightened series of dramatic events), and the moral (the compulsion to confess).

Questions for Discussion

1. How would you describe the narrator of the story? How does your description compare or contrast with what he would like to have you believe about him?

2. What disease is the narrator referring to in the first paragraph?
3. What caused the narrator to murder the old man? Was his reason valid?
4. What narrative devices does Poe use to heighten the suspense of the tale? Give examples.
5. Poe believed in the existence of the "spirit of perverseness" within every man. How is this revealed in the story?
6. Do you feel the confession at the end of the tale is necessary? Why? What is Poe's purpose in presenting this confession?

Topics for Writing

1. Discuss the significance of the light and dark imagery in "The Tell-Tale Heart."
2. Consider the effect of premeditation in "The Tell-Tale Heart."
3. Discuss the use of sight and sound as dramatic devices in "The Tell-Tale Heart."
4. Write an essay analyzing the dichotomy between the narrator's view of himself and our view of him in "The Tell-Tale Heart."
5. Explore reality versus illusion in "The Tell-Tale Heart."
6. **RESPONDING CREATIVELY** Rewrite the story from the point of view of the police officers or from the point of view of the old man.
7. **RESPONDING CREATIVELY** Consider the events that might result from the action of this story, and write a sequel presenting these developments.

Related Commentary

See page 127.

Suggested Readings

Adler, Jacob H. "Are There Flaws in 'The Cask of Amontillado'?" *Notes and Queries* 199 (1954): 32–34.
Buranelli, Vincent. *Edgar Allan Poe.* 2nd ed. Boston: G. K. Hall, 1977.
Baudelaire, Charles P. *Baudelaire on Poe: Critical Papers.* University Park: Pennsylvania State UP, 1952.
Carlson, Eric W., ed. *Critical Essays on Edgar Allan Poe.* Boston: G. K. Hall, 1987.
Carlson, Eric W. *Introduction to Poe: A Thematic Reader.* Glenville, IL: Scott, 1967.
Dillon, John M. *Edgar Allan Poe.* Brooklyn, NY: Haskell, 1974.
Fletcher, Richard M. *The Stylistic Development of Edgar Allan Poe.* New York: Mouton, 1974.
Gargano, J. W. "'The Cask of Amontillado': A Masquerade of Motive and Identity." *Studies in Short Fiction* 4 (1967): 119–26.
———. *The Masquerade Vision in Poe's Short Stories.* Baltimore: Enoch Pratt, 1977.
Hammond, J. R. *An Edgar Allan Poe Companion: A Guide to Short Stories, Romances, and Essays.* Savage: B and N Imports, 1981.
Knapp, Bettina L. *Edgar Allan Poe.* New York: Ungar, 1984.
Levin, Harry. *The Power of Blackness: Hawthorne, Poe, Melville.* Columbus: Ohio UP, 1980.

Mabbott, Thomas Olivle, ed. *Collected Works of Edgar Allan Poe.* Cambridge, MA: Harvard UP, 1978.

May, Charles E., ed. *Edgar Allan Poe: A Study of Short Fiction.* Boston: Twayne, 1990.

Muller, John P., and William J. Richardson, eds. *The Purloined Poe: Lacan, Derrida, and Psychoanalytic Reading.* Baltimore: Johns Hopkins UP, 1988.

Pitcher, E. W. "Physiognomical Meaning of Poe's 'The Tell-Tale Heart.' " *Studies in Short Fiction* 16 (1979): 231–33.

Robinson, E. A. "Poe's 'The Tell-Tale Heart.' " *Nineteenth Century Fiction* 19 (1965): 369–78.

Symons, Julian, ed. *Selected Tales.* New York: Oxford UP, 1980.

Tucker, B. D. "Tell-Tale Heart and the Evil Eye." *Southern Literary Journal* 13 (1981): 92–98.

KATHERINE ANNE PORTER

He (p. 710)

"He" was included in Porter's collection *Flowering Judas,* published in 1930. Like the photographs from the 1930s taken in the American South by Dorothea Lange and Walker Evans for the Works Progress Administration, which can serve as eloquent illustrations of the lives of poor families, it describes the poverty-stricken lives of many rural Americans like the Whipple family in Porter's story.

The Whipples' struggle to feed and clothe their family is made more difficult by the fact that their second son is mentally defective. (They have two normal children, their daughter Emly and their son Adna.) This boy doesn't have a name. He is referred to as "He" or "Him" or "His," always with a capital "H," signifying His special status in the family. The extraordinary quality of the story is the result of the way it is told. The third-person-singular narration is channeled through the point of view and characteristic language of Mrs. Whipple, who is her son's primary caretaker and who is deeply emotionally involved in his welfare. "His" interior life is blocked to us, because he never talks, but Mrs. Whipple tells us everything she thinks and feels and elicits comments from family and neighbors around her; we participate in the tragedy of the boy's life through her responses.

With such a subject, it would be extremely easy for Porter's story to slip into sentimentality given the reader's direct access to Mrs. Whipple's feelings. What makes the story effective is Porter's unflinching honesty in dramatizing the social and economic background of the characters and her brilliant use of Mrs. Whipple's language, both of which keep the narrative solidly positioned on the hard nub of truth. (A generation later Flannery O'Connor took Porter's work as a model for her use of colloquial speech rhythms and dialogue in her short fiction.)

For example, the Whipples' neighbors say behind their backs that it would be much better for the family if the second son died ("'A Lord's pure mercy if He should die,' they said"), yet to their faces "everybody said, 'He's not so bad off. He'll be all right yet. Look how He grows!'"

Mrs. Whipple does the best she can to love and protect her second son. Taking care of Him becomes a way to repel the bad luck visited upon the family.

His well-being is a sign that she and the family will survive this bad luck so long as He keeps going. She also believes that no matter how badly things go for the family, her good care of her second son is a way to show the world that the Whipples may be whipped, but not beaten. The neighbors who speak ill of her boy really are judging her entire family. As Mrs. Whipple says, "I get sick of people coming around saying things all the time."

Even a visit from her brother's family, whom she loves, isn't a happy occasion. Mr. Whipple resents the fact that they must kill a suckling pig for them in order to put on the appearance of doing well. He ruins his wife's pleasure in recollecting the visit by suggesting that the guests were critical of the family: "Who knows what they had in their minds all along?" Mrs. Whipple's response is to defend the way she has cared for her second son: "They can't say He wasn't dressed every lick as good as Adna — oh, honest, sometimes I wish I was dead!"

The family's fortunes continue to slide during the development of the story. Mrs. Whipple says, "We're losing our hold. Why can't we do like other people and watch for our best chances? They'll be calling us poor white trash next." Adna and Emly leave home to take jobs to earn much-needed money, and he gets sick. Even after four months' worth of medical bills, Mrs. Whipple manages to remain optimistic. Her refusal to accept the reality of the situation continues nearly until the end, when He begins to cry as the wagon leaves the Whipple residence on the way to the County Home. When He breaks down, she begins to cry too, and Porter lets us share her internal anguish as she relinquishes her boy: "There was nothing she could do to make up to Him for His life. Oh, what a mortal pity He was ever born."

Questions for Discussion

1. What is Mr. Whipple's educational background? Mrs. Whipple's? How much better educated will Emly and Adna be?
2. What opportunities do the Whipples have to make money and prosper?
3. Why does Mrs. Whipple take her brothr's visit so seriously? Why didn't Mr. Whipple want to kill the suckling pig?
4. Why does Mrs. Whipple box His ears? How does she feel afterwards?
5. What is the relationship between Mr. and Mrs. Whipple?
6. Why is Mrs. Whipple so nervous when she sees Him leading the bull? Is this a foreshadowing of His sickness later in the story?

Topics for Writing

1. Describe Mrs. Whipple's personality. Is she a good or an overprotective mother?
2. Analyze how Porter dramatizes the economic hardship of the Whipple family in "He" and makes it an integral part of the story.

Suggested Readings

Bayley, Isabel. *Letters of Katherine Anne Porter.* New York: Atlantic Monthly P, 1990.
Bruccoli, Matthew J., ed. *Understanding Katherine Anne Porter.* Columbia: U of South Carolina P, 1988.

Demouy, Jane Krause. *Katherine Anne Porter's Women: The Eye of Her Fiction.* Austin: U of Texas P, 1983.

Hendrick, Willene, and George Hendrick. *Katherine Anne Porter.* Boston: Twayne, 1988.

Mooney, Harry J. *The Fiction and Criticism of Katherine Anne Porter.* Rev. ed. Pittsburgh: U of Pittsburgh P, 1990.

Nance, William L. *Katherine Anne Porter and the Art of Rejection.* Chapel Hill: U of North Carolina P, 1964.

Plimpton, George, ed. *Women Writers at Work: The* Paris Review *Interviews.* New York: Penguin, 1989.

Porter, Katherine Anne. *The Collected Essays and Occasional Writings.* New York: Harcourt Brace, 1970.

———. *Flowering Judas.* New York: Harcourt Brace, 1930, 1958.

Stout, Janis P. *Strategies of Reticence: Silence and Meaning in the Works of Jane Austen, Willa Cather, Katherine Anne Porter, and Joan Didion.* Charlottesville: UP of Virginia, 1990.

Tanner, James T. F. *The Texas Legacy of Katherine Anne Porter.* Denton: U of North Texas P, 1990.

Unrue, Darlene H. *Truth and Vision in Katherine Anne Porter's Fiction.* Athens: U of Georgia P, 1985.

ALIFA RIFAAT

Distant View of a Minaret (p. 718)

The first two-thirds of this short story describe an older married couple in bed having sex together in the morning. The story is told in the third person, from the wife's point of view. During the twenty or so years of their marriage, she has become accustomed to her husband's indifference to her own sexual pleasure. The one time she insisted that he continue after his own orgasm, he had pushed her away, protesting "Are you mad, woman? Do you want to kill me?"

The wife sublimates her sexual frustration into her Muslim devotions, praying several times each day and receiving an almost sensual pleasure from her prayers. "Each prayer had for her a distinct quality, just as different foods had their own flavours." This religious sublimation and her devotion to her teenage son give her the emotional gratification she finds in her marriage, along with her sense that she has served her husband's needs without rebelling from her role as a dutiful wife.

The husband's words echo ironically at the end of the story, when the wife returns to the bedroom with his morning coffee and finds that he has suffered a fatal heart attack. She tells her son to go for a doctor, and while she waits for them to return, she calmly pours herself a cup of hot coffee. Now that her years of service to her unappreciative husband are over, she can finally begin to live for herself.

Questions for Discussion

1. Why does Rifaat take such pains in telling us about the husband's sex life in the first part of the story — that he consciously chose not to give his wife pleasure and that he went to prostitutes?
2. What does the wife think about as she submits to her husband's embrace? What does this tell you about her character?
3. Is the wife a sympathetic or unsympathetic character? Could she be a practicing Christian, or is her adherence to the Muslim faith important in this story?
4. What role does the setting play in the story? How does the location of the apartment where the family lives in Cairo add to our understanding of the wife's apparently unlimited store of patience?

Topic for Writing

1. Compare and contrast Rifaat's story with Chopin's "Story of an Hour."

LESLIE MARMON SILKO

Yellow Woman (p. 722)

This story is told in the first person and presented episodically in several sections. It takes place over two days, beginning the morning Yellow Woman wakes up beside the river with Silva, the stranger she has spent the night with. The story ends at sundown the next day, when she returns to her family in the Pueblo village.

"Yellow Woman" is built on different traditions from those in the cultural background of most American students. Silko writes fiction that preserves her cultural heritage by re-creating its customs and values in stories that dramatize emotional conflicts of interest to modern readers.

As Yellow Woman narrates the story of her abduction and return to her family, the reader comes to share her mood and her interpretation of what has happened. As a girl she was fascinated by the stories her grandfather told her about Silva, the mysterious kachina spirit who kidnaps married women from the tribe, then returns them after he has kept them as his wives. These stories were probably similar to the imaginary tales passed down in an oral tradition whose origins are lost to contemporary American folklorists. Silko has created their modern equivalent, her version of how they might be reenacted in today's world. The overweight, white Arizona rancher is familiar to us, as is the Jell-O being prepared for supper, and we have no difficulty imagining the gunnysacks full of freshly slaughtered meat bouncing on the back of Yellow Woman's horse.

The dreamlike atmosphere Silko creates in "Yellow Woman" makes such realistic details protrude sharply from the soft-focus narrative. Yellow Woman doesn't think clearly. She seems bewitched by the myths her grandfather told her, and her adventure following the man she calls Silva holds her enthralled. At the end she says, "I thought about Silva, and I felt sad at leaving him; still, there was something strange about him, and I tried to figure it out all the way back home." We are not told what — if anything — she does figure out.

Instead, action takes the place of thought in the story. Yellow Woman looks at the place on the riverbank where she met Silva and tells herself that "he will come back sometime and be waiting again by the river." Action moves so swiftly that we follow Yellow Woman as obediently as she follows her abductor, mesmerized by the audacity of what is happening. There is no menace in Silva, no danger or malice in his rape of Yellow Woman. The bullets in his rifle are for the white rancher who realizes he has been killing other men's cattle, not for Yellow Woman — or for us.

Questions for Discussion

1. Why is Yellow Woman so eager to believe that she and Silva are acting out the stories her grandfather told her?
2. How does Silko structure the opening paragraphs of the story to help the reader suspend disbelief and enter the dreamlike atmosphere of Yellow Woman's perceptions?
3. Why does Silko tell the story through the woman's point of view? Describe the Pueblo Indian woman we know as Yellow Woman. Is she happy at home with her mother, grandmother, husband, and baby? Why is Yellow Woman's father absent from the story?
4. Are there any limitations to Silko's choice to tell the story through Yellow Woman's point of view? Explain.
5. Why doesn't the narrator escape from Silva when she discovers him asleep by the river as the story opens? What makes her decide to return home the next day?

Topics for Writing

1. **RESPONDING CREATIVELY**   Tell the story through a third-person omniscient narration.
2. Compare "Yellow Woman" with an Indian folktale about the kachina spirit who kidnapped married women.
3. **CONNECTIONS**   Compare Silko's "Yellow Woman" and Oates's "Where Are You Going, Where Have You Been?" as rape narratives.

Related Commentary

Leslie Marmon Silko, Language and Literature from a Pueblo Indian Perspective, p. 910.

Suggested Readings

Allen, Paula Gunn. *The Sacred Hoop: Recovering the Feminine in American Indian Traditions.* Boston: Beacon, 1986.

————, ed. *Spider Woman's Granddaughters: Traditional Tales and Contemporary Writing by Native American Women*. Boston: Beacon, 1989.

Graulich, Melody, ed. *"Yellow Woman."* Women, Text and Contexts Series. New Brunswick, NJ: Rutgers UP, 1993.

Hoilman, Dennis. "The Ethnic Imagination: A Case History." *Canadian Journal of Native Studies* 5.2 (1985): 167–75.

Nelson, Robert M. *Place and Vision: The Function of Landscape in Native American Fiction*. New York: P. Lang, 1993.

Sands, Kathleen Mullen. "Indian Women's Personal Narrative: Voices Past and Present." *American Women's Autobiography: Fea(s)ts of Memory*. Ed. Margo Culley. Madison: U of Wisconsin P, 1992.

Silko, Leslie Marmon. *Almanac of the Dead*. New York: Simon, 1991.

AMY TAN

Two Kinds (p. 731)

"Two Kinds," which was first published in the February 1989 issue of *The Atlantic Monthly*, is a story from Amy Tan's best-selling book *The Joy Luck Club*. It is a skillfully written story that will probably pose no difficulty for most students; plot, characters, setting, and theme are immediately clear. The narrator states what she's "learned" from her experience in her final paragraph: She has come to realize that "Pleading Child" and "Perfectly Contented" are "two halves of the same song."

Looking back to her childhood, the narrator appears to be "perfectly contented" with her memories. Her interpretation of her relationship with her mother is presented in a calm, even self-satisfied way. After her mother's death, she tunes the piano left to her in her parents' apartment. "I played a few bars [of the piano piece by Robert Schumann], surprised at how easily the notes came back to me." The painful memory of her fiasco as a piano student has dissipated. Now she is her own audience, and she is pleased with what she hears. There is no real emotional stress in "Two Kinds"; the girl has had a comfortable life. She has survived her mother and can dispose of her possessions as she likes. She is at peace with her past, fulfilling her mother's prophecy that "you can be best anything."

The mother earned her right to look on the bright side of life by surviving tremendous losses when she left China. Her desire to turn her daughter into a "Chinese Shirley Temple" is understandable but unfortunate, since it places a tremendous psychological burden on the child. A discussion about this story might center on parents' supporting children versus "pushing" them to succeed in tasks beyond their abilities or ambitions.

Still, the narrator doesn't appear to have suffered unduly from her mother's ambitions for her. By her own account she was more than a match for her mother in the contest of wills on the piano bench. After her wretched performance at the recital, the daughter refuses to practice anymore. Her mother shouts, "Only two kinds of daughters. . . . Those who are obedient and those who follow their own mind! Only one kind of daughter can live in this house. Obedient daughter!" The girl answers by saying the unspeakable: "I wish I'd never been born! I wish I were dead! Like [the mother's twin baby girls lost in China]." This ends the conflict, but the narrator goes on to tell us that she was unrelenting in victory: "In the years that followed, I failed her many times, each time asserting my will, my right to fall short of expectations. I didn't get straight *As*. I didn't become class president. I didn't get into Stanford. I dropped out of college." She tells us that only after her mother's death can she begin to see things in perspective, when she is free to create her version of the past.

Since most students in class will be of the age when they are also asserting their will against parents in a struggle to take control of their lives, they will probably sympathize with Tan's narrator and accept her judgments uncritically. Will any reader take the mother's side?

Questions for Discussion

1. Why is the setting of this story important? What do you learn from it about the experience of Asian immigrants in their first years in the United States?
2. What advantages are offered to the child? What disadvantages?
3. How typical is Tan's story of the mother-daughter conflict? Explain.
4. Explain the meaning of the last paragraph of the story.

Topics for Writing

1. **CONNECTIONS** Compare and contrast the theme of initiation in Ellison's "Battle Royal" and Tan's "Two Kinds."
2. **CONNECTIONS** Analyze the use of dialect in Wright's "The Man Who Was Almost a Man" and Tan's "Two Kinds."
3. **CONNECTIONS** Compare and contrast the mother in Tan's "Two Kinds" with Olga, the protagonist of Chekhov's "The Darling."

Related Commentary

Amy Tan, In the Canon, for All the Wrong Reasons, p. 916.

Suggested Readings

Tan, Amy. *The Joy Luck Club.* New York: Ballantine, 1989.
———. "The Language of Discretion." *The State of the Language.* Ed. Christopher Ricks. Berkeley: U of California P, 1990.

Leo Tolstoy

The Death of Ivan Ilych (p. 741)

No one who comes to "The Death of Ivan Ilych" from a direction other than that of *War and Peace* and *Anna Karenina* is likely to share the opinion of some Tolstoy scholars that it is parable-thin in its evocation of life, providing only a transparent surface of detail through which Tolstoy's allegorical intentions are exposed. The story is studded with brilliantly realistic representations of experiences that the reader encounters with a twinge of sometimes embarrassed recognition — Peter Ivanovich's struggle with the pouffe, for example. But it is nonetheless a product of the period following Tolstoy's religious crisis and a

story written by one whose explicit theory of art rested on a utilitarian moral didacticism.

The story's effectiveness depends on Tolstoy's avoiding, until the last possible moment, preaching the sermon that, as the headnote suggests, he eventually means to preach. The opening section places us in the shoes of Peter Ivanovich, causing us to sympathize with the desire to look away from death, at the same time that it subjects that desire to a devastating satiric attack. Then, by returning to a long chronological survey of Ivan Ilych's life, Tolstoy forces us to do exactly the opposite of what Peter Ivanovich does: to confront death and its meaning in an extended and excruciatingly matter-of-fact account. What we see is not a life, but a death — or a life viewed as death. For Ivan Ilych's life, as he eventually comes to realize, is a slow but accelerating process of dying. The narration, however, decelerates, so that the reader may expect it to be nearly over around section VI, whereas in fact there are six more (albeit shorter) sections to come, containing a series of painful revelations that burst through the screen Ivan Ilych has built up to hide himself from reality.

Tolstoy tortures the reader just as Ivan Ilych is tortured, so that the precept finally advanced by the story arrives as the answer to the reader's fervent need. Ivan Ilych is not a particularly bad man; and — bad or good — all men, as Gerasim remarks, come to the same spot. Tolstoy makes this recognition virtually intolerable by his vivid rendering of Ivan Ilych's suffering. Then he offers a way out by proposing that one simple motion of the soul toward charity can release the sufferer from his mortal anguish. Tolstoy prepares us for this revelation by stressing the relief Ivan Ilych finds in the kindness of Gerasim, whose health, strength, and repose are bound up with his simple acceptance of sickness and death as necessary parts of life. Some critics have claimed that Tolstoy's art fails to encompass the illumination Ivan Ilych receives at the end, which rests on doctrines extrinsic to the text; but at least it can be said that he avoids sentimental piety by providing for an ironic interpretation when he caps Ivan Ilych's triumphant assertion "Death is finished. . . . It is no more!" with the paradoxical conclusion "He drew in a breath, stopped in the midst of a sigh, stretched out, and died."

The preoccupations and activities of Ivan Ilych and his peers during Ilych's lifetime in the society portrayed by Tolstoy contrast sharply with those of the unselfish peasant Gerasim. They are directed to no constructive end, serving only to gratify the ego with a sense of power and to hide the fear of death under a surface awareness of pleasure and propriety. Ivan Ilych is never more content than when manipulating the inert objects which are so plentiful in the story — as when decorating his new house — and he does his best to relate to people as he relates to things, insulating himself from true human contact. After he has received his death blow from the quite inert knob of a window frame, however, Ivan Ilych experiences a similar dehumanizing treatment by the doctors, his wife, and his friends, none of whom can bear to face the implications of his evident mortality. As his sickness steadily reduces him to a state of infantile dependency, Ilych comes to recognize first his own powerlessness and then the error in his strategy of living. Finally, as the coffin-womb he has built for himself falls away and he is reborn into the light of spiritual understanding, he sees the fundamental truth he has worked so hard to deny: The feelings of others are as real as his own. At this moment, moved by pity for his wife and son, he at last finds something worthwhile to do; and, in doing it, he attains the sense of ease and "rightness" that has previously eluded him. That the single positive act of Ivan Ilych's life is to die may be seen as either a grim irony or an exciting revelation, depending on the perspective from which the reader views it. But either way the conclusion of the story embodies the kernel of Tolstoy's social theme. As Edward Wasiolek puts it, "Death for Tolstoy now, as the supremely shared experience, is the model of all solidarity, and only the profound consciousness of its significance can bring one to the communion of true brotherhood."

WILLIAM E. SHEIDLEY

Questions for Discussion

1. How does the authorial voice qualify our view of Ivan Ilych's survivors' reactions to his death in section I?
2. Evaluate Peter Ivanovich's view of Ivan Ilych's son when he meets him near the end of section I.
3. Comment on the implications of Ivan Ilych's hanging a medallion bearing the motto *respice finem* (consider your end) on his watch chain.
4. What is wrong with Ivan Ilych's marriage? with his work? with his ambitions?
5. By examining the authorial comments in sections III and IV, define the attitude toward Ivan Ilych that Tolstoy asks the reader to share. Does this attitude change?
6. Consider the opening sentence of section VI. Is this section a low point in the story? If so, what kind of rise ensues?
7. Why does Ivan Ilych find relief in having his legs supported by Gerasim?
8. What is the effect of the shift to the present tense about one-third of the way through section VIII?
9. In section IX, Ivan Ilych complains to God in language similar to that of Job. Compare and contrast their plights.
10. What is the meaning of Ivan Ilych's reversion to childhood shortly before his death?
11. How might Ivan Ilych's dream of the black sack be interpreted?

Topics for Writing

1. Stop after reading section I and write a paragraph or two on the theme and tone of the story as you understand them so far. After reading the rest of the

story, write a paragraph evaluating your original response. Write an essay examining the opening section as a story in itself, but one fully understood only after reading sections II–XII.

2.   Consider bridge as an epitome of the life Ivan Ilych and his friends try to live.

3.   Discuss Tolstoy's use of symbolic, descriptive details in "The Death of Ivan Ilych."

4.   Using "The Death of Ivan Ilych" as the basis of your knowledge of society, write a manifesto calling for revolution or reform.

5.   **RESPONDING CREATIVELY**   Write a sermon, using the demise of Ivan Ilych Golovin as your occasion.

Related Commentary

Leo Tolstoy, Chekhov's Intent in "The Darling," p. 919.

Suggested Readings

Christian, R. F. *Tolstoy: A Critical Introduction.* Cambridge: Cambridge UP, 1969. 236–38.

Greenwood, E. B. *Tolstoy: The Comprehensive Vision.* New York: St. Martin's, 1975. 118–23.

Simmons, Ernest J. *Introduction to Tolstoy's Writings.* Chicago: U of Chicago P, 1968. Esp. 148–50.

Wasiolek, Edward. *Tolstoy's Major Fiction.* Chicago: U of Chicago P, 1978. Esp. 165–79.

JOHN UPDIKE

A & P (p. 783)

Although Updike was a precociously successful writer who spent his apprenticeship living in New York City and writing for *The New Yorker* magazine, much of the strength of his writing stems from his ability to take the reader back to the atmosphere of the small town where he grew up. "A & P" showcases this ability. This story about a nineteen year old at a checkout counter in an A & P supermarket skillfully sustains the point of view of a teenage boy from a small-town working-class family.

The incident the story describes is slight. What gives "A & P" its substance is the voice of the narrator. He is obviously what the author thinks of as an ordinary teenager, impatient with old people, not interested in his job, and deeply aroused by girls. The longest descriptive passage — almost a third of the story itself — dwells on the body of one of the girls; as the story's slight action unfolds, the bodies of that girl and one of her friends are mentioned several times again. The narrator's adolescent desire and adoration are amusingly played off his clumsy bravado and the idiom of sexist stereotypes he is trying to master. "You never know for sure how girls' minds work (do you really think it's a mind in there or just a little buzz like a bee in a glass jar?)." His view of adult women is no less callow: "We're right in the middle of town, and the women generally put on a shirt or shorts or something before they get out of the car into the street. And anyway these are usually women with six children and varicose veins mapping their legs and nobody, including them, could care less."

It is probably true that when the story was written, in the late 1950s, its attitudes were not considered unusual. Today we have to ask ourselves whether the deplorable sexism is redeemed by the artfulness of the story, the technique Updike brings to constructing his narrator's voice.

Questions for Discussion

1. What does the language of the story tell us about the narrator's social background?
2. Are there any details in the story that place it in a specific part of the United States, or could it be happening anywhere within a few miles of a beach? Explain.
3. Is the boy's discomfort with older people limited to women, or is he also uncomfortable with men? Is there anyone in the store he is comfortable with? Explain.
4. Do you think Updike shares the narrator's attitudes?

Topics for Writing

1. Analyze the strengths and the limitations of the first-person narrative in "A & P."
2. **CONNECTIONS** Consider "acting like a man": the bag boy in Updike's "A & P" and Dave in Wright's "The Man Who Was Almost a Man."
3. **CONNECTIONS** Compare and contrast adolescent narrators in Updike's "A & P" and Joyce's "Araby."

Related Commentary

John Updike, Kafka and "The Metamorphosis," p. 927.

Suggested Readings

Cantor, Jay. "On Giving Birth to One's Own Mother." *TriQuarterly* 75 (Spring–Summer 1989): 78–91.
Detweiler, Robert. *John Updike.* Rev. ed. Boston: G. K. Hall, 1987.
Fleischauer, John F. "John Updike's Prose Style: Definition at the Periphery of Meaning." *Critique: Studies in Contemporary Fiction* 30.4 (Summer 1989): 277–90.
Greiner, Donald J. *The Other Updike: Poems, Short Stories, Prose, Play.* Columbus: Ohio UP, 1981.
Luscher, Robert M. "John Updike's Olinger Stories: New Light among the Shadows." *Journal of the Short Story in English* 11 (Autumn 1988): 99–117.

Lyons, E. "John Updike: The Beginning and the End." *Critique* 14.2 (1972): 44–59.

Newman, Judie. *John Updike*. New York: St. Martin's, 1988.

Samuels, C. T. "Art of Fiction: John Updike." *Paris Review* 12 (1968): 84–117.

Seib, P. "Lovely Way through Life: An Interview with John Updike." *Southwest Review* 66 (1981): 341–50.

Taylor, Charles C. *John Updike: A Bibliography*. Ann Arbor, MI: Books Demand UMI, 1989.

Thorburn, David, and Howard Eiland. *John Updike: A Collection of Critical Essays*. New York: Prentice-Hall, 1979.

Updike, John. *Hugging the Shore*. New York: Random House, 1983.

———. *Picked-Up Pieces*. New York: Knopf, 1976.

———. *Too Far to Go*. New York: Ballantine, 1979.

Wilhelm, Albert E. "Rebecca Cune: Updike's Wedge Between the Maples." *Notes on Modern American Literature* 7.2 (Fall 1983): Item 9.

———. "The Trail-of-Bread-Crumbs Motif in Updike's Maples Stories." *Studies in Short Fiction* 25.1 (Winter 1988): 71–73.

ALICE WALKER

Everyday Use (p. 789)

In this very accessible but powerful story, Alice Walker deals with issues that college readers should find thought-provoking and relevant to their lives. It is a story about family, heritage, and personal pride, and the way that one young woman's search for identity causes her to devalue the very aspects of her past that are most important. While searching for objects and symbols to enshrine as reflections of her zealous racial pride, Dee overlooks the human beings whose strength and courage she should really be interested in preserving and emulating.

Dee has always been seen, by herself and others, as different from her family and the people around her. She is smart, ambitious, wanting more out of life than her family seems to have. Of course, there is nothing wrong in any of this, and as many young people do, Dee moves away to find herself and a better life. The irony arises after she finds this new life. Then, her need to feel a connection to a past, a people, and a history asserts itself, and Dee searches for her identity in a socially trendy fashion, reaching back to African tradition in hairstyle, clothing, and name, "Wangero." The problem is that in "reaching back" to Africa, she reaches right past her own relatives, whose lives she considers common, ignorant, and unimportant.

This is illustrated most powerfully by her rejection of her birth name, which, she tells her mother contemptuously, is a name "after the people who oppress me." Her mother, puzzled, reminds her that she was named after her aunt, who was named after her mother, who was named after her mother . . . and reflects that the name could probably be traced back beyond the Civil War to slave days. You would think that a young woman who is so interested in preserving her "heritage" would show some interest in these women whose name she bears and whose lives of struggle and oppression she truly springs from, but Dee doesn't care at all. Dee is interested only in pieces of history that are aesthetically appealing and will enhance her life by making her (or her surroundings) look good. The stories of dead women, who lived (in Dee's view) in ignorance, poverty, and passive acceptance of oppression have no value for her.

Dee's shallowness and her superficial vision of family history are again displayed as we watch her select objects from her mother's house to take away as mementos. She takes the churn top and dasher, which her mother obviously still puts to practical use, without even asking permission, because she needs a centerpiece for a table. She places no value on the function of these objects or on another person's need for them, only on her own appreciation of their "artistic" qualities. Her mother allows her to have her way, but finally stands up to her and says no when she tries to take the handmade quilts. These quilts have been promised to Maggie, the rather pathetic younger sister who has always lived in Dee's shadow. Here, Mrs. Johnson's protective instincts are aroused, as she sees that Maggie will give in to Dee as she has always done unless her mother prevents it. She knows that Maggie is the one who will really value the quilts, putting them to "everyday use," as they were intended.

It is Maggie who is really in touch with her heritage, who has a "memory like an elephant" and who knows the family history because she knew and loved the people who created it. Maggie and her mother still live the same kind of life that their ancestors lived, in the same place, with the same kind of house, furniture, and food (which "Wangero" is so condescendingly "delighted" with). Dee, who is frenetically searching for objects that will make her feel connected to her roots, is smugly convinced that only she "understands her heritage." But, in reality, she doesn't understand anything about her family and in fact, has always looked down upon them all. Maggie is the one who deserves the family heirlooms, as she and her mother are the ones who really understand their meaning and value their creators.

Questions for Discussion

1. Describe the mother in this story. What kind of person is she? How does she seem to feel about Dee? about Maggie?
2. How did Dee relate to her family before she left home? What role did she assume for herself? Does this change after she leaves home?
3. How do you feel about Dee? Do you sympathize with her desire to "improve" herself and her family? Where do you think she goes wrong?
4. Discuss the relationship between Maggie and Dee.
5. Why has Dee assumed African dress, hairstyle, and name? How would you characterize the attitudes of her and her new husband/boyfriend toward their race? positive or negative? honest or simply "politically correct"?
6. Discuss Dee's mother's and sister's reactions to her new persona, "Wangero." Do you sympathize with them?
7. How would you describe the way that Dee reacts to the food and objects in her mother's house?
8. Why does Mrs. Johnson decide to stand up to Dee and not allow her to take the quilts at the end of the story?
9. Why do you think Maggie is so content at the end?

Topics for Writing

1. Discuss Dee's final comment to her mother that she (the mother) "doesn't understand" her heritage.
2. **RESPONDING CREATIVELY**   Argue with Mrs. Johnson, and try to convince her that Dee/Wangero deserves the quilts.
3. Discuss the positive and negative aspects of Wangero's and Hakim-a-barber's search for identity.

Related Commentaries

Cheryl B. Torsney, "Everyday Use": My Sojourn at Parchman Farm, p. 922.
Alice Walker, "Zora Neale Hurston: A Cautionary Tale and a Partisan View," p. 930.

Suggested Readings

Banks, Erma Davis, and Keith Byerman. Alice Walker: *An Annotated Bibliography 1968–1986.* New York: Garland, 1989.
Bell, Roseann P., Bettye J. Parker, and Beverly Guy-Sheftall, eds. *Sturdy Black Bridges: Visions of Black Women in Literature.* New York: Anchor, 1979.
Bloom, Harold. *Alice Walker.* New York: Chelsea House, 1990.
Byerman, Keith, and Erma Banks. "Alice Walker: A Selected Bibliography, 1968–1988." *Callaloo: An Afro-American and African Journal of Arts and Letters* 12.2 (Spring 1989): 343–45.
Byrne, Mary Ellen. "Welty's 'A Worn Path' and Walker's 'Everyday Use': Companion Pieces." *Teaching English in a Two-Year College* 16.2 (May 1989): 129–33.
Cooke, Michael. *Afro-American Literature in the Twentieth Century: The Achievement of Intimacy.* New Haven: Yale UP, 1984.
Davis, T. M. "Alice Walker's Celebration of Self in Southern Generations." In *Women Writers of the Contemporary South.* Ed. Peggy Whitman Prenshaw. Jackson: UP of Mississippi, 1984. 83–94.
Erickson, P. "Cast Out Alone/To Heal/and Re-create/Ourselves: Family Based Identity in the Work of Alice Walker." *College Language Association Journal* 23 (1979): 71–94.
Evans, Mari, ed. *Black Women Writers (1950–1980): A Critical Evaluation.* New York: Anchor, 1984. 453–95.
Mariani, Philomena, ed. *Critical Fictions: The Politics of Imaginative Writing.* Seattle: Bay Press, 1991.
Petry, Alice Hall. "Alice Walker: The Achievement of the Short Fiction." *Modern Language Studies* 19.1 (Winter 1989): 12–27.
Stade, G. "Womanist Fiction and Male Characters." *Partisan Review* 52 (1985): 265–70.
Winchell, Donna Haisty. *Alice Walker.* Boston: Twayne, 1990.

David Foster Wallace

Incarnations of Burned Children (p. 796)

Wallace has written a true horror story, not one inhabited by witches and goblins, or by robotic, space-age monsters. His horror story describes what could happen to ordinary, flesh-and-blood people during a bad day on Earth. "Incarnations of Burned Children" appeared in his collection *Oblivion* (2004). As the critic Laura Miller stated in a Salon review, the book is "relentlessly trained on the things people do and say to bear the unbearable."

The mother and father of the toddler who just overturned the pot of boiling water on himself aren't given names in the story. They are just "Daddy" and "Mommy." The third-person narrator stands apart at some distance from the scene of the accident, observing it objectively, unable to help even though the reader feels like imploring him to phone 911 immediately so that medics can bring something to sooth the child or at least put him out of his agony.

Wallace's story is one long scream caught in a paragraph that goes on for three printed pages. The narrator focuses on the father's frantic efforts to help his young son and his furious anger at his wife for allowing the accident to happen, while she dissolves into hysterics, "talking singsong at the child's face." Music is the only sound possible to the father at this unbearable moment — "Break your heart inside and something will a child is the twangy song the Daddy hears again as if the radio's lady was almost there with him."

Questions for Discussion

1. In focusing on the father's actions, Wallace doesn't describe the accident that scalds the toddler. Why does he leave this out of the story?
2. In which way are Daddy and Mommy typical young parents? How does Wallace describe the differences in their characters as the story progresses?
3. The toddler survives the accident, but how does it affect him for the rest of his life?
4. Who besides the toddler is screaming in this story? Whose scream continues the longest?

Topics for Writing

1. This story is very long on feeling and very short in length. Write a poem based on the incident Wallace is describing.
2. Analyze the function of the door that Daddy is hanging at the beginning of the story. How does it help Wallace pace his narrative?

Eudora Welty

A Worn Path (p. 800)

Try not to force the Christian or mythological schemes of allegory the story supports until you encourage students to savor the beauty of the literal narration. Phoenix Jackson is an embodiment of love, faith, sacrifice, charity, self-renunciation, and triumph over death in herself, quite apart from the typological implications of her name or the allusions to the stations of the cross in her journey. Phoenix transcends her merely archetypal significance just as she transcends the stereotype of old black mammies on which she is built. Welty accomplishes this act of creation by entering fully into the consciousness of her character. There she discovers the little child who still lives within the old woman and causes her to dream of chocolate cake, dance with a scarecrow, and delight in a Christmas toy. Phoenix is right when she says, "I wasn't as old as I thought," but she does not merit the condescension of the hunter's exclamation, "I know you old colored people! Wouldn't miss going to town to see Santa Claus!" Even in her greatest discomfort, lying in the weeds, losing her memory, getting her shoes tied, "stealing" a nickel, or taking one as a handout, Phoenix retains her invincible dignity, an essential component of the single glimpse we receive of her triumphant homeward march, bearing aloft the bright symbol of life she has retrieved through her exertions.

In her comments on the story (included in Part Two, p. 932), Welty implies that the meaning of Phoenix's journey is that of any human exertion carried out in good faith despite the uncertainty of the outcome: "The path is the thing that matters." In keeping with this theme, Welty repeatedly shows Phoenix asserting life in the face of death. Her name itself, taken from the mythical bird that periodically immolates itself and rises reborn from its ashes, embodies the idea. (She even makes a noise like "a solitary little bird" in the first paragraph.) Phoenix makes her journey at the time of the death and rebirth of the year; her own skin color is like the sun bursting through darkness; she overcomes discouragement as she tops the hill; she extricates herself from a thorn bush (of which much may be made in a Christian allegorical interpretation); she passes "big dead trees" and a buzzard; she traverses a field of dead corn; she sees a "ghost" that turns out to be a dancing scarecrow; she is overcome by a "black dog" but rescued by a death-dealing hunter whose gun she faces down and whom she beats out of a shiny nickel; and she emerges from a deathlike trance in the doctor's office to return with the medicine her grandson needs to stay alive. Phoenix's strength lies in the purpose of her journey, and her spirit is contagious. The hunter, the woman who ties her shoes, and the doctor's attendant all perform acts of charity toward her, and lest the reader overlook the one word that lies at the heart of Welty's vision, the nurse says "Charity" while "making a check mark in a book."

Questions for Discussion

1.   Notice Phoenix's identification with "a solitary little bird." What other birds does she encounter on her journey? Explain their implications.
2.   What techniques does Welty use to suggest the laboriousness of Phoenix's trip?

3.   Before she crosses the creek, Phoenix says, "Now comes the trial." Does she pass it? How? To what extent is this event a microcosm of the whole story? Are there other microcosmic episodes?

4.   What effect do Phoenix's sequential reactions to the scarecrow, the abandoned cabins, and the spring have on the reader's view of her?

5.   What is your opinion of the hunter? What conclusion might be drawn from the fact that even though he kills birds and patronizes Phoenix, he helps her in a way he does not know?

6.   Interpret the passage that begins with Phoenix bending for the nickel and ends with her parting from the hunter.

7.   Describe Natchez as Phoenix perceives it. Is it a worthy culmination for her journey?

8.   In her comments reprinted in Part Two (p. 932), Welty remarks that Phoenix's victory comes when she sees the doctor's diploma "nailed up on the wall." In what sense is this moment the climax of the story? What is different about the ensuing action from the action that leads up to this moment? Are there any similarities?

9.   How does Phoenix describe her grandson? What is Welty's reason for using these terms?

10.   Explain the irony in the way the nurse records Phoenix's visit.

Topics for Writing

1.   Explain why many readers think that Phoenix Jackson's grandson is dead.

2.   Discuss the symbolism of birds in "A Worn Path."

3.   After your first reading of "A Worn Path," write a paragraph giving your opinion of Phoenix Jackson. Then study some symbolic interpretations of the story (such as those by Ardelino, Isaacs, and Keys, cited in Suggested Readings). Reread the story and write another assessment of the central character. Does she bear up under the freight of symbolic meaning the critics ask her to carry? Does her relation to these archetypes help to account for your original response?

4.   **RESPONDING CREATIVELY**   In Part Two, read Welty's account of how she came to write "A Worn Path." Following her example, write an account of what you imagine to be the day's experience of someone you catch a glimpse of who strikes your fancy. Use the intimate interior third-person limited-omniscient point of view that Welty employs for Phoenix Jackson.

Related Commentary

Eudora Welty, Is Phoenix Jackson's Grandson Really Dead?, p. 932.

Suggested Readings

Ardelino, Frank. "Life out of Death: Ancient Myth and Ritual in Welty's 'A Worn Path.' " *Notes on Mississippi Writers* 9 (1976): 1–9.

Bloom, Harold. *Eudora Welty.* New York: Chelsea House, 1986.

Desmond, John F. *A Still Moment: Essay on the Art of Eudora Welty.* Metuchen, NJ: Scarecrow, 1978.

Isaacs, Neil D. "Life for Phoenix." *Sewanee Review* 71 (1963): 75–81.

Keys, Marilynn. "'A Worn Path': The Way of Dispossession." *Studies in Short Fiction* 16 (1979): 354–56.

Kieft, Ruth M. *Eudora Welty.* Rev. ed. Boston: G. K. Hall, 1987.

MacNeil, Robert. *Eudora Welty: Seeing Black and White.* Westport, CT: Greenwood, 1990.

Phillips, Robert L., Jr. "A Structural Approach to Myth in the Fiction of Eudora Welty." *Eudora Welty: Critical Essays.* Ed. Peggy Whitman Prenshaw. Jackson: UP of Mississippi, 1979. 56–67, esp. 60.

Preenshaw, Peggy W., ed. *Eudora Welty: Thirteen Essays.* Jackson: UP of Mississippi, 1983.

Schmidt, Peter. *The Heart of the Story: Eudora Welty's Short Fiction.* Jackson: UP of Mississippi, 1991.

Turner, W. Craig, and Lee Harding, eds. *Critical Essays on Eudora Welty.* Boston: G. K. Hall, 1989.

Welty, Eudora. *The Eye of the Story.* New York: Vintage, 1990.

———. *One Writer's Beginnings.* New York: Warner, 1984.

TOBIAS WOLFF

Say Yes (p. 808)

Wolff narrows the scope of "Say Yes" to zoom in on a seemingly ordinary evening in the life of a long-married couple. The unremarkable sequence of events nevertheless leads to the erotically charged atmosphere of the final paragraph. Through the routine domestic gestures of washing and drying dishes, attending to a cut finger, taking out garbage, mopping the floor, and magazine reading, Wolff manages to reveal much about the inner lives of these people. Their namelessness emphasizes their ordinariness.

A conversation about interracial marriage sets the story in motion. Early in the dialogue, after suggesting that interracial marriage is a bad idea (without being able to fully articulate his reasons), the husband, observing his wife's expression, realizes he should back off from the subject but instead presses forward. These two know each other intimately — know how to needle, cajole, hurt, and apologize in subtle and not-so-subtle ways. in fact, this very intimacy — as with most marriages — carries negative as well as positive meanings. The husband's insistence that "a person from their culture and a person from our culture could never really know each other" reflects back on the couple's own relationship, leading the reader to question the extent to which *any* two people can know each other. Taking out the garbage and observing the night stars, the husband reflects on his marriage. Ashamed of fighting, he realizes the depth of the intimacy he shares with his wife as well as the transitoriness of their relationship with an intensity that affects him physically. This epiphany transforms at least his short-term behavior. Where normally he would "heave rocks" at the two dogs that topple his garbage, in this instance he lets them go unharmed.

Back in the house, he apologizes in the terms of the earlier discussion of interracial marriage, which now becomes a fantasy when he affirms that he'd marry her even if she were black. This openness to unexplored possibilities recharges the erotic life of the couple. When his wife enters the room in the darkness, "his heart pound[s] the way it had on their first night together," as if they were strangers.

Questions for Discussion

1. Why doesn't the husband "keep his mouth shut" when he knows he should?
2. What do you think the husband means when he says, "A person from their culture and a person from our culture could never really know each other"? Do you agree? What are some advantages and disadvantages of intracultural versus intercultural romantic relationships?
3. Why does the husband not "heave rocks" at the dogs that topple his garbage on this occasion, as he normally would?
4. In the final paragraph, why is the husband so excited? Does he experience a positive, erotic excitement, or does he realize that he doesn't know his wife as well as he thought he did?
5. Why is the question "Would you have loved me if I had been black?" so important to the wife?
6. To whom does the title apply? Who is expected to say yes?

Topic for Writing

1. Discuss the role of domestic details in advancing characterization in "Say Yes." What do these details reveal about this couple and their marriage?

Suggested Readings

Wolff, Tobias, *Back in the World: Stories.* Boston: Houghtn, 1985.
——. *The Barracks Thief and Other Stories.* New York: Bantam, 1984.
——. *In the Garden of the North American Martyrs: A Collection of Short Stories.* New York: Ecco, 1981.
Woodruff, Jay, ed. "In the Garden of the North American Martyrs." *A Piece of Work: Five Writers Discuss Their Revisions.* Iowa City: U of Iowa P, 1993.

RICHARD WRIGHT

The Man Who Was Almost a Man (p. 813)

Dave Saunders dislikes being laughed at, and his discomfort at becoming an object of amusement for accidentally shooting old Jenny, the mule, precipitates his final step into manhood. Although the anecdote around which Wright builds the story is comical enough, the reader probably should accede to Dave's wish to be taken seriously, for the fate that lies ahead of this young man as he rolls toward his unknown destination atop a boxcar with nothing in his pocket but an unloaded gun is likely to be grim.

At the same time, however, Dave's self-esteem and independence deserve respect. At the beginning of the story he dissociates himself from the field hands and fixes on his ambition to declare his manhood by owning a gun. Throughout the story the idea that *boys* do not have guns recurs, and Dave not only wants a gun but also chafes at being called "boy" by his parents and at being treated as a child. Just before he goes out to master the gun and hop a freight, Dave grumbles, "They treat me like a mule, n then they beat me." His resolution to escape his inferior status will involve not only leaving home but taking potshots at the facade of white society just as he wants to shoot at "Jim Hawkins' big white house" in order "to let him know Dave Saunders is a man." The question Wright leaves hanging for the reader as his story trails off into ellipses is whether Dave has killed the mule in himself or whether he himself, like Jenny, may become the victim of his own wild shots.

WILLIAM E. SHEIDLEY

Questions for Discussion

1. Explain the pun in the last sentence of the first paragraph.
2. Define our first impression of Dave. What reasons do we have to admire him? to laugh at him? to pity him?
3. What does it take to be a man in the world of the story? Is a gun enough? How does one get a gun?
4. What is ironic about the way Dave gets the money to buy his gun?
5. How is Dave treated by his father? Why does Ma say of the gun, "It be fer Pa"?
6. With the gun under his pillow, Dave feels "a sense of power. Could kill a man with a gun like this. Kill anybody, black or white." What does Dave still have to learn before he can be called a man? How does the story bring it home to him?
7. Explain what happens the first time Dave fires the gun. What does he do differently the next time?
8. Why does Wright describe the death of the mule in such detail?
9. Explain why being laughed at is so painful for Dave. What might enable him to join in and laugh at himself?
10. Comment on the possible implications of Dave's remark "They treat me like a mule, n then they beat me," both within the story and in a broader social and historical context. Does Dave's killing the mule have a symbolic significance?
11. Where might Dave be headed as he hops on the Illinois Central? What might he find at the end of his journey?
12. Why is the title not "The Boy Who Was Almost a Man"?

Topics for Writing

1. Examine the tone of Wright's story.
2. Discuss the treatment of Wright's social themes in "The Man Who Was Almost a Man." (See the story's headnote.)
3. **RESPONDING CREATIVELY** Write a sequel to Wright's story, another episode in the life of Dave Saunders — something that happens on the train ride or when he arrives in New Orleans or Chicago or wherever. Try to sus-

tain and develop as many themes and motives already present in Wright's story as you can, but make the material your own by imagining what you think happens, not necessarily what you guess Wright would have written. Decide whether to adopt Wright's style and point of view or employ a different mode of narration. Remember that the story is set during the Great Depression.

Related Commentary

Richard Wright, Reading Fiction, p. 934.

Suggested Readings

Felgar, Robert. *Richard Wright.* Boston: Twayne, 1980.
Hakutani, Yoshinobu, ed. *Critical Essays on Richard Wright.* Boston: G. K. Hall, 1982.
Margolies, Edward. *The Art of Richard Wright.* Carbondale: Southern Illinois UP, 1969.
McCall, Dan. *The Examp'e of Richard Wright.* New York: Harcourt, 1969.
Reilly, John M. *Richard Wright: The Critical Reception.* New York: Burt Franklin, 1978.
Wright, Richard. *Uncle Tom's Children.* New York: Harper, 1989.

THEMATIC INDEX

Story Pairs

1. Crane, *The Open Boat,* and *The Sinking of the* Commodore [A short story masterpiece and the newspaper narrative on which it is based]

2. Hemingway, *Hills Like White Elephants,* and Banks, *Black Man and White Woman in Dark Green Rowboat* [A short story masterpiece retold as if it took place today]

On Writing

Atwood, *Happy Endings*
García Márquez, *A Very Old Man with Enormous Wings*

Munro, *Miles City, Montana*
Paley, *A Conversation with My Father*

Fantasy and the Supernatural

Borges, *The Circular Ruins*
Cheever, *The Swimmer*
García Márquez, *A Very Old Man with Enormous Wings*
Gilman, *The Yellow Wallpaper*
Hawthorne, *Young Goodman Brown*

Jackson, *The Lottery*
Kafka, *A Hunger Artist*
Kafka, *The Metamorphosis*
Lawrence, *The Rocking-Horse Winner*
Silko, *Yellow Woman*

Childhood

Bambara, *The Lesson*
Cisneros, *The House on Mango Street*
Faulkner, *That Evening Sun*
Jewett, *A White Heron*

Lahiri, *When Mr. Pirzada Came to Dine*
Lawrence, *The Rocking-Horse Winner*
Tan, *Two Kinds*

Adolescence and Initiation

Anderson, *Hands*
Cather, *Paul's Case*
Díaz, *How to Date A Browngirl, Black-girl, Whitegirl, or Halfie*
Ellison, *Battle Royal*
Erdrich, *The Red Convertible*
Joyce, *Araby*

Mohr, *Tell the Truth*
Oates, *Where Are You Going, Where Have You Been?*
Updike, *A & P*
Wright, *The Man Who Was Almost a Man*
ZZ Packer, *Drinking Coffee Elsewhere*

Identity and Renewal

Alexie, *The Lone Ranger and Tonto Fistfight in Heaven*
Anderson, *Hands*
Baldwin, *Sonny's Blues*
Carver, *What We Talk About When We Talk About Love*
Cather, *Paul's Case*
Chopin, *Désirée's Baby*
Conrad, *Heart of Darkness*
Divakaruni, *Mrs. Dutta Writes a Letter*

García Márquez, *A Very Old Man with Enormous Wings*
Hawthorne, *Young Goodman Brown*
Jewett, *A White Heron*
Kafka, *The Metamorphosis*
Kincaid, *Girl*
Maupassant, *The Necklace*
Oates, *Where Are You Going, Where Have You Been?*
O'Brien, *The Things They Carried*

Flannery O'Connor, *Everything That Rises Must Converge*
Flannery O'Connor, *Good Country People*
Flannery O'Connor, *A Good Man Is Hard to Find*

Silko, *Yellow Woman*
Woolf, *Say Yes*
Wright, *The Man Who Was Almost a Man*

Love, Marriage, and Infidelity

Atwood, *Happy Endings*
Banks, *Black Man and White Woman in Dark Green Rowboat*
Carver, *What We Talk About When We Talk About Love*
Cheever, *The Swimmer*
Chekhov, *The Darling*
Chopin, *Désirée's Baby*
Chopin, *The Story of an Hour*
Faulkner, *A Rose for Emily*
Gilman, *The Yellow Wallpaper*

Hawthorne, *Young Goodman Brown*
Hemingway, *Hills Like White Elephants*
Hurston, *Sweat*
Joyce, *The Dead*
Mason, *Shiloh*
Maupassant, *The Necklace*
Munro, *Miles City, Montana*
Rifaat, *Distant View of a Minaret*
Silko, *Yellow Woman*
Wolff, *Say Yes*

Parents and Children

Cather, *Paul's Case*
Divakaruni, *Mrs. Dutta Writes a Letter*
Faulkner, *That Evening Sun*
Jen, *Who's Irish?*
Kafka, *The Metamorphosis*
Kincaid, *Girl*
Lahiri, *When Mr. Pirzada Came to Dine*
Lawrence, *The Rocking-Horse Winner*
Flannery O'Connor, *Everything That Rises Must Converge*

Flannery O'Connor, *Good Country People*
Olsen, *I Stand Here Ironing*
Paley, *A Conversation with My Father*
Porter, *He*
Tan, *Two Kinds*
Walker, *Everyday Use*
Wallace, *Incarnations of Burned Children*
Welty, *A Worn Path*
Wright, *The Man Who Was Almost a Man*

War and Revolution

Achebe, *Civil Peace*
Bierce, *An Occurrence at Owl Creek Bridge*
Conrad, *Heart of Darkness*
Gordimer, *Some Are Born*

Mukherjee, *The Management of Grief*
O'Brien, *The Things They Carried*
Frank O'Connor, *Guests of the Nation*

Looking at the Wall

Alexie, *The Lone Ranger and Tonto Fistfight in Heaven*
Allende, *An Act of Vengeance*
Baldwin, *Sonny's Blues*
Banks, *Black Man and White Woman in Dark Green Rowboat*
Bierce, *An Occurrence at Owl Creek Bridge*
Borges, *The Circular Ruins*
Carver, *Cathedral*
Carver, *Errand*
Carver, *What We Talk About When We Talk About Love*
Conrad, *Heart of Darkness*
Crane, *The Open Boat*
Divakaruni, *Mrs. Dutta Writes a Letter*
Gordimer, *Some Are Born*

Faulkner, *That Evening Sun*
Ha Jin, *Saboteur*
Hemingway, *Hills Like White Elephants*
Jackson, *The Lottery*
Joyce, *The Dead*
Kafka, *A Hunger Artist*
Kafka, *The Metamorphosis*
Mansfield, *The Fly*
Maupassant, *The Necklace*
Melville, *Bartleby, the Scrivener*
Oates, *Where Are You Going, Where Have You Been?*
Flannery O'Connor, *Everything That Rises Must Converge*
Flannery O'Connor, *A Good Man Is Hard to Find*

GUIDE TO COMMENTARIES

Writers on Writing

Writers on Other Writers

Chinua Achebe
An Image of Africa: Conrad's "Heart of Darkness," p. 827

Willa Cather
The Stories of Katherine Mansfield, p. 847

Kate Chopin
How I Stumbled upon Maupassant, p. 858

Julio Cortázar
On the Short Story and Its Environs, p. 859

Bobbie Ann Mason
On Tim O'Brien's "The Things They Carried," p. 885

Herman Melville
Blackness in Hawthorne's "Young Goodman Brown," p. 889

Frank O'Connor
Style and Form in Joyce's "The Dead," p. 901

Leo Tolstoy
Chekhov's Intent in "The Darling," p. 919

John Updike
Kafka and "The Metamorphosis," p. 927

Alice Walker
Zora Neale Hurston: A Cautionary Tale and a Partisan View, p. 930

Biographical and Historical Contexts

James Baldwin
Autobiographical Notes, p. 841

Robert H. Brinkmeyer Jr.
Flannery O'Connor and Her Readers, p. 975

Raymond Carver
On Writing, p. 941
Creative Writing 101, p. 946

Ann Charters
Translating Kafka, p. 851

Stephen Crane
The Sinking of the Commodore, p. 861

Ralph Ellison
The Influence of Folklore on "Battle Royal," p. 864

Sally Fitzgerald
Southern Sources of "A Good Man Is Hard to Find," p. 987

Charlotte Perkins Gilman
Undergoing the Cure for Nervous Prostration, p. 870
Why I Wrote "The Yellow Wallpaper," p. 872

Zora Neale Hurston
How It Feels to Be Colored Me, p. 873

Tom Jenks
The Origin of "Cathedral," p. 956

Sarah Orne Jewett
Looking Back on Girlhood, p. 880

Jamaica Kincaid
On "Girl," p. 884

Olga Knipper
Remembering Chekhov, p. 952

Flannery O'Connor
From "Letters, 1954–55," p. 964

Leslie Marmon Silko
Language and Literature from a Pueblo Indian Perspective, p. 910

Amy Tan
In the Canon, for All the Wrong Reasons p. 916

Henri Troyat
Chekhov's Last Days, p. 953

Eudora Welty
Is Phoenix Jackson's Grandson Really Dead?, p. 932

Richard Wright
Reading Fiction, p. 934

Critics on Writers

Wayne C. Booth
A Rhetorical Reading of O'Connor's "Everything That Rises Must Converge," p. 984

Sandra M. Gilbert and Susan Gubar
A Feminist Reading of Gilman's "The Yellow Wallpaper," p. 867

Dorothy Tuck McFarland
"On Good Country People," p. 980

Arthur M. Saltzman
A Reading of "What We Talk About When We Talk About Love," p. 957

A. O. Scott
Looking for Raymond Carver, p. 959

Cheryl B. Torsney
"Everyday Use": My Sojourn at Parchman Farm, p. 922

SHORT STORIES ON FILM AND VIDEO

Sherman Alexie
The Lone Ranger and Tonto Fistfight in Heaven
Movie Title: *Smoke Signals*
89 min., color, 1998
Cast: Adam Beach, Evan Adams
Directed by Chris Eyre
Distributed by Miramax Pictures Home Video

Ambrose Bierce
An Occurrence at Owl Creek Bridge
Movie Title: *An Occurrence at Owl Creek Bridge*
27 min., b&w, 1962
Cast: Roger Jacquet, Ann Cornaly, Anker Larsen, Stephanie Fey
Directed by Robert Enrico
Distributed by New York Film Annex

Raymond Carver
What We Talk About When We Talk About Love
Movie Title: *Short Cuts*
189 min., color, 1993
Cast: Jennifer Jason Leigh, Tim Rob-bins, Madeleine Stowe, Frances McDormand, Peter Gallagher, Lily Tomlin, Andie McDowell, Jack Lemmon, Lyle Lovett, Huey Lewis, Matthew Modine, Lili Taylor, Christopher Penn, Robert Downey Jr.
Directed by Robert Altman
Distributed by Columbia Tristar Home Video

Willa Cather
Paul's Case
Movie Title: *Paul's Case*
52 min., color, 1980
Cast: Eric Roberts, Michael Higgins, Lindsay Crouse
Directed by Lamont Johnson
Distributed by Moneterey Home Video

John Cheever
The Swimmer
Movie Title: *The Swimmer*
94 min., color, 1968
Cast: Burt Lancaster, Janet Langard
Directed by Frank Perry
Distributed by Goodtimes Home Video

Kate Chopin
The Story of an Hour
Movie Title: *Kate Chopin's The Story of an Hour*
24 min., color, 1982
Originally released as a major motion picture in 1982
Cast: Gwendolyn Coleman, Laura Lanfranchi, Shannon Baker, Paul Zakrzewski
Directed by Marita Simpson
Distributed by ISHTAR Films

Movie Title: *The Joy that Kills*
56 min., color, 1999
Cast: Frances Conroy, Jeffrey De Munn, Rosalind Cash
Directed by Tina Rathborne
Distributed by Films for the Humanities

Movie Title: *Five Stories of an Hour*
25 min., color, 1991
Four dramatic renditions of Kate Chopin's "The Story of an Hour," in addition to her original story
Cast: Zoe Wanamaker, Julian Cartside, Jilly Blond
Directed by Paul Kafno, Greg Lanning, David Hodgson
Distributed by Films for the Humanities

Joseph Conrad
Heart of Darkness
Movie Title: *Heart of Darkness*
120 min., color, 1993
Made for television
Cast: Tim Roth, John Malkovich, James Fox
Directed by Nicholas Roeg

Distributed by Turner Home Entertainment Company

Movie Title: *Apocalypse Now*
153 min., color, 1979
Cast: Martin Sheen, Marlon Brando, Robert Duvall
Directed by Francis Ford Coppola
Distributed by Paramount Home Video

Stephen Crane
The Open Boat
Movie Title: *The Open Boat*
29 min., b&w, 1965
Part of the "American Story Classics" series
Distributed by Film Video Library

William Faulkner
A Rose for Emily
Movie Title: *A Rose for Emily*
27 min., color, 1983
Cast: Angelica Huston, John Carradine
Distributed by Pyramid Media

Gabriel García Márquez
A Very Old Man with Enormous Wings
Movie Title: *A Very Old Man with Enormous Wings*
90 min., color, 1991
In Spanish with English subtitles
Cast: Daisy Granados, Asdrubal Melendez, Luis Alberto Ramirez, Fernando Birri
Distributed by Orion Home Video

Charlotte Perkins Gilman
The Yellow Wallpaper
Movie Title: *The Yellow Wallpaper*
14 min., color, 1977
Cast: Sigurd Wurschmidt, Tom Dahlgren, Susan Lynch
Distributed by Women Make Movies

Nathaniel Hawthorne
Young Goodman Brown
Movie Title: *Young Goodman Brown*
44 min., color, 2000
Cast: John p. Ryan, Tom Shell, Judy Geeson, Dorothy Lyman
Directed by Peter George
Distributed by Films for the Humanities & Sciences

Movie Title: *Young Goodman Brown*
30 min., color, 1971
Distributed by Pyramid Media

Shirley Jackson
The Lottery
Movie Title: *The Lottery by Shirley Jackson*

19 min., color, 1980
Distributed by Encyclopedia Britannica Educational Corporation

Sarah Orne Jewett
A White Heron
Movie Title: *A White Heron*
26 min., color, 1978
Distributed by New Letters on the Air

James Joyce
The Dead
Movie Title: *The Dead*
82 min., color, 2000
Cast: Angelica Huston, Donal McCann, Helena Carroll, Cathleen Delany
Directed by John Huston
Distributed by Artisan Home Entertainment

Franz Kafka
A Hunger Artist
Movie Title: *A Hunger Artist*
23 min., b&w, 1983
Distributed by Film Ideas

Movie Title: *The Metamorphosis of Mr. Samsa*
10 min., color, 1991
Animation
Directed by Caroline Leaf
Distributed by National Film Board of Canada

D. H. Lawrence
Odour of Chrysanthemums
Movie Title: *Odour of Chrysanthemums*
24 min., color, 1995
Cast: Jack Shepherd, Philip Jackson
Written and Presented by Graham Martin
Distributed by Films for the Humanities & Sciences

The Rocking-Horse Winner
Movie Title: *The Rocking-Horse Winner*
91 min. b&w, 1949
Cast: John Mills, Valerie Hobson
Directed by Anthony Pelessier
Distributed by Home Vision Cinema

Guy de Maupassant
The Necklace
Movie Title: *The Necklace by Guy de Maupassant*
20 min., color, 1980
Distributed by Encyclopedia Britannica Education Corporation

Movie Title: *The Necklace*
22 min., color, 1982
Directed by Bernard Wilets
Distributed by Barr Films

Herman Melville
Bartleby, the Scrivener
Movie Title: *Bartleby*
28 min., color, 1969
Distributed by Encyclopedia Britannica
    Education Corporation

Movie Title: *Bartleby, the Scrivener*
79 min., color, 1970
Cast: Paul Scofield, John McEnery
Directed by Anthony Friedman
Distributed by The Video Catalog

Movie Title: *Bartleby by Herman Melville*
38 min., color, 1990
Cast: Patrick Cambell, James Westerfield
Directed by Larry Yust
Distributed by Encyclopedia Britannica
    Education Corporation

Movie Title: *Bartleby, the Scrivener*
59 min., color, 1988
A teleplay by Israel Horovitz
Cast: Nicholas Kepros, Joel Colodner
Distributed by Films for the Humanities

Joyce Carol Oates
Where Are You Going, Where Have You Been?
Movie Title: *Smooth Talk*
92 min., color, 1985
Cast: Laura Dern, Treat Williams, Mary
    Kay Place, Levon Helm
Directed by Joyce Chopra
Distributed by Vestron Video

Flannery O'Connor
Good Country People
Movie Title: *Good Country People*
32 min., color, 1975
Cast: Johnnie Collins III, Shirley Slater,
    June Whitley Taylor
Directed by Jeffrey E. Jackson
Distributed by Valley Video

Frank O'Connor
Guests of the Nation
Movie Title: *Guests of the Nation*
58 min., color, 1981
Cast: Frank Coverse, Richard Cottrell,
    Charlie Stavola
Directed by John Desmond
Distributed by Broadway Theatre Archive

Edgar Allan Poe
The Cask of Amontillado
Movie Title: *The Cask of Amontillado*
29 min., b&w, 1965
Part of the "American Story Classics"
    series

Distributed by Film Video Library

The Tell-Tale Heart
Movie Title: *The Tell-Tale Heart*
30 min., b&w, 1980
Cast: Alex Cord, Sam Jaffe
Distributed by Churchill Films

Amy Tan
Two Kinds
Movie Title: *Joy Luck Club*
139 min., color, 2000
Cast: Tsai Chin, Kieu Chinh, Lisa Lu
Directed by Wayne Wong
Distributed by Hollywood Pictures Home
    Video

Leo Tolstoy
The Death of Ivan Ilych
Movie Title: *The Death of Ivan Ilych*
60 min., color, 1995
Part of The Living Literature: The Classics
    & You Series
Directed by Tony Labriola
Distributed by Insight Media

John Updike
A & P
Movie Title: *A & P*
31 min., color, 1999
Cast: Sean Patrick Hayes, Randy Oglesby,
    Amy Smart
Directed by Bruce R. Schwartz
Distributed by Films for the Humanities &
    Sciences

Eudora Welty
A Worn Path
Movie Title: *A Worn Path*
32 min., color, 1994
Cast: Cora Lee Day, Conchata Ferrell, Jodie
    Markell, Brad Dourif
Directed by Bruce R. Schwartz
Distributed by Films for the Humanities &
    Sciences

Richard Wright
The Man Who Was Almost a Man
Movie Title: *Almos' a Man*
39 min., color, 1977
Cast: LeVar Burton
Directed by Stan Lathan
Distributed by Moneterey Home Video